LAND GRAB

Land Grab

Green Neoliberalism, Gender, and Garifuna Resistance in Honduras

KERI VACANTI BRONDO

THE UNIVERSITY OF
ARIZONA PRESS
TUCSON

THE UNIVERSITY OF ARIZONA PRESS

www.uapress.arizona.edu

Library of Congress Cataloging-in-Publication Data
  Land grab : green neoliberalism, gender, and Garifuna resistance in Honduras /
Keri Vacanti Brondo.
    pages cm
  Includes bibliographical references and index.
  ISBN 978-0-8165-3021-2 (cloth : alk. paper) 1. Garifuna (Caribbean people)—Land
tenure—Honduras. 2. Garifuna (Caribbean people)—Honduras—Government relations.
3. Garifuna (Caribbean people)—Cultural assimilation—Honduras. 4. Garifuna
women—Honduras—Social conditions. 5. Garifuna women—Honduras—Economic
conditions. 6. Honduras—Ethnic relations . 7. Honduras—Politics and government.
I. Title.
  F1505.2.C3B76 2013
  305.80097283—dc23
                                                              2012046600

Publication of this book is made possible in part by the proceeds of a permanent
endowment created with the assistance of a Challenge Grant from the National
Endowment for the Humanities, a federal agency.

18 17 16 15 14 13   6 5 4 3 2 1

Contents

Illustrations

Acknowledgments

This book emerges from over a decade of fieldwork, and the intellectual foundation was laid even earlier. Thus, my list of influences and debts of gratitude are enormous, and I simply cannot acknowledge all of those who contributed to this work's development. The most important words of gratitude go to the Hondurans who collaborated on this research. I thank the people of Sambo Creek, Corozal, San Antonio, Nueva Armenia, Rio Esteban, East End, and Chachahuate who welcomed me into their lives and shared their stories. I apologize that I cannot thank each of you by name, but I wish to honor the anonymity that I promised.

I also thank the government officials and NGO staff people from the various organizations in La Ceiba and Tegucigalpa who shared their knowledge through formal interviews and enabled me to conduct archival research in their offices. I promised most of you anonymity as well, but you know who you are, and I greatly appreciate your insights. The work would not have been possible without the support over the years from core members of La Organización Fraternal Negra Hondureña (OFRANEH) and La Organización de Desarrollo Etnico Comunitario (ODECO) who served as research facilitators, teachers, and inspirational leaders. Daniel and I thank our expatriate friends along the coast, for their companionship and allowing us a glimpse into their lives in Garifuna territory. Over the years we remained close with one matrifocal household in particular in Sambo Creek; the matriarch served as a surrogate mother to me, her daughters, my sisters, and their sons, our children's playmates. I hope that I have done justice to the words and actions of all the Hondurans who shared their wisdom with me, and I take full responsibility for any errors or misrepresentations in the stories I present here.

The research would not have been possible without the support of many institutions. Fulbright IIE provided ten months of fieldwork in 2002; further fieldwork in the early 2000s was supported through Michigan State

University's (MSU) Department of Anthropology via a National Science Foundation Ethnographic Training Grant, MSU's Center for Latin American and Caribbean Studies (CLACS) through a Tinker Foundation Travel Grant. Operation Wallacea supported my travel and in-country expenses in 2005 and 2006, and the College of Arts and Sciences, Fresh Connections, and the Department of Anthropology at the University of Memphis provided research and travel expense support in 2011. I thank the following journals for granting rights to reproduce portions of previously published work: portions of the book appeared in *Conservation and Society* (2011, 9.2), *Journal of Latin American and Caribbean Anthropology* (2010, 15.1), *Journal of International Women's Studies* (2007, 9.1), and *Ecological and Environmental Anthropology* (2007, 3.1). A small part of chapter 9 originally appeared in *Cengage Learning's Anthropology Coursereader* by Wadsworth/Cengage Learning. I am especially grateful for Allyson Carter's assistance in guiding me through the publication process with the University of Arizona Press.

This book has its roots in my dissertation at Michigan State University, where my committee—Laurie Medina (chair), Anne Ferguson, Bill Derman, and Antoinette WinklerPrins—helped me to formulate my research questions and challenged me to grow as a scholar. Marietta Baba provided significant support in seeing through to completion my dissertation and providing opportunities to expand my engagement with applied anthropology. Scott Whiteford and Lynne Goldstein also provided guidance and support over my time at MSU. Other colleagues from MSU whom I wish to thank include: Inez Adams, James Bielo, Jennifer Brewer, Holly Dygert, Robert Edmondson, Tara Hefferan, Suzanne Kent, Christine LaBond, Kate Patch, Zakia Posey, Sue Schneider, Raju Tamot, Victor Torres, Shannon Vance, Michael Walker, and Aaron and Jill Whiteford. I am particularly grateful for my friendship and professional relationship with Suzanne Kent, who shares my passion for unpacking the gendered effects of development and globalization, who assisted in research in the Cayos Cochinos in 2005, and who has provided unwavering support to our family for the last decade.

Research in the Cayos Cochinos Marine Protected Area and its dependent communities was supported by Operation Wallacea, through which I worked with many wonderful international scholars and local translators. I thank the research and administrative staff from Operation Wallacea and the Honduran Coral Reef Fund for their assistance between 2005 and 2007. I am especially indebted to Adoni Cubas and Tony Ives, who shared their social networks and passion for collaborative conservation in Garifuna communities, and to Natalie Bown, research collaborator extraordinaire, whose areas of expertise in fisheries governance helped round out my own understandings and analysis of resource rights and conservation in the Cayos Cochinos. I also thank the student members of Opwall social science teams from 2005 and 2006: Claire Cass, Tom Cooke, Ria Harding, Caroline Morgan, Ewan Ritchie, and Tara Sabi. Anisha Grover, Monica Kar, and Tara Sabi kindly shared their photographs from the field for use in this book.

I thank my anthropology colleagues at the University of Memphis for the nurturing and supportive environment that enabled the production of this manuscript. The receipt of the College of Arts and Sciences Early Career Research Award in 2010 and a Professional Development Award in 2011 allowed me the time to travel and write. I am very grateful to the university for making these investments in an early career scholar.

I would like to thank Linda Bennett, Natalie Bown, Harry Brondo, Tara Hefferan, Kathryn Hicks, Tony Ives, Suzanne Kent, Katherine Lambert-Pennington, and Daniel Vacanti for reviewing earlier versions of the book's chapters and providing helpful feedback. Sara Bridges and Chris Mueller also played important roles in listening to me work through some of the book's contents on our long runs. Sarah Donovan provided outstanding support through the final copyedit stage.

Over the years, three other scholars have made substantial intellectual contributions to my work: Mark Anderson, Dario Euraque, and Helen Safa. Dario Euraque taught me the complexities of Honduran ethnic history, and its relationships to power. Helen Safa encouraged me to move beyond my romantic tendencies in approaching analyses of women's lives, and to celebrate the power of women's activism. Mark Anderson not only provided the foundation for the work that I pursued on the north coast but also taught me how to be a good teacher and colleague. From the very start of my dissertation work, Mark has provided open access to any data that could bolster my own work, thoroughly constructive feedback on writing, and steadfast support for my research endeavors. I am eternally grateful.

On a personal note, I am deeply indebted to my family. Little do non-academics realize when taking up with one how much of academia will spill over into their lives. My parents, Harry and Valerie Brondo, and grandparents Thaler and Brondo taught me the value of hard work and a strong will, and I thank them for being proud of me even when they may not have understood my career choice. Kurt Brondo and Jamie Hardy, thank you for sharing time over the years in Honduras, and for your genuine interest in the future of residents on the north coast and islands. Sharon Vacanti and Grace Burge, thank you for your providing care for Keegan and Amalie over the years as I wrote. To my daughter Amalie, who was "writing her own dissertation" when she was two years old (or so she said)—your joy for life and concern for equity and inclusion is inspirational. To Keegan "Kiki" Vacanti, your life is the life of this book, from making your first trip to Honduras in my womb, to turning one and two years old in Sambo Creek, and to finally reuniting with your old friends in 2011 for a game of *futból* on the coastal beaches. Lastly, Daniel (DJ) Vacanti—no words can capture all you have given to support this project. Closing this book means opening a new chapter to our lives. I dedicate this book to you, to our children, and to the *hijos del pueblo garifuna*.

LAND GRAB

Introduction

Death and a (Land?) Motive

June 2002

We woke up that morning as any other morning in our temporary home, a two-room rental just outside of the official borders of Sambo Creek, a Garifuna community 20 kilometers outside the city of La Ceiba. Our home was one of the growing number of hotel/restaurants that cater to tourists, well-to-do beach day trippers from the city of La Ceiba, foreign and national tourists, missionaries and other long-term visitors to the coast. Keegan, aged 23 months, was hungry to nurse and served as our alarm clock. Daniel and I rose to make breakfast and coffee, with Keegan ducking in and out of the kitchen cabinet door under the sink, playing peek-a-boo. While Keegan and I readied for our day, Daniel headed out with his coffee in hand to the outdoor beach restaurant, to see if anyone had the daily newspaper or was around to visit. Our family of three were often the only weekday residents of this hotel. As long-term occupants who helped the all-Garifuna staff in the restaurant when needed, we became privileged to both the voices and positions of the expatriate and elite mestizo population who occupied and/or visited the coast, and to the unique relationships developed between Garifuna employees and their mestizo and foreign employers.

Before Keegan and I made it outside that morning, Daniel was already back, alarmed by news of a murder in which Aubert,[1] our friend and Canadian landlord, was being held as an accomplice in a jail in La Ceiba. The incident involved two mestizo night watchmen from our hotel, Francisco and Manuel. While one was napping, the other deserted work, taking with him two guns from the hotel/restaurant. Manuel awoke Aubert and together they drove over to the center of Sambo Creek to find Francisco, taking a shotgun with them in the truck.

1

They found Francisco by the *salon* (the community gathering center on the beach), with a packed suitcase. When confronted to return the two guns, Francisco allegedly pointed one at Aubert's head. Aubert pleaded with him, and when Francisco did not pull back, Manuel reached behind Aubert's head and shot Francisco. The two men then got out of the car to see if Francisco was still alive; his skull had been smashed into hundreds of pieces by the shotgun's force. The two went back to Aubert's property to call the police, and once the police arrived, they all returned to the scene. Witnesses from Sambo Creek alleged to the details of the crime, and both men were imprisoned and remained there awaiting trial throughout the year 2002.

As other mornings, I headed out to the center of the pueblo, distraught over what I learned that morning, and curious to hear how Sambeños were responding. Daniel and Keegan stayed behind. What I discovered when I began speaking with my friends in central Sambo Creek was that a number of people were awake watching footage from the World Cup when they heard a car pull up. According to gossip across the town, eyewitnesses concurred that all three men (Manuel, Aubert, and Francisco) arrived in the same car. Witnesses alleged that Manuel pushed Francisco onto the street while Aubert remained in the vehicle, and then Manuel shot Francisco in the head. Everyone was asking "Why? Why bring him to the center of the pueblo to murder him?" Various rumors circulated. In one account, Aubert and his wife, Eva, were said to be involved in drug trafficking and that Francisco might have seen something he should not have. The alleged rationale for murdering Francisco in the busiest section of the community was that Aubert and Eva wanted to send a message to the community, demonstrating their position of power. Rumors such as this one about cause quickly dissipated, but concerns about violence introduced by outsiders who came to control local resources did not.

The day of the shooting, a Garifuna friend shared, "Keri, now you can see why we don't want people from outside here; they bring violence to our *pueblo*." She provided her evidence: the series of local murders in Sambo Creek that were connected to foreigners. One had been on "the German's" land;[2] two died outside La Champa (a mestizo-owned restaurant); and now this one, in the center of the community. Belinda cried, "Now we don't know what to do for our own safety," but then she reassured me saying, "Don't worry, Keri. Everyone knows you aren't connected to this incident and that you only rent from them." Consesa, another friend, disagreed, stating that Francisco's family was not from Sambo Creek and that if someone came up to Sambo seeking revenge—which he argued was very likely, considering how most mestizos are violent—they would see Daniel's white skin and mistake him for Aubert. Consesa argued that under informal Honduran politics, Aubert, as a wealthy boss, was held responsible for Manuel's actions. Thus, revenge would not be sought on Manuel's family, but rather on Aubert's. Foreign and elite mestizo patrons of the restaurant reported hearing community members on the radio saying that Francisco's family declared they "should kill one of their [Eva and Aubert's] kids so they know how it feels."

Eva visited Francisco's family, paying her regrets for what had transpired, and helped the family financially with funeral arrangements and to offset the hardship of losing a working family member. She also continued to support Manuel's family while he remained in jail, paying for a private cell, as well as for his legal services.

In the days that followed, we heard gossip that there were people from Sambo Creek at the jail crying out in protest that "the Canadians should go home and stop taking all their land." Land thus became tied to the murder, and the murder added fuel to Sambeños' claims against foreigners. Before this incident, I had already been hearing stories about how outsiders (mestizos and foreigners) had transformed the community in negative ways. They were criticized for introducing new forms of land tenure—specifically, they privatized and guarded their lands, thus disallowing passage on land that had historically been communal. They cut down coconut, mango, and *nance* fruit trees—or claimed those remaining on their property as private— significantly reducing harvesting opportunities for Sambeños. Moreover, outsiders were charged with the introduction of violence in association with the protection of their private landholdings. A number of outsiders (mestizos included) who owned land in Sambo Creek hired armed guards to watch their property and, in the past, had killed trespassers on their lands.

We heard from hotel/restaurant patrons that one of the eyewitnesses who claimed to see Aubert order Manuel to shoot Francisco had been involved in a series of land occupations, efforts to recuperate what they believed was Garifuna ancestral territory that had been irregularly obtained by mestizos or other outsiders. One of the targeted plots was owned under clear title by Eva and Aubert. The Sambeños who attempted to reclaim that plot peacefully retired when they learned it was under title. Patrons and colleagues of Eva and Aubert believed that the man was seeking revenge, and they encouraged her not to close the restaurant (even for one day). One friend shared, "They [the community] have been trying to get them to leave here and take this land because they don't want it to be in the hands of a white man. To leave now, would mean they won."

While some Sambeños may have felt that Eva and Aubert should return to Canada, it would be unfair to suggest that this was a consensus across the community. The three had pleasant relationships with many Sambeños, formulated largely as patron-employee relationships. The depth of these relations is revealed by the fact that all but one of their Garifuna employees came to the hotel at sunrise after hearing of the murder, approximately four to five hours before their work shift began (the only employee who didn't come was on vacation). The tearful women cried for days. When I saw Leslie, my closest friend who worked for them that early afternoon, she just walked over and hugged me, at a loss for words. The women never doubted Aubert's innocence and were torn up that some Sambeños were spreading rumors about him.

While not wanting to abandon our foreign and mestizo friends in this crisis, but concerned at the possibility that our Garifuna friends' suggestions that Keegan or Daniel could be at risk were valid, we left Sambo Creek to conduct comparative research in two additional communities. After six weeks away, we returned to Sambo Creek. Upon our return, I asked Zita, a close Garifuna friend, whether she'd heard anything more about the murder of Francisco being tied to the land claim in Sambo Creek. She had not, and she said to me, "Maybe it is all in their head." Maybe Zita was onto something. Perhaps the discourse and practices of foreign expats and mestizo business owners in the area were being shaped by recent attempts by Sambeños to recuperate land. Maybe the recent open wounds from having land "invaded" shifted the way in which they processed and understood events. I noticed in reviewing all of my field notes and post-murder interviews that the only people who linked land and this murder were "outsiders" (foreigners and mestizos living in the community). Although people reported to me that Garifuna community members were making radio declarations about land, these were all foreign immigrants; I never heard these declarations myself. Garifuna people *did* react to the murder, but the way in which they reacted was by talking about violence. Native Sambeños did not want wealthy foreigners and mestizos on their lands, because they have demonstrated violent behavior in what had been considered a *tranquilo* Garifuna community. In that same discussion with Zita after my return, she continued her thought, saying, ". . . ever since that murder happened, I've felt that it was dangerous for you to keep living there, because you have the same skin color as Aubert, and you can be killed in revenge . . . once the indios get something in their head, it doesn't go away. It's dangerous." Thus, my Garifuna friends in Sambo Creek feared that my family would be caught in the middle of mestizo revenge, while my foreign and mestizo friends feared our being caught in the middle of Garifuna revenge. The history of interethnic conflict created by unequal access to resources based on racial hierarchies produced (articulated, invented) by those in political and economic power provides the backdrop for how both everyday practices and uncommon events are understood and interpreted in Garifuna communities. This history will be developed in the first few chapters; for now, we will cross the Caribbean Sea 15 kilometers to the Cayos Cochinos, a set of two main islands and thirteen smaller cays forming extensive coral reefs at the southernmost part of the Mesoamerican Barrier Reef System.

An Island Rave

June 2005

Three years after Francisco was killed, I sat on the porch of the cabin I shared with seven other white European and American researchers, debating with myself whether or not I really wanted to join the party. It was Friday night, and the rave-like music pumping out of the speakers on the dock could be heard across the island. After a long week of rising early for underwater collection of data on marine life and reef quality, and forest sweeps for the pink boa and other terrestrial life, the researchers and student research tourists from Operation Wallacea (Opwall) let their hair down. Opwall is a private conservation expedition organization that has been granted accommodations for the summer months on Cayo Menor, the second-largest island in the Cayos Cochinos marine protected area, where the MPA's managing agency, the Honduran Coral Reef Fund (HCRF) research station is located.

Opwall volunteers familiar with these parties had shored up mass quantities of alcohol for this occasion and spent the week bringing newbies up to speed on what to expect, sharing stories of surprisingly raunchy party behavior from years past. I walked tentatively out and found a wallflower place, sitting down on the wooden box where life jackets and other diving supplies were stored. Bodies were moving all around me. The female students and researchers had dressed up for the evening, wearing something other than a swimsuit for the first time in a week. The reputedly "craziest" of all the male researchers had on a sarong and nothing else, as he clutched a bottle of Flor de Caña (a Nicaraguan brand of rum popular in Honduras) and danced with several female research volunteers.

The laughter among the group was infectious. It was the kind of intimacy that develops through such rites of passage as volunteer research tourism

(Lyons and Wearing 2008a), where students are immersed in another culture and setting, living in close proximity in small groups and relying on one another to accomplish goals. Having spent the days off Chachahuate, the island on the cay inhabited by the Garifuna, or in the Garifuna settlement of East End on the larger island of Cayo Mayor, I hadn't formed those bonds with the Opwall team. I watched as the few mestizo HCRF staff members baited the white Opwall volunteers into a punta dance-off. The punta is an African-influenced dance constituted by rapid movements of the hips and buttocks, traditionally performed at wakes, holidays, and other cultural events by female dance troupes dressed in matching long, colorful, flowing dresses and head wraps that represent their community of origin (typically, punta music is played by an all-male drum and conch shell band). Punta and punta rock has become exceedingly popular with Hondurans of all ethnic-racial backgrounds, and it appears at national celebrations of cultural heritage (see Anderson 2009:24–25). Today, young dancers from Honduras and abroad perform it as an erotic and seductive competitive dance.

I watched this strange scene of mestizo elite and foreigners moving so confidently, pounding their place into the dock. It was similar to how they assertively navigated the waters and islands, how they could move wherever and whenever they wanted during this research season, as if they *belonged* here, as if they *owned* the natural surround and its resources. Meanwhile, the Garifuna, who had inhabited the area since 1797, were becoming increasingly restricted—in 2004 the Cayos Cochinos Marine Protected Area (CCMPA) Management Plan came into effect, for an initial five-year period (2004–9). Conservation measures meant that Garifuna access to particular fishing zones and island territory would be restricted and supervised by the HCRF. In addition to its specific conservation aims, the CCMPA management plan sought to encourage eco- and research tourism as income generators for natural resource conservation. Ecotourism was also advocated as an alternative to replace fishing as a primary economic strategy for the Garifuna population.

Earlier that evening, Garifuna from Chachahuate and East End were invited to the island to prepare a traditional barbeque and put on a "cultural performance" for the research tourists. The Garifuna cooks prepared barbeque chicken, fried plantains, and beans and rice. They earned less than what was paid to the regular HCRF chef per plate (of often similar food). After the performance of drumming and dance, the Garifuna were shuttled off, expected to return to their settlements and not mingle with the

Figure I.1 Contradictions in rights to resources: dive boat alongside traditional fishing boat. Photo by Monica Kar

research volunteers.[3] Now, here we were slightly more than 1.25 nautical miles away, dancing the *punta*, drinking our Salva Vidas ("lifesaver," a local beer), and exchanging scuba stories of marine life, views that the Garifuna could not be caught gathering, given the management plan regulations. What historical dynamics and policy changes lead a place to become so exclusionary, catering to single 20–30-year-old foreign research volunteers, when it had been a source of household subsistence for the Garifuna?

The above vignettes are underscored by national and international economic development policies and environmental management driven by neoliberalism. Neoliberalism is a set of political and economic strategies that presumes human well-being can be best enhanced through encouraging efficient economic markets, free trade, and strong property rights; by privatizing public services; engaging in massive governmental deregulation; and limiting the role of the state (Edelman and Haugerud 2005; Harvey 2005). At the turn of the new millennium, such free-market universalism dominated global development policy, replacing past approaches of modernization, redistribution with growth, and meeting the basic needs of the poor (Edelman and Haugerud 2005:8). In a book concerned with the relationship between gender, development policy, and rights to resource management, a brief review of shifts in development theory and practice, and feminist political ecology is in order.

While historians of development theory (e.g., Edelman and Haugerud 2005; Peet 1999; Rist 1997) trace the roots of the concept to the Enlightenment and the Age of Reason, for brevity and relevance to the topic at hand, my review begins after World War II. Post–WW II expectations of "development" were based on Rostow's (1960) "stages of economic growth," which assumed that through development interventions, postcolonial states could "catch up" to the consumption levels of industrialized nations by copying the same steps that industrialized models followed. In the late 1970s, with the realization that developing nations were not advancing to "take off," Rostow's modernization theory was replaced with a "basic needs" approach, in which development programs were designed to simply meet the needs of the poor without attempting equity with wealthier nations. Then the structural adjustment programs of the 1980s ended up worsening any advances toward meeting basic needs by hitting the world's poorest the hardest, through the implementation of conditionalities that called for free-market policies and cuts to state-run social services (Edelman and Haugerud 2005). By the late 1980s, the only approach to development that states could agree on was to eliminate development policy and let the market rule (Edelman and Haugerud 2005:8).

Important advances have been made in theorizing development, including Marxist, feminist, and poststructural critiques, leading us to redefine what "development" might actually look like if achieved. Most conceptualizations of development have a base expectation of progress, but progress need not always be defined in terms of economic growth. In recent years development has come to be understood as improved well-being or "development as freedom" (Sen 1999), replacing the unidimensional economistic views of development as measured by increases to GDP or other rates of return (Edelman and Haugerud 2005:1). While international organizations such as the World Bank, Inter-American Development Bank, and UN agencies may well now be measuring "development" in terms of indicators of health, life expectancy, education, or literacy, the notion of development as the freedom to achieve a standard of well-being still exists alongside of programs and policies that remain informed by a neoclassical view of development, currently under the form of economic neoliberalism. Hence, my study asks: can "freedom," understood as well-being, be achieved under the structures of neoliberalism? I ground this question in the context of Garifuna relationships to territorial (land and sea) control and self-determination.

This book is informed by feminist political ecology. Political ecologists focus on the uneven distribution of access, control, and management of resources on the basis of class and ethnicity (Igoe 2004; Peet and Watts 1993; Stonich 2000). Feminist political ecologists add gender as a critical variable in shaping these relationships to resources, which interacts with other variables such as race, ethnicity, culture, caste, and class (Rocheleau, Thomas-Slayter, and Wangari 1996:4). The approach I take is to unearth the structural causes of inequalities, and the means by which power impinges on the abilities of some actors to shape the future of resource use and management.

I am particularly concerned with the critical role of gender within two key domains: *gendered environmental rights and responsibilities* (i.e., access and control of property and resources, and legal and customary rights) and *gendered environmental politics and grassroots activism* (i.e., the growth of women's involvement in collective struggles over natural resources) (Rocheleau, Thomas-Slayter, and Wangari 1996:4–5). With regard to gendered environmental rights and responsibilities, I am concerned with access, procurement, and managerial control of natural resources as they apply to productive resources (land, water, trees, and animals, but in my case, especially land). As Rocheleau and colleagues (1996: 10) point out, not only is there a gendered division of resources, but there is also a gendered division of power over the preservation, protection, and restoration of environments and the regulation of actions of others. In the two cases in focus here, development policies and agrarian reforms have transformed women's control and access to resources along the coastline. The gendered process looks different for Garifuna women, mestizo women, and foreign expats, and class plays a significant role in shaping environmental rights and responsibilities. With regard to gendered environmental politics and grassroots activism, my focus lies in the role of women in Garifuna ethnic federations lobbying for women's environmental sustainability as central to cultural sustainability, and the role women have played in localized land recuperation efforts in the north.

The global restructuring of economies, ecologies, and politics has brought about profound changes in the relationships of individuals as stakeholders and actors to resource use and allocation and to environmental management (Rocheleau, Thomas-Slayter, and Wangari 1996). Over the past couple of decades, a "green developmentalism" (McAfee 1999) or "green neoliberalism" (Hanson 2007) has emerged that involves a set of "institutions, discourse, and practices that facilitate objectification and commodification of nature's values . . . [making] efficient use and exchange of 'natural capital'" (Hanson 2007:247–248). I am concerned with two forms of green neoliberalism, two arenas in which neoliberal policies have altered local interactions with resources—(1) neoliberal agrarian legislation and (2) neoliberal conservation policies—and their relationship to tourism development and power.

My engagement with neoliberal agrarian legislation attends to the implications the reregulation of community land has for Honduras's Garifuna population. Following Igoe and Brockington (2007:437), I employ the label "reregulation" in lieu of what advocates of neoliberal policies call "deregulation," because reregulation better captures the fact that under neoliberal land reforms, such as those discussed in this book, states transform previously untradable things into tradable commodities, removing regulations that impede market competition. Two examples of the ways in which land can be reregulated include the privatization of communal or state-owned property and the distribution of collective land titles to rural communities, both of which have occurred in Honduras. Collective land titling programs are used to bring rural communities into the market, enabling communities to enter into business ventures with outside investors (Lemos and Agrawal 2006:437). The reregulation of land assigns new value to areas that had not been directly territorialized.

Territorialization involves the marking of territories "within states for the purposes of controlling people and resources" (Igoe and Brockington 2007:437). Who and what becomes controlled, who is benefiting, and how these patterns are gendered are important considerations. Lemos and Agrawal (2006:312) warn that, unfortunately, reregulation and decentralization can easily be used by those in power to enhance their own political positions and landholdings. In Honduras's Garifuna communities, territorialization has led to reduced women's land rights for the sake of a real estate boom associated with tourism development and other investment opportunities for elite mestizos and investors. To quote Phillips (2011:222), "Where there is land conflict in Honduras, there are human rights issues."

By "neoliberal conservation" I am referring to the decentralization of environmental governance, or the shift in responsibility for natural resource management from state to local institutions, and the new forms of commodification and commercialization of nature that emerge in these contexts in order to fund conservation efforts. While proponents of neoliberal conservation efforts believe that inequities in relationships to natural resources can be fixed through market-based solutions, the critical literature on neoliberal conservation demonstrates this model of resource management does very little to improve the local economies or the relationships of local peoples to local resources (Brockington, Duffy, and Igoe 2008; Büscher and Whande 2007; Igoe and Brockington 2007). Rather, such commodification and commercialization assigns new values to resources, values that typically then become available to outsiders or local elites who are already in positions of political and economic power (vis-à-vis the majority local population). Numerous case studies have shown that in such contexts, national and transnational individuals and groups are the main benefactors of neoliberal conservation efforts (see, for example, Fortwangler 2007; Hitchcock 1995; Igoe and Brockington 2007).

One of the most common approaches to improving inequities that emerge within neoliberal conservation contexts is the development of tourism—especially ecotourism. Tourism has become a favorite development approach for multilateral lending agencies, including the World Bank, the Inter-American Development Bank, and the International Monetary Fund (IMF), and is a central strategy of economic growth pursued by many developing nations. Tourism—and ecotourism in particular—has a "neoliberal appeal" in that it is a nontraditional export industry that has the potential for growth in an environmentally sustainable manner (Brockington, Duffy, and Igoe 2008:131–132). International tourism has been growing steadily for the past several decades, and the United Nations World Tourism Organization (UNWTO) forecasts continued growth through the 2010s. According to the UNWTO (2011), international tourist arrivals grew by nearly 7 percent, totaling 940 million travelers, and generating $919 billion in export earnings.

Tourism is often proposed to serve as a central source of revenue to maintain protected areas. Protected areas are "all national parks, game reserves, national monuments, forest reserves and the myriad other places and spaces for which states provide special protection from human interference" (Brockington, Duffy, and Igoe 2008:1). As of 2008, there were over 120,000 protected areas in the world, covering 12.2 percent of the Earth's land and 5.9 percent of the sea (World Database on Protected Areas 2011).[4] Protected areas can include or exclude human inhabitation. In some cases human populations are displaced when an area comes under protected status; in other cases people may remain living within the protected area, but their activities and interactions with the natural surround will come under surveillance to ensure sustainable use of local resources. At times the local population will be involved in the development and enforcement of management plans, regulations on resource extraction, and compliance measures; and in other cases, they will not.

Ecotourism is proposed within protected area management plans both as a means to achieve conservation and as an alternative livelihood strategy for communities living within the boundaries or impact zones of a protected area. The International Ecotourism Society (TIES 2011) defines ecotourism as "responsible travel to natural areas that conserves the environment and improves the well-being of local people." TIES further claims that ecotourism should be ("is about") "uniting conservation, communities, and sustainable travel," such that activities that are pursued under the ecotourism umbrella should be respectful of the local environment *and* culture, provide positive experiences for both hosts and guests, raise awareness, and have direct financial benefits for the local population and for conservation (TIES 2011).

Two other types of tourism enterprises that are expanding within protected areas are voluntourism and research tourism. Volunteer tourism, or voluntourism, refers to holidays that focus on "aiding or alleviating the material poverty of some groups in society, the restoration of certain environments or research into aspects of society or environment" (Wearing 2002:240). Research tourism captures the field trips individuals take in order to pursue research projects, often in conjunction with a holiday. Research tourists could be "gap year" students who are interested in working on a senior scholar's project for an honors thesis or master's project, or volunteers unaffiliated with a university who simply wish to combine a learning opportunity with travel to a new destination. As one can see from the definitions above, each of these three forms of tourism—ecotourism, research tourism, and voluntourism—can, and often do, overlap. Organizations like Operation Wallacea (mentioned in the second opening vignette) are part of the emerging sector of organizations that coordinate research volunteer tourist expeditions that purport to apply scientifically based research projects to contribute to sustainable development in host countries. These organizations sit at the nexus of research, volunteer, and ecotourism.

While each of these three forms of tourism is informed by notions of ethical travel, unfortunately there are all too many examples of their ill effects on local populations. Case studies have found failure to make significant investment in local communities (e.g., Duffy 2002), unequal distribution of revenues among local populations (e.g., Bookbinder et al. 1998; Igoe and Croucher 2007; Vivanco 2001), heightened (rather than reduced) pressure on natural resources due to the presence of tourists (e.g., Puntenney 1990), conflicts over land use, management, and compliance (e.g., Bookbinder et al. 1998; Guerrón-Montero 2005; Hoffman 2009), and the introduction of new values and practices between people and their natural surround (e.g., Macintyre and Foale 2007; West and Carrier 2004).

While there is little evidence that local people and the environment fare better as a result of neoliberal projects, it is unlikely that such policies will be reversed. Governments simply do not have the resources to renationalize land and water or to detach themselves from global trading networks (Liverman and Vilas 2006:356–357). As such, constructive research endeavors might search for institutional solutions to help mediate the negative social and environmental effects of free trade and declining governmental roles (Liverman and Vilas 2006:357).

It is within this vein that this book emerges. While a significant portion of this book reveals the same patterns of inequality consistent with political-ecology critiques of neoliberal environmental governance, the conclusion attends to the possibilities for more equitable relationships to resources that have been created through the emergence of transnational indigenous, environmental, and feminist mobilizations, as well as potential for voluntourism partnership models.

Outline of the Book

The book's main chapters take up questions of *roots* (native status), *rights* (to access and manage natural resources, including land), and *belonging* (attitudes and practices regarding one's place) within the context of neoliberal conservation and development. Chapters 1 and 2 provide the historical context for understanding contemporary identity politics as they interact with development policy on the north coast and Cayos Cochinos.

Chapter 1 begins with a brief ethnohistorical account of the Garifuna, their settlement in Honduras, and their relative exclusion from Honduran national identity through to the mid-1900s. Throughout this time the fruit industry and labor movement played a key role in defining the Garifuna place (or lack thereof) within Honduras's racial-ethnic hierarchy. While the banana companies, local elites, and military dominated significant tracts of coastal lands, the Garifuna still maintained relative control over their functional habitat (cultivation plots, marine resources, and forest).

Chapter 2 describes how in the decades following the decline of the banana industry, as the coastal population blossomed and the coastline was transformed to accommodate new export products, the Garifuna began losing territorial control to more powerful interest groups. Between the 1950s and 1980s, the Garifuna began to organize as Afro-Honduran autochthonous people, asserting their rights as equal citizens within the nation-state. But as the nation-state joined the global march toward a neoliberal economic development agenda in the 1980s and beyond, an Afro-Honduran ethnic status became insufficient to combat the effects of deregulatory agrarian legislation on the Garifuna population, and an afro-indigenous identity emerged in its place.

Chapters 3 and 4 explore the gendered impacts of Honduras's neoliberal agrarian legislation and national development priorities. Drawing on ethnographic research in Sambo Creek, the chapters demonstrate how the process of territorialization along the north coast has been overtly gendered. Chapter 3 provides an introduction to the community of Sambo Creek, and its demographic transition as Garifuna labor migration expanded and mestizos moved into the community, displacing Garifuna from their ancestral cultivation lands.

Chapter 4 documents how Garifuna women's rights have become increasingly restricted through the delineation of new territorial boundaries under the privatization of communal land and the distribution of collective land titles. Not only are new values assigned to previously untradable goods, thus bringing new market-oriented actors to the coast, but women are assigned different values in their own communities. Their responsibilities and relationships to territory are redefined by neoliberal discourse and practice, further disenfranchising them within their households and communities. In addition to the limitations set on women's rights to territory as shaped by contemporary development models, relationships to resources are also being reshaped as youth livelihood interests evolve in response to transnational forces.

Chapter 5 focuses on Garifuna ethnopolitics and grassroots activism. I compare and contrast the two main organizations that represent the Garifuna, the Organización Fraternal Negra Hondureña (OFRANEH) and the Organización de Desarrollo Etnico Comunitario (ODECO), showing that each differs in its approach to coastal development strategies and the related struggles over territorial control and natural resource management. While both organizations are informed by global discourses of human rights and equality, OFRANEH is pointed in its role in promoting black indigeneity. I apply the notion of "place-making" to show how OFRANEH articulates an indigenous place within the Honduran nation, and in so doing, it resists the forces of neoliberalism. In contrast, I show how ODECO's strategy of working within the structures of neoliberalism creates a "discursive blur" (Büscher 2008:229–230), obscuring the local reality of neoliberal policies. Finally, this chapter presents Sambo Creek's attempts to "rescue" ancestral land, tracing peoples' multiscale efforts from local land occupations, to national work with OFRANEH, to the filing of an international petition with the Inter-American Commission on Human Rights (IACHR).

Chapter 6 looks at the effects of the production of Garifuna indigeneity at the local level. The chapter asks, How do ordinary members of the dominant majority population (mestizos) respond to the emergence of multicultural rights? How do mestizo and creole inhabitants attempt to "make place" (Muehelbach 2001) and demonstrate their rights to territory within a Garifuna community? The stories of Sambeños' reactions to the 2001 land occupations reveal how landed mestizos also react through identity construction. Faced with the internationalization of Garifuna indigeneity and national legislation that opened spaces for mobilizations based on Garifuna cultural rights, (some) mestizos at the local level (re)constructed their own ethnic identities in response, harking back to forms of *mestizaje* that protected their place within the racial hierarchy and denied Garifuna rights as Hondurans.

Chapters 7 and 8 look at another example of roots, rights, and belonging through a case study of Cayos Cochinos Marine Protected Area. In these chapters I explore the effects of and Garifuna resistance to the 2005–9 preservationist conservation management plan for the CCMPA, which emerged as part of Honduras's neoliberal development agenda. Chapter 7 discusses the development of a hybrid environmental governance model for the Cayos Cochinos MPA and the relationships created between the Garifuna community and research tourists that emerged from a market-oriented approach to conservation. Emphasis is placed on the CCMPA management plan's objective for the MPA-reliant communities to transition from fishing dependence to eco- and research tourism, and the fractures created within Garifuna communities as a result of these livelihood transitions. Chapter 8 assesses the potential for Garifuna resistance to lead to a restructuring of resource governance in favor of community-based management. The chapter is grounded in an evaluation of the relationship between "research voluntourism" and the Garifuna right to self-determination. By examining the discourse (marketing) and practice (ethnographic reality) of Opwall's "social and environmental responsibility programme," the chapter takes up the question of whether voluntourism can in fact contribute to the development of rights-based management within a neoliberal development context.

Chapter 9 explores the relationship between Garifuna indigeneity, development agendas, and gendered rights and activism after the 2009 coup d'état that deposed President Manuel Zelaya. The chapter analyzes how, in the post-coup environment, multiculturalism as an official discourse of equality has become incorporated into a neoliberal development agenda to consolidate power along gendered lines, serving as a "limit point" (Fischer and Benson 2006) to social change.

The final chapter attends to landscapes of power, from the power of positionality and narrative to that of ideology, counterideology, and resistance movements in Honduras's streets and across the globe. The chapter considers the potential for self-determination, and conservation and development with justice, within a post-coup neoliberal environment of instability and deepening poverty.

This book asks, Can "freedom" ever be achieved under the structures of neoliberalism? Freedom comes in many forms, often creating friction as distinct groups of people cross paths in grounded space in pursuit of their individual and collective rights. In her study of global interaction and conflict surrounding Indonesian rain forests, Anna Tsing (2005) encountered a range of interest groups similar to the interlocutors in this study. In framing her analysis of "freedom," Tsing (2005:245) writes that "the freedom of middle-class students to roam in wild nature contrasts with the struggle of activists for communal empowerment." Her observation about engagement with Indonesian rain forests resonates with the divergent interests in Honduran coastal territory, once managed largely as common territory of the Garifuna population. From this point Tsing (2005:245) asks, "Can any cause for justice emerge from these differences?" The answer is probably more yes than no. Through her concept of friction, a "metaphorical image . . . [that] reminds us that heterogeneous and unequal encounters can lead to new arrangements of culture and power," Tsing (2005:5) moves us beyond thinking about solidarity and the quest for social justice as necessitating homogeneity among likeminded individuals. Change does not always emerge because people think and act alike. In fact, differences — "friction" — can lead to productive collaborations for social justice.

In the coming pages, we will meet a variety of characters—including afro-indigenous activists, Sambeño women seeking to eke out a modest living, foreign entrepreneurs, artisanal fishermen, conservation nongovernmental organization (NGO) leadership, and student research tourists, among others—each exercising their "freedom" to interact with Garifuna ancestral territory in pursuit of their own well-being, or that of a larger community. The majority of these actors believe they are "doing the right thing" for themselves, their families, and for their communities, and even at times for the future of humanity (with environmental stewardship or national development priorities in mind). Some of these actors are misguided, and a few you might even find intentionally menacing, but most are in pursuit of a "just" world (even when their views and goals may be underwritten by romantic understandings of indigeneity or ill-advised visions of economic advancement). Tsing's attention to friction brings out the "sticky" nature of ethnographies of global interconnection (which, today, all ethnographies indeed are). I advise you, the reader, to pay attention to the friction that surrounds the future of Garifuna territory. Consider the possibilities for social change and justice as various actors intersect and engage with their freedom to self-determination, their freedom to own and manage environmental resources, and their freedom to protest against land dispossession.

We know not what the future holds, but what we do know well is that neoliberal globalization provides the backdrop for all contemporary studies of conservation, development, and territorial rights. Ethnographic studies of neoliberalism are ubiquitous; some might even say the literature is overworked. As such I would like to position this book not as another critique of neoliberalism, but as one that engages the potential for social transformation—for "freedom"—under neoliberalism.

The contemporary development model (neoliberalism) ensures continued and accelerated control of local resources by powerful nations and individuals. The potential for social transformation lies in identifying first and foremost the voices from the margins, those most disproportionately affected by neoliberal economic globalization—hearing their stories and locating their points of articulation with other global networks and actors. Like Keck and Sikkink (1998), I believe there is potential in the power of social mobilization and especially with the ever-expanding transnational mobilizations that enable the world's citizens to witness and advocate from a distance (Ribeiro 1998). The concluding chapter attends to the "counterpunches" of Garifuna activists, who fearlessly call out political processes responsible for the widening gulf between haves and have-nots, those institutions and individuals responsible for disenfranchising Garifuna, and especially Garifuna women and youth. In the new millennium their efforts are bolstered by the unfortunate fact that the middle is now joining the bottom, instead of the trickle-down effect promised in the 1980s as nations worldwide embraced free-market liberal economic policies and structural adjustment programs.

This struggle is nothing new. It is the history of Garifuna peoples in Honduras. Our current moment in history is quite bleak, marked by global warming, water scarcity, food insecurity, warfare and increased global military spending, and financial crises; the list goes on. In many ways it feels like we have reached the edge of humanity. For many Garifuna women and children, the crushing reality of post-coup Honduras is one of despair, unrest, and insecurity. Yet people maintain their ability to act, and actions *can* be transformative in nature; they can lead to a reconfiguration of power relationships. Tsing (2005:266, 267) writes, "Finding hope has become more difficult in recent years. . . . [But] hope is most important when things are going badly in the world." Like Tsing's, my narrative is one of hope within a good deal of despair.

ONE

Identity, Labor, and the Banana Economy

Identity, power, and control of resources are intimately related. This statement crystallizes as the next few chapters tell the story of the Garifuna's diminishing control over coastal territories as the region and its natural resources became increasingly coveted by those with social, economic, and political power.

Identity is a social product, and people create their identity/ies through interactions with others as situated and symbolic beings. Individuals become "subjects" by occupying positions with meanings attached to them and recognizing the meaning attached to that identity category (Foucault 1979; Laclau and Mouffe 1985). For example, individuals who occupy the subject position of "Garifuna," a category that is recognized as unique and "cultural," begin to take meaning from their positioning within that identity category, as well as to transfer meaning back to that identity category. These processes further validate the notion that "being Garifuna" means something significantly different from "being mestizo" or "being Honduran."

Categories of people, who are identified and positioned in particular ways, receive differential access to resources and opportunities (Medina 2004:13). Garifuna identity categories have shifted over time, and these shifts are linked to the changing economic development approaches pursued in the coastal region. The Garifuna were excluded from Honduran national identity for a significant part of their time in the nation-state, but in the last few decades there have been efforts to integrate the area and its people into the Honduran nation, because both are seen as having economic potential. Both the Garifuna's culture and ancestral lands and natural resources are objectified within the discourses and practices of a "green developmentalism" (McAfee 1999) or "green neoliberalism" (Hanson 2007). Hence, identity politics are intimately tied to environmental governance models, the creation and implementation of agrarian law, and protected area management strategies, as well as resistance to neoliberal legislation and conservation models. As a stage-setter, this chapter lays the groundwork for what scholars of identity politics have long argued: identity and ethnic classifications are remarkably complex and susceptible to change.

Garifuna Ethnogenesis

The Garifuna are descendants of an intermixture of marooned African slaves and native Amerindians (Carib and Arawakan) groups that inhabited the Greater Antilles and parts of the South American mainland as early as 200 BC. While the Arawak economy was based on cassava (i.e., yuca) farming, hunting, and fishing, the Caribs were fishermen and warriors, but not agriculturalists. By around AD 1000, scholars theorize, resource scarcity forced some Arawakan groups to move down the Orinoco River to the Caribbean Sea and its islands. The Carib Indians later followed the path of the Arawaks, first trading with them, and then eventually conquering the Arawak-speaking groups that were already living on the islands (González 1988). Pushing the Arawaks onto smaller islands, the Carib arrivals took Arawakan women as wives and either killed or enslaved the men. Descendants of the ensuing generations of Carib men and Arawakan women became known as the Island Caribs (Cayetano and Cayetano 1997).

There are at least three accounts of how Africans became integrated into Carib society: (1) as shipwrecked slaves from the mid-seventeenth century, (2) as pre-Columbian early explorers (Van Sertima 1976), and (3) gradually, as escaped slaves and free blacks.[1] Ethnohistorians deny that there was a singular shipwreck that brought Africans to mix with the Island Caribs. Nancie González, the leading Garifuna ethnohistorian, shows that soon after their initial contact with Europeans, the Island Caribs began to absorb both European and African individuals into their society (González 1988). These individuals were either captured or simply adopted into the Island Carib society. González argues that the adoption of "others" was probably simply an extension of how they interacted in the past with other Amerindian groups. The extent of this integration eventually led to the creation of a new society that appeared to be racially and culturally distinct from the Island Carib. By 1700, or perhaps slightly earlier, this new society and culture began to be referred to by the British as the "Black Caribs," as opposed to the "Red" or "Yellow" Caribs (González 1988). The Black Caribs shared customs of the Island Caribs and intermarried with them. The Carib language served as a lingua franca for the Africans, who came from several different tribes. From this base, the Black Caribs incorporated Yoruba, French, and English words into their Arawak-Carib vocabulary, producing the Garifuna language. They later added Spanish words.

The fertile land of St. Vincent attracted both the British and the French, who each wanted to establish plantations on the island. In 1719 French settlers began to set up small tobacco, cotton, and sugarcane plantations on the island, but they did not attempt to force the Caribs off their land. The British wanted to set up large-scale plantations, which required removing the Caribs from the land. This conflict over land led to 32 years of war, with the French partnering with the Caribs against the British. By 1795 the British overpowered the Caribs, burning their homes, canoes, and crops, and in 1796 the latter finally surrendered. Upon surrender the British separated the Caribs according to color, sending the "yellow" (lighter-skinned) people back to St. Vincent, and deported almost two thousand Black (darker-skinned) Caribs to Roatan (an island off the coast of Honduras), likely separating family members from one another. The British made this distinction because they believed the lighter Caribs were of a different political and ethnic group than the Black Caribs, and thought them to be basically benign (González 1988:23).

A large percentage of the Black Caribs deported to Roatan soon chose to cross to the Central American mainland, arriving first in Trujillo and then spreading along the Atlantic coastline to establish settlements in Nicaragua, Honduras, Guatemala, and Belize. González (1988) cites the move from Roatan to the mainland as the point of Garifuna ethnogenesis. She claims that as they moved about seeking a better life, they absorbed other peoples' culture traits and emerged as a "neoteric" society. González's work reveals a complex genealogy of intermixture with West Indian, Miskito, and mestizo peoples of Central America, in addition to the Island Caribs. Today, Honduras has the largest Garifuna population in Central America, estimated at approximately 250,000, or 2 percent of the country's population. Forty-eight Garifuna communities dot the country's north coast.

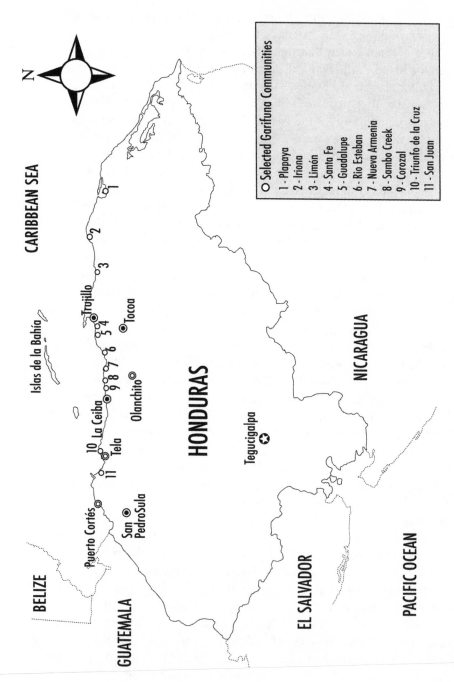

Figure 1.1 Honduras, with selected Garifuna communities. Map by Juan Mejia

Coastal Isolation, the Banana Economy, and Garifuna Displacement from Agricultural Lands

When the Garifuna arrived from Roatan to the north coast in 1797, they found a sparsely populated new homeland. The indigenous population had been decimated by warfare, disease, slavery, and dislocation (England 2006:37), and few Spaniards or ladinos wished to settle in a region with a seemingly inhospitable climate and unproductive landscape (England 2006:37–38). The sparse population had made this region particularly vulnerable to pirate attacks, and thus the landscape was marked by forts laying Spanish claim to the territory. Trujillo was one of the earliest of such forts, established in the 1500s. It had been destroyed by English and Dutch pirates in the mid-seventeenth century and remained nearly deserted for many years. By 1799 the first two mainland settlements—Rio Negro and Barrio Cristales—were established near Trujillo. Other early arrivals moved east and west along the coastline, establishing new villages at the mouths of rivers. In such locations, the Garifuna were able to exploit both marine and forest resources, reproducing many of the cultural traditions of their St. Vincent ancestors. Plots were located away from housing settlements, accessed on foot or by canoe. Women were the main cultivators of land, with male support in clearing and harvesting (England 2006:40).

In the 1890s the coast began its transformation into a central seat of US-owned banana companies and their plantations. Apart from the Garifuna, few lived in the region where the banana plantations were established. (Miskito settlements were in southeastern Honduras, bordering Nicaragua, and not near the territories that were transformed into plantations.) The Garifuna, who had a reputation for being industrious, strong, and hardworking, were incorporated into the fruit industry, hired to work as plantation laborers, as dock workers, and in railroad construction (González 1988).

In 1899 the United Fruit Company (UFCO) added Honduras as a new supply site for banana production, with the intention that the country would serve as an important link and spread the industry throughout Central America. The three major fruit companies that eventually came to dominate the Honduran coast were (1) the Vaccaros Brothers (later named the Standard Fruit Company), which operated in the region of La Ceiba, (2) the United Fruit Company near Tela and Trujillo, and (3) Cuyamel Fruit (taken over by the United Fruit Company in the late 1920s), which operated in the region of Puerto Cortes. The government granted them huge land subsidies for each kilometer of railroad track they constructed. While the government expected that the companies would eventually build a national rail system that linked the capital with the largely inaccessible Caribbean coast (Merrill 1993), they instead used the railroads to reach new coastal lands and transform them into expansive plantations. By the start of World War I, the banana companies had been granted 416,500 hectares (about 1,029,194 acres) of fertile land on the north coast (Ruhl 1984:39). As a result, the three companies eventually came to control the majority of good land on the Caribbean coast, owning 75 percent of all Honduran banana groves. Bananas accounted for 66 percent of all Honduran exports in 1913, making the companies extremely powerful players in Honduran politics. During the first half of the twentieth century, managers of the United Fruit Company and the Standard Fruit Company were perceived of as exerting as much power (if not more) as the Honduran President (Merrill 1993).

According to Euraque's (2003) review of historical documents, the Garifuna were important pioneers in the coastal communities of Tela (the seat of UFCO administration), La Ceiba (the home of Standard Fruit operations), and Trujillo (a major United Fruit center) and were actually some of the earliest banana growers. His research shows that by 1900, the Garifuna owned *ejidal* (community) land in Tela and that it remained in Garifuna hands into the 1910s. Moreover, historical records from Tela cite some Garifuna by name as early "capitalists," owning much of the land occupied by other Garifuna and West Indians in the black area of Tela (Euraque 2003:238). Similar reconsiderations of La Ceiba's history have found that Garifuna also held significant economic power there from the 1870s through the early 1920s.

While the Garifuna were landowners, they were arguably "community capitalists," not capitalists in the sense of individuals seeking self-advancement and profit. Their fundamental cultural orientation was and continues to be counterproductive to income generation through land exploitation. Rather than being ruled by the market, Garifuna buy and sell land through customary pricing (England 2006:48). Sale prices are based on a common understanding of what is fair, and anyone who goes above that price is socially stigmatized (England 2006:48). Land had also been exchanged through relationships of generalized reciprocity, and anyone practicing negative reciprocity was duly stigmatized. Without private title, use rights to communal land were sealed through the act of clearing the land in preparation for cultivation. Together these practices indicate that land historically was seen as a free resource, and very few Garifuna sought profit maximization through agricultural production or private ownership (England 2006:48).

Figure 1.2 Women on way to harvest. Photo by Keri Brondo

As the banana industry grew in success, corrupt officials on the coast began expropriating large tracts of land to either keep for themselves or sell to foreign companies. Burns (2005) cites an example from Trujillo in which Colonel Gustavo Alvarez, a local military commander, expropriated 2,000 hectares (approximately 4,942 acres) of Garifuna land and distributed it among wealthy landowners despite Garifuna protests. Garifuna were forced to abandon both residential areas and agricultural lands in the Tela area and nearby La Ceiba. Powerful ladinos sought governmental permission to access and exploit territory they deemed underutilized by the Garifuna, dismissing Garifuna production as "miniscule plantings" of the "moreno race" (historical sources quoted in Anderson 2009:83).

Ladinos with power used the Garifuna's culturally sanctioned tradition of a gendered division of labor in natural resource management against them to further justify their removal from coastal land (Anderson 2009:84). Garifuna men were positioned as "lazy savages," leaving the majority of agricultural work to women (their "beasts of burden") while they took to the sea to fish or to the forest to hunt (Anderson 2009:84). As Anderson

(2009:84) notes, those in power did not recognize the division of labor as culturally endorsed but instead used it to confirm the Garifunas' savage status and justify their displacement from prime agricultural lands.

Historically, the Garifuna practiced shifting agriculture, using fields for a certain number of years and then leaving them fallow while the soil recovered and became fertile again. The traditional gendered division of agricultural labor is such that men are typically responsible for preparing the soil through tilling, slashing, and burning, while women sow, care for, and harvest the crops. That said, in practice, some men also participate in sowing, caring for, and harvesting the crops. Once harvested, women had historically been solely responsible for the two-day processing of yuca, which involves peeling, grating, drying, and baking into *casabe* (i.e., cassava bread). The strict gendered division of labor has changed with the introduction of presses, and men can be found leeching the root of its poisonous starch and then grating the yuca.

Between the 1870s and the 1930s, the north coast territories experienced major population growth. By the 1930s, 20 percent of the country's population resided in coastal departments (compared to less than 5 percent during the nineteenth century) (Euraque 1998:155). The Garifuna communities—whose overall population had remained relatively constant between 1797 and 1935, ranging between 1 and 5 percent of the country's total population (Euraque 2003:242)—soon began to suffer from mestizo and foreign encroachment, as more and more individuals moved to the area in search of labor opportunities and economic growth. The banana companies also attracted foreigners from a variety of locations. British were hired into management, Arabs and Armenians became involved as merchants, and West Indians were hired as laborers.

The black British West Indian population grew significantly in the late nineteenth and early twentieth centuries, when the fruit companies expanded. People of African descent were considered the most effective workers in the industry because of their resistance to diseases like malaria, and they were known for having superior strength and endurance (Anderson 2000:131). The fruit companies favored West Indians because they were already skilled in banana cultivation, spoke English, had higher literacy levels, and were already acclimated to white authority and racism (Bourgois 1989). As such, West Indians became the answer to a perceived labor shortage, and they soon were the majority of Honduras's plantation workers. According to governmental reporting, in 1929 there were about 10 thousand West Indian workers in Honduras (Echeverri-Gent 1992:283). Moreover, British officials noted that companies actively

Figure 1.3. Woman grating *yuca*. Photo by Tara Sabi

Figure 1.4 Press in Rio Esteban, 2006. Photo by Tara Sabi, 2006.

recruited more workers than they could employ, resulting in a labor surplus and competition between workers of different identities and nationalities (Anderson 2000).

Garifuna Exclusion: The Black Threat and Indo-Hispanic National Identity

Work in the banana industry soon became a critical area of employment for Hondurans, and the national elite started pressuring the banana companies to hire Hispanic Hondurans. When mining, one of the nation's other principal export industries (albeit quite small in contrast to banana exports), declined in 1910, the pressure to find jobs for Hispanic Hondurans increased (Echeverri-Gent 1992:298). The overabundance of West Indian immigrants became a point of contention between the Hispanic Honduran population, the Honduran government, and the fruit companies. With the companies recruiting more West Indian workers than they could employ, the Hispanic Honduran population began to perceive the immigrants as stealing jobs from the "sons of the nation" (Anderson 2000:132). This growing resentment created a racist labor movement in which Hispanic Hondurans pushed for anti–West Indian policies (Echeverri-Gent 1992:298).

The movement grew throughout the first half of the twentieth century, becoming a widespread campaign against the immigrant blacks employed by the US-based fruit companies. Honduran papers were filled with letters and editorials protesting the presence of foreign blacks and calling for an immigration law to prohibit their entrance (Anderson 2000:112–113). British colonial officials who were stationed in Honduras documented the growing anti-black sentiment. For example, in the British correspondence reviewed by Echeverri-Gent (1992:300), British officials reported Hondurans declaring, "If the government doesn't get rid of [West Indian workers] they won't hesitate to do it themselves in bloodshed." Another document noted that "feelings on the North Coast are very strong against these coloured men, and a very strong article was recently published against the unwelcome immigration of coloured people, who, so the writer wished to point out, work for less wages than the native workmen, and consequently were robbing him of employment" (Echeverri-Gent 1992:300). All levels of society singled black workers out; even artisans in Tegucigalpa protested their presence (Echeverri-Gent 1992:304). Froylan Turcis, an elite from Tegucigalpa, published a series of editorials about the "unnecessary immigrants," citing the "danger" of racial mixture (Euraque 2003:243). The concern over immigration centered on the perceived moral and physical threat that blacks represented as a "race" (Anderson 2000). The following quote from one of the well-respected Honduran intellectuals of the time who was involved in the campaign against black immigrants is illustrative of this sentiment.

> But there is something worse in this African importation. There exists, each time more effective, each time more growing, the danger that over the course of years Honduras will be nothing but a nation of *mulattos*. Because the herd of blacks that the companies import, today in one form, tomorrow in another, making use of all kinds of excuses, are degenerating in alarming manner the Honduran race. [Protección a los nacionales, *El Pueblo*, March 10, 1931 (quoted in Anderson 2000:113)]

The national racist messages from the capital filtered down to the local level on the coast, influencing local officials—and police in particular, who frequently harassed black workers (Anderson 2000:135). Echeverri-Gent's (1992) historical review found reports of targeted racial violence. Great Britain maintained foreign offices in coastal towns to oversee their West Indian colonial subjects. While British authorities documented a series of abuses, they seem to have offered little direct (physical) protection to the West Indians. For example, in the 1910 "*La Masica*" incident, a Honduran officer and the men under his command gratuitously killed three and wounded three other West Indians who worked for Vaccaros Brothers. In 1912 a West Indian who refused to do forced labor in La Ceiba had a dead body "tied to his neck and both were dragged along by chain fastened to his hands" (British report quoted in Echeverri-Gent 1992:299). British authorities pressed these cases and formally demanded compensation for the death of its colonial subject in the latter incident. The case was submitted to the king of Spain for arbitration, and in 1917 the king ruled in favor of Great Britain (Echeverri-Gent 1992:299). The courts found Honduran officials and the fruit companies at fault for the death. Great Britain likely expected that the Honduran government would suffer political and economic costs, which in turn would lead it to pressure local officials into improving their relations with the British West Indian labor. Unfortunately, the ruling did not have this outcome, and the racially charged violence continued.

Several administrations attempted to curb West Indian immigration altogether as a means to eliminate the racial tensions. In 1914 British correspondence reported that the Honduran government planned to stop labor recruitment from the West Indies. In 1916 they threatened to deport West Indian workers, and in September of that year, the Ministry of War issued orders that no black workers were to disembark (Echeverri-Gent 1992). Then, in 1917, the Honduran government requested that the UFCO repatriate its black labor force. The company refused, telling the Honduran government that if it wanted to deport the black workers, it would have to do so itself. In 1921 President Lopez Gutiérrez prohibited the entry of black British subjects, stating that they were unfairly replacing Honduran labor (Echeverri-Gent 1992:300–330).

In 1923, the Federación Obrera Hondureña (Federation of Honduran Workers, or FOH), which was established by artisans from Tegucigalpa, introduced legislation seeking to prohibit the importation of Negroes, Africans, and coolies (East Indians), to deport all those who had been brought in by the companies, and to issue identification cards to all "Negroes" and "coolies" (Euraque 1998:157, 2003:244). The banana companies and embassies of the United States and Britain opposed the bill as well as subsequent bills, and all failed to pass. However, Honduran officials supported the antiblack movement and the deportation of West Indians, and in 1924, several ships with West Indian immigrants were sent back to their ports of origin without being allowed to dock (Echeverri-Gent 1992:301).

The movement against blacks gained significant momentum in this decade due to massive immigration of Salvadorans who came to Honduras in search of land and jobs. By the end of the decade there were over twelve thousand Salvadoran immigrants, representing 10 percent of the labor force. These immigrants were incorporated into the labor movement, serving as key activists united with mestizo Hondurans as Hispanic Central Americans against West Indians. By the mid-1920s the movement became violent, resulting in armed mobs in the streets of Trujillo in July 1924. Strikes broke out on plantations, with mestizo workers threatening black workers with machetes if they did not leave the country. Two black workers were killed, and many others were stabbed. British foreign officials began patrolling the area in an attempt to protect the black workers, because, according to British historical records, these violent outbreaks appeared to have received support from Honduran local officials. The support of local officials made it difficult for the banana companies to pacify the strikers. In an effort to avoid a massacre, the companies boarded over a thousand black workers onto a Norwegian steamboat (Echeverri-Gent 1992). Tensions continued and in 1929 Hispanic Honduran laborers began organizing to "take matters into their own hands" (British official quoted in Echeverri-Gent 1992:303) in Trujillo, Tela, and La Ceiba.

By the 1930s, although racism did not disappear, two events caused the influx of "new blacks" to slow. First, the 1929 immigration law institutionalized racism by restricting the arrival of a variety of identified "races" (*negro, árabe, china, turca, siria, Armenia, palestina, coolie*) by charging the immigrants heavy—and therefore unaffordable—entrance fees and deposits (Euraque 2003). At the same time, the depression and banana disease caused recession among the fruit companies, further slowing immigration. In the 1930s, much of the West Indian population was reduced; many returned home or migrated to other countries (Anderson 2000:136). However, the discrimination against West Indian blacks on the coast certainly had an impact on the treatment and representation of the Garifuna.

The Garifuna were the first stable black population employed by the banana companies, and their labor remained critical for longer than most other historical records suggest. Although the Garifuna probably did not make up the majority of the four thousand or so workers in the banana economy between the 1890s and 1910s, given their numerical presence on the coast, it is likely that their numbers in the industry were higher than early records stated (Euraque 2003). Specifically, Euraque (2003) argues that the banana companies probably confused black West Indians with Garifuna in their official counts. In her account of Garifuna ethnohistory, González (1988) also notes their importance in the banana economy between the 1890s and 1930s but claims that in those later years, the Garifuna left plantation and dock work and returned to their communities, leaving the work to the newly recruited West Indians, Indios, and mixed-race Hondurans. Euraque agrees that there probably was an exodus of Garifuna labor beginning around the late 1910s and early 1920s, as it coincided with the Salvadoran immigration.

Euraque (2003:239) argues that given their coastal numbers, the "black threat" articulated in the 1920s labor movement and directed toward the British West Indians was likely an outgrowth of the internal and local threat posed by the Garifuna population to the national elite. Specifically, he suggests that as the original occupants of the rich coastal lands, the Garifuna were perceived as a threat to the Hispanic Honduran growers who sought to extend their holdings in the 1910s and 1920s. Euraque claims that the threat of limited access to the coastal economy was one of the causes behind the creation of an Indo-Hispanic nationalist identity discourse in the 1920s.

The triumph of a mestizo Honduras by the 1930s was the ideological result of a process of social and economic change that brought foreign capital and foreign immigrants to Honduras's north coast and threatened, on many levels, the elites' domination of their country. Elites and the Honduran state were too weak politically and economically to challenge or reject foreign capital; thus, they attempted to reassert their dominance, at least in the ideological sphere, by asserting a national unity based on a homogeneous Honduran mestizo race and excluding, in particular, the West Indian immigrants brought in by the banana companies but also the indigenous north coast Garifuna populations, and by the early twentieth century, *mestizo* came to represent a particular kind of "mixed" person, that is, a person of "Indian" and "Spanish" miscegenation, and hence different from the broader range of miscegenation suggested by the term *ladino* (Euraque 1998:152, 155). The newly created national identity categories thus emerged in response to the threat posed by the Garifuna as original occupants of coastal territories, and purposefully excluded blacks (West Indians and Garifuna) in order to maintain the position of power for Hispanic elites.

Two key symbolic events signaled this reimagining and recategorization of the nation's populace. First, in 1926, the Honduran legislature named the national currency the lempira, after an indigenous leader who died resisting the conquest, thus making an Indian a national hero and symbol of Honduran identity. Then, in 1930, Honduras reflected this transformation in its official census data, declaring that the majority of the population was mestizo. For Euraque (1998), these two events signaled the state construction of an indo-Hispanic nation, introducing a new pride in having an indigenous racial heritage and separating Hondurans as a unified group from both US and British elites. Importantly, this indo-Hispanic mestizaje denied and negated the presence of blackness within Honduras. Given the Garifuna's historical control over coastal territories, the state's positioning (or exclusion) of Garifuna subject identity in this fashion makes sense.

Since the beginning of the nineteenth century, given that the locus of the political and economic elite was concentrated inland, the Garifuna had de facto control over significant tracts of land in the coastal region. With the beginning of the banana plantations, blacks—both the Garifuna and the imported British West Indians—held the corner on the coastal labor market, because the US fruit companies perceived them as "better workers." Antiblack resentment grew as Hispanic Hondurans felt they were passed over for employment in favor of "non-Hondurans." While elite Honduran politicians had an interest in seeing coastal land remain available for the banana companies (because they received economic support in return), they also had an interest in unifying the nation against the US companies that dominated the region. Euraque argues that the emergence of an Indo-Hispanic mestizaje that negated the presence of blackness in the Honduran mestizo identity, while highlighting the contributions of Indians, was linked to elite attempts at exerting their power and control over the coastal economy. Once the coast became a major source of revenue, and industries such as mining began to decline, elites turned their attention to the region. The Garifuna became a threat to elites because they occupied and utilized prime resources; and because they shared phenotypic similarities with the black West Indians, they suffered discrimination from Hispanic Central Americans who were competing with them for high-paying jobs in the banana industry. The denial of blackness in the Honduran national identity gave reason to deprive the Garifuna of land and commercial opportunities in coastal towns such as Tela and La Ceiba. As blacks, they were not considered to be true members of the Honduran state. They did not "belong" and therefore did not have rights to the land.

The way in which the fruit companies classified the Garifuna further supported the notion that they were not true Hondurans. Employee statistics from the Standard Fruit Company in 1915 included six categories of workers: *Hondureños, Morenos, Italianos, Americanos, Negros Americanos y de Jamaica,* and *Diferentes Naciones*; the Garifuna were included as *Morenos* (Anderson 2009:86). This categorization meant that they were identified as a group *separate* from the Honduran nation, not as a subcategory (such as *Moreno Hondureño*) or as having a nation of their own (Anderson 2009: 87). Hence, they were positioned in an ambiguous state, neither fully Honduran nor fully foreign (because their natal country was unclear to mestizo Hondurans).

With the denial of a national identity and given the typical conflation of Garifuna with other blacks and the association of blackness as a signal of backwardness and a threat to the Honduran nation, the Garifuna occupied a precarious position of racial-cultural "other" within the Honduran nation-state. They remained at the bottom of both the racial and class hierarchies on the coast, below the racial-cultural class of the mestizos and foreign immigrants who ran commerce and industry, and in a lower labor class than the West Indians within the fruit companies (Anderson 2009:86–89).[2]

Since their arrival in Honduras in 1797, the Garifuna have been positioned and have positioned themselves within particular subject categories. The Garifuna historically controlled much of the north coast through de facto ownership as occupants and users of coastal lands and were met with little to no interference from the political and economic elite through the 1800s. Their presence on the coast was inconsequential to the nation-state until the growth of the banana industry, when they entered into an economic relationship with the dominant classes of Honduran and foreign society as employees. While the banana companies, local elites, and military dominated significant tracts of coastal lands, the Garifuna were still able to continue cultivating their individual plots for the better part of the twentieth century, because the area's population density remained relatively low.

As Hispanic Hondurans realized the economic value of work or trade in bananas, blacks came to be positioned as stealing jobs from "the sons of the nation," which led the political elite to spearhead a new nationalist identity in the 1920s. This new identity privileged indigenous and European heritages, and not African heritage. Blackness was denied as part of the emergent Indo-Hispanic mestizo populace's identity, because blackness represented the foreign others (British West Indians) who held coveted positions in the banana industry. Thus, through the creation and deployment of this type of national identity, those in power attempted to maintain control over key coastal resources and limit the ability of blacks to access resources and opportunities. This new form of mestizaje attempted to eliminate class boundaries between mestizos, unifying the elite with the poor, and supported the mobilization of poor, jobless mestizos against coastal blacks.

The next chapter reviews how in the decades following the decline of the banana industry, the Garifuna began to articulate an Afro-Honduran autochthonous ethnic identity, asserting their rights as equal citizens within the nation-state. As the historical power holders marched toward a neoliberal economic development model in the 1980s and beyond, an Afro-Honduran ethnic status became insufficient to combat the effects of deregulatory agrarian legislation on the Garifuna population, and an afro-indigenous identity emerged in its place. As the identity politics literature demonstrates, indigeneity, like other racial-ethnic categories, is constructed and susceptible to change; and "blacks" can also be indigenous in the Americas (Anderson 2007, 2009; French 2009; Greene 2007a, 2007b; N'gweno 2007; Safa 2006, 2005). The next chapter links the shift toward neoliberal development policy and growth of the tourism industry to the formation of Garifuna indigeneity, the emergence of which has afforded the Garifuna certain resource rights not granted to other racial-ethnic populations.

TWO

Development and Territorialization on the North Coast

This chapter provides an account of changing political-economic structures in Honduras and on the north coast from the 1950s to the 1990s, and their relationship to developments in Garifuna activism. In the 1950s the organized labor movement changed from an antiblack movement to one that explicitly addressed racial discrimination against blacks. This shift in the labor movement, combined with the emergence of civil rights discourse, created new articulations of identity, and the Garifuna began to assert themselves as Afro-Hondurans, and therefore an equal part of the Honduran citizenry. In the decades to follow, the rights the Garifuna built up through alliances with other ethnic minorities would become threatened as the Honduran nation-state joined the global march toward neoliberal governance. The economic development policies of the 1980s forward—especially those in the agricultural sector—permanently altered Garifuna communities, their relationships to ancestral territories, and cultural autonomy. Garifuna activism expanded in reaction to issues of land and resource control, bolstered by a strategic identification of the Garifuna as an ethnic group similar to Honduras's recognized indigenous groups.

Shifts in the Coastal Economy and Population: 1950s–80

Between 1930 and 1961, the Honduran population more than doubled, reaching 1,875,000. From 1945 to 1969, some 300,000 Salvadoran peasants (about 7 percent of the Salvadoran population) migrated to Honduras in search of land and labor. By the late 1960s these Salvadorans constituted 12 percent or more of the Honduran population. The mountainous nature of the country, combined with the fact that a significant number of Hondurans relied on agriculture because there were very limited labor options, meant that Honduras was facing a land shortage by the 1960s. Families were forced to subdivide their plots for their children, resulting in the inability of farmers with smaller plots to leave their fields fallow, which reduced the soil fertility and lessened productivity (Ruhl 1984:39). By 1965, a total of 63,120 rural families (26 percent of the rural population) were landless. Land conflicts with the Salvadoran immigrants grew in the west of the nation, resulting in a brief war in July 1969 (Norsworthy and Barry 1993).[1]

In addition to the population growth, the dominant development paradigm, "modernization," reached Honduras in the 1960s and 1970s, altering the Garifuna's de facto coastal land ownership. In an effort to "modernize" the agricultural sector, international lending institutions offered credit to landowners willing to invest in large-scale mechanized production of export crops (England 2006:110). Credit for agricultural modernization was theoretically available to all Hondurans, but in practice only large landowners of the elite class with military and political connections could take advantage of the credit (Durham 1979; England 2006; Stonich 1993). Mechanized cotton production in southern Honduras expanded through the elite classes, pushing peasant sharecroppers (who were bought out or evicted from their lands) from southern Honduras to the sparsely populated north coast in search of land and alternative livelihoods (England 2006:111).

In the 1970s beef and sugar became major exports, causing land pressures to intensify (Ruhl 1984:40). The country's cattle production more than tripled between 1950 and 1980, and elite landowners expanded their coastal landholdings, exacerbating land inequities. Land for the expanding cattle industry became available when the banana companies began returning some of their land to the government in the 1950s. Cattle ranching can occur in a wide range of ecological conditions, and even the marginal lands and forests on the coast were taken over for this purpose.

Without any government-directed land reform in place in the early 1970s, poor Hondurans turned to illegal squatting as a means to gain land. There was growing unrest in the highlands as thousands of landless peasants engaged in illegal occupations on unused lands, attempting to push the government into resurrecting its 1962 agrarian reform law. There had been extremely slow progress with land distribution since the 1962 law was passed, and growing frustration among peasant groups.

In 1974 Hurricane Fifi destroyed 60 percent of Honduras's agricultural production, and the banana companies abandoned many more of their plantations. The north coast became a resettlement area for landless and jobless mestizo peasants, and the region experienced a major population increase. Resettlement was encouraged through the passage of new agrarian legislation that would further modernize the agricultural sector. The 1974 agrarian reforms were intended to convert large and small landholdings into large and medium-scale commercial enterprises. Unused national and private lands were to be redistributed to peasant cooperatives and associative enterprises that had access to credit and technical assistance (England 2006:111). However, rather than threaten the agrarian bourgeoisie, the National Agrarian Institute (Instituto Nacional Agrario, or INA) instead encouraged displaced peasants to migrate to areas where land tenure was unclear—the north coast and La Mosquitia. The INA's very understanding of development enabled the large-scale expropriation of Garifuna lands. Viewing the subsistence agricultural practices of the Garifuna and other indigenous populations as unproductive and backward, and thus lacking a "social function" (i.e., agricultural production for the market or cattle ranching, resource extraction), the INA justified the expropriation of Garifuna territory (England 2006:112).

Thousands of peasants were brought to the coast via the INA's Bajo Aguán colonization project. The banana companies abandoned the Aguán River Valley, and the INA brought 45,000 families to the region to work in cooperatives dedicated to bananas, pineapple, grapefruit, and coconut (Jones 1990). By 1978 nearly 30 percent of the 45,000 families had abandoned the area, and many of them settled on land in the Cordillera Nombre de Diós region (Jones 1990). This mountain range is located in the department of Atlántida, bordering the coastal Garifuna communities. Sambeños cultivated mountain land as recently as 1980. The influx of land-seeking ladinos to the north coast forced the Garifuna into legalizing their holdings as individual private owners, as unclaimed lands were under threat of expropriation and redistribution by the INA. Since the INA did not recognize the Garifuna practice of fallowing fields and mixed-crop swidden agriculture as a "social function" use of the land (England 2006:48), the Garifuna lost significant tracts of coastal land that had been utilized and maintained for over a century through generational use rights.

Garifuna Migration and Black Autochthony

Migration has long been a part of Garifuna society, beginning with seasonal migration in Central America in the 1800s and early 1900s, and expanding to include migration to the United States since the 1950s. Research on Garifuna migration (e.g., England 2006; González 1988; Kerns 1983) suggests that poverty was not a motivating force behind their labor migration until recent decades. Rather, the Garifuna used migration to obtain industrial goods and supplement their already adequate subsistence economy (England 2006:33). Garifuna migration to the United States grew immensely after the decline of banana production, and returning migrants brought ideas back with them to the Honduran coast, including those associated with political mobilization in the United States.

In the 1950s the north coast became a center for newly created labor unions and political parties that centered on protecting the proletariat (Anderson 2000:164).[2] The newly defined labor movement championed workers' rights against foreign capitalist domination. It was at this point that the *negro* (Garifuna and English-speaking blacks) gained a voice in the labor movement (Anderson 2000; Centeno Garcia 1997).

In 1958 Honduras's first black organization, La Sociedad Cultural Abraham Lincoln, was formed. This organization closely identified with the civil rights movement in the United States and focused on combating racism in schools, public places, and the workplace (Centeno Garcia 1997:84). The organization's identification with the US political climate demonstrates the close ties Honduran blacks had with the United States. Unfortunately, the achievements of La Sociedad Cultural Abraham Lincoln were short-lived, as a military coup in the early 1960s forced "leftist" organizations to disband. However, its leaders continued to remain politically active internationally, forming transnational alliances on the basis of an African diasporic identity. Civil rights and black identity had become powerful political tools, and it was around this time that Honduran Garifuna began to identify and represent themselves as "Afro-Honduran."

In 1977 former key leaders of the Sociedad Cultural Abraham Lincoln formed OFRANEH. Garifuna activists began to call attention to the discriminatory practices of the Honduran political and economic elite, noting how the national elite had positioned the Garifuna as "other" or non-Honduran, thus limiting their access to resources and opportunities. These activists recast the Garifuna subject in a way that made explicit their unique identity category (as "black" and "native") and their historical presence in Honduran territory.

In the 1980s, Garifuna identity took on a new form, as activists cast the Garifuna as both "black" and "autochthonous." Most dictionaries define *autochthonous* as either "native" or "indigenous," thus complicating analysis of the differences between the two. However, the *Oxford English Dictionary* gives a more elaborate definition of the word, explaining that autochthonous beings are "any of the earliest known dwellers in a region" or "human being living in his or her place of origin." In Spanish, the word has the same connotations of deep rootedness to a particular place. An autochthonous identity signifies a "native" identity but does not have the same racial connotations as *indigenous*, in that *indigenous* is typically used to describe the descendants of the original inhabitants of the Americas (i.e., those encountered by Columbus) (see also Anderson 2009:12–13). By the late 1980s, Honduran Garifuna realized that by asserting an autochthonous identity they could make primordial claims similar to those of indigenous groups, while still maintaining their racial identification as black.

From this time period on, autochthony served as an umbrella identity under which all native peoples, regardless of phenotype, origin, and identity, can (and do) unite to make demands on the government. The proposed Law for the Protection of Autochthonous Ethnic Groups provides an example. In July 1987, Garifuna, Miskito, Xicaques, Pech, and English-speaking blacks proposed this law. Within it were a series of demands, including the reclamation and titling of lands, the right to control resources located within their territories, the right to bilingual and bicultural education, recognition of traditional forms of organization, and the guarantee of political participation in the National Congress (Anderson 2009:122). Although the Law for the Protection of Autochthonous Ethnic Groups did not pass, it outlined the key struggles of Honduras's autochthonous groups. The Garifuna experience as marginalized "other" is similar to that of indigenous groups, and therefore all groups share common goals and positions vis-à-vis national and international powers. The successful recasting of the Garifuna as black autochthonous peoples was solidified through the creation of institutionally recognized government committees, including the Comité Asesor para el Desarrollo de las Etnias Autóctonos de Honduras (the Council for the Support of the Development of Indigenous Groups in Honduras), or CADEAH, and the Confederación de Pueblos Autóctonos de Honduras (the Confederation of Indigenous Peoples of Honduras), or CONPAH, which was formed in 1992.

Development in Garifuna Territory: 1980s and Beyond

It sounds like a strong statement, but Honduras is a country that does not have its own economic policy. The real policy comes from the International Monetary Fund (IMF), the World Bank, the Inter-American Development Bank (IDB) and the three main bilateral aid agencies, among them the US Agency for International Development (USAID). Economic debate . . . is not part of Honduran democracy. (Calderón et al. 2002:10).

Throughout the 1980s Honduras was largely a puppet of Washington and US-directed policies. The state was surrounded by turmoil in Nicaragua, El Salvador, and Guatemala, and it was selected to serve as a stable platform for US interventionism in the region (Norsworthy and Barry 1993). Huge amounts of US aid and military troops flooded the country, serving to maintain economic stability in Honduras, while enabling the US to conduct counterinsurgency operations to destabilize Nicaragua. When the United States withdrew its military aid in 1989, Honduras's economy plummeted. The effects on unemployment and livelihoods were brutal. By 1995 employment in the agricultural sector had dropped to 37 percent, down from 57 percent in 1980 (England 2006:117). The rural population was living on less than two hectares of land, earning approximately $70 per year. The urban population did not fare much better, making a living in the informal sector or in poorly paid service jobs. By 1991 only 10 percent of the Honduran population held secure employment in the formal sector (England 2006; Merrill 1993).

A new economic elite with close ties to USAID began to organize itself in the 1980s, creating the foundation for a full-scale transformation to state-sponsored neoliberalism in the 1990s. Throughout the 1980s, key business leaders established a variety of think tanks and private-sector associations. The focus of these emerging associations was on creating a different way of doing business, including the development of new economic-sector activities such as the promotion of nontraditional exports under neoliberal social and economic policies (Robinson 2003:125). These capitalist groups extended their reach into both state and civil society, and as the decade progressed, they moved into direct political mobilization, including the establishment of their own party faction, the Rafael Callejas Nationalist Movement (Robinson 2003:127). Callejas came from one of the wealthiest families in the country and was an agricultural economist, banker, and investor (Robinson 2003:127).

The full-on turn to neoliberalism occurred in 1989 when Callejas (1990–94) was elected to presidency. Within weeks of his election, Callejas introduced an economic reform package that he had negotiated prior to his election with the World Bank, USAID, and the Inter-American Development Bank. The Structural Adjustment Program included the devaluation of the lempira by 50 percent, tax increases on consumption, elimination of price controls, tariff reductions and abolitions, cuts to the public-sector workforce, and the advancement of privatization (Robinson 2003:129). Accompanying these economic reforms was the increase of transnational capital through the entry and immediate expansion of *maquiladoras*. Both the state and private-sector consortiums (through which Callejas was backed) opened several new export processing zones ("free zones") in the early 1990s. The expansion of the maquiladora industry solidified the transition of Honduran elite from a landed oligarchy to a business elite. The 1990s were marked by deteriorating socioeconomic conditions, rising crime, and growing proletarianization as a new working class of service workers and maquiladora employees emerged and expanded. These symptoms associated with the ever-widening gap between rich and poor that characterize neoliberal globalization were all the more apparent in the face of conspicuous consumption by the new upper classes and elite (Robinson 2003:132).

The subsequent administrations of Carlos Roberto Reina (1993–97) and Carlos Roberto Flores Facusse (1998–2002) continued structural adjustment programs. During Reina's presidency, the government endorsed a program of the Facusse Group (one of the prominent families within the new business elite) called "the Great National Transformation Project" (Gran Proyecto de Transformación, or GPTN). This program created a "Super Free Trade Zone" that made virtually every part of the country open to transnational investors and enabled major expansion of nontraditional exports and tourism (Robinson 2003:129).

Ricardo Rodolfo Maduro Joest (2002–6) continued efforts to meet the demands of multilateral lending agencies, and under his administration, Honduras received some debt relief. However, it was during the Maduro administration that Honduras ratified the US Central America Free Trade Agreement, further spreading neoliberal economic logic and Central American integration.

The turn to dependence on multilateral aid agencies and their mandated development policies had serious effects on Garifuna landholding. Beginning in the 1990s, several neoliberal agrarian legislative acts were passed to "modernize" the agricultural sector and promote diversification in the coastal economy, including the development of the tourism industry.

Before 1992 none of Honduras's Garifuna communities held definitive land titles. The first titles to be granted to Garifuna communities were titles of occupation, issued by the INA in the 1970s when their communities attempted to formalize holdings to avoid further ladino encroachment. However, titles of occupation are not secure documents; they merely state that a group of people occupies the land. They do not grant ownership of that land to those people. Titles of occupation include only the areas in which homes and community infrastructure are constructed. Thus, cultivation lands, harvest lands, and territories of spiritual significance are not included in the titles.

Despite significant levels of mestizo encroachment on Garifuna cultivation territory, their ancestral properties were somewhat protected under Article 107 of the Honduran Constitution. Article 107 of the (1982) Honduran constitution states

> The land belonging to the State, the municipalities, communities or private property located in the areas bordering other states, or in the littoral of both seas, in an extension of 40 kilometers inland and in the islands, keys, reefs, sand banks, (etc.) may only be owned, possessed, or had under any title, by Hondurans by birth or by companies formed entirely by Honduran shareholders and by institutions of the state. [Author's translation from Spanish][3]

Because the land occupied by the Garifuna falls within 40 kilometers of the coast or cays, the article, by default, protects them from the threat of foreign ownership of that land. Yet savvy investors still get around this by pursuing joint ventures with Honduran partners, and expatriates have gained control over other properties through marriage arrangements with local women.

In 1990, recognizing that the constitutional prohibition of foreign property ownership was a barrier to the development of tourism and the economic potential of Honduras's coastal and island areas, the Honduran Congress passed Decree Law 90/90, which enabled foreigners to purchase properties in areas designated by the Ministry of Tourism to be tourism zones. Under the decree, foreigners were authorized to purchase up to 3,000 square meters for residential use in urban areas, and unlimited amounts in urban or rural areas for tourism or other development projects.[4] Since the passing of Decree 90/90, the purchase of land in coastal zones and the Bay Islands has boomed (Stonich 2000). People have also found legal means to get around the limit on 3,000 square meters for residential properties, such as forming Honduran stock corporations in which they name Hondurans as the original shareowners.

The passage of Decree 31-92, the Law for the Modernization and Development of the Agricultural Sector (Ley para la Modernizacion y Desarrollo del Sector Agricula, or LMA), in 1992 further facilitated the privatization of coastal lands. The LMA promoted foreign and domestic investment in agriculture by accelerating land titling and enabling land cooperative members to break up their holdings into small plots to be sold as private lands. The LMA was originally drafted by USAID and had three principal objectives: (1) to eliminate state intervention in the agrarian sector, (2) to limit expropriations and promote private ownership, and (3) to promote new foreign and domestic investment in agriculture (because the law was intended to increase the amount of secure [legally titled] land available on the market). As a result, many smallholders suffering from economic hardship chose to sell their land to wealthier landowners and to the giant banana producers, who desperately wanted to expand their landholdings (Norsworthy and Barry 1993). The companies needed additional land to increase production and meet an anticipated new demand from the European Union (Merrill 1993).

Like the agrarian reforms of the 1970s that defined agricultural resources in terms of "social function" (which meant agricultural productivity or resource extraction), the LMA further marginalized smallholders and the subsistence strategies of indigenous peoples. But this time the tenets of neoliberalism prevailed, and the legislation privileged the law of supply and demand, creating a market in land and transitioning the countryside to capitalist agriculture. Juan Ramón Martínez, the former president of the INA who resigned from his post in opposition to this law, argued that it is "fundamentally a counter agrarian reform designed to halt land access by *campesinos*, derailing the capacity to develop their organizations either as unions or economically, and passes the management of the agrarian conflict from the government to private individuals" (quoted in Norsworthy and Barry 1993:78).

The LMA legalized the process of land privatization in favor of investment, providing an impetus for the increased privatization of land that the Garifuna had historically utilized by foreigners interested in tourism and housing development. According to Garifuna activists, the lack of definitive property titles led national and international businessmen, military, and politicians to harass Garifuna into abandoning their land as well as strategically declare ancestral harvest and cultivation lands for tourism development.

ILO 169, Garifuna Activism and Communal Titling Initiatives

In 1994 Honduras became a signatory of the 1989 Convention (No. 169) Concerning Indigenous and Tribal Peoples in Independent Countries of the International Labor Organization (commonly referred to as ILO 169). ILO 169 was written to pressure nation-states to enact special legislation for the rights of "indigenous and tribal peoples" to land, bilingual education, political and economic autonomy, and fair labor practices. Ratifying ILO 169 into law created a legal mechanism through which the Garifuna could make claims to territory both currently and traditionally occupied, as well as officially declaring the state's role in securing land rights for the Garifuna and ensuring that traditional law and rights be protected.

ILO 169's definition of the groups protected by the convention is rather loose, applying to tribal peoples, indigenous peoples, and peoples present prior to colonization who have continued to retain "traditional" cultural institutions. The convention states that it applies to

(a) Tribal peoples in independent countries whose social, cultural and economic conditions distinguish them from other sections of the national community, and whose status is regulated wholly or partially by their own customs or traditions or by special laws or regulations; (b) Peoples in independent countries who are regarded as indigenous on account of their descent from the populations which inhabited the country, or a geographical region to which the country belongs, at the time of conquest or colonisation or the establishment of present State boundaries and who, irrespective of their legal status, retain some or all of their own social, economic, cultural and political institutions (International Labor Organization 1989).

Honduras's ratification of the ILO 169 convention was a direct result of the successful mobilization of groups who built alliances on the basis of a shared autochthonous identity. On October 12, 1992 (El Día de la Raza), indigenous and Garifuna organizations marched on the capital, making the first of many public calls demanding that the government ratify and implement the ILO Convention. CONPAH, ODECO, and OFRANEH continued to lobby President Callejas's administration. Finally, in 1994, under President Reina, ILO 169 was ratified into law. At this time, an attorney-general of the ethnic groups (Fiscal de las Etnias) was established to represent and protect the rights of ethnic groups vis-á-vis the state and powerful private interests. ILO 169 created a legal mechanism through which the Garifuna could contest neoliberal agrarian legislation, as the nation-state became tasked with recognizing collective rights. Garifuna leaders cite Honduras's ratification of it as a defining moment for Garifuna land claims.

The preamble of ILO 169 recognizes the right of indigenous peoples to maintain control over their institutions, ways of life, economic development, identities, languages, and religions within their state's frameworks

(Anaya 1996: 48). Land is central, because without control over territory, indigenous peoples have no control over economic development. Moreover, land is tied to the maintenance of cultural identity. The second part of the convention (i.e., Articles 13–19) deals explicitly with indigenous land rights. Article 13 declares that governments respect the cultural and spiritual value that indigenous peoples attach to their lands, territories, or both and, in particular, the collective nature of that relationship. The remaining articles make clear that indigenous peoples be afforded their rights not just to land occupied by them, but also to areas that they had traditionally accessed for subsistence and other activities. Governments are tasked with safeguarding and guaranteeing the protection of indigenous rights to ownership and are called upon to adopt "adequate procedures . . . within the national legal system to resolve land claims by the peoples concerned" (International Labor Organization 1989).

When Honduras signed ILO 169 into national law in 1994, it may have served to legitimize Garifuna land claims, but it did not implore the INA to work aggressively to title Garifuna lands. Between 1993 and 1995, and arguably only because of Garifuna lobbying, only 14 of the 48 Garifuna communities obtained definitive titles. Moreover, the titles that communities received did not cover their historical landholdings, and any part of a community's land that was deemed appropriate for housing construction or tourism development was redefined as property of the state under Decree 90/90. The Garifuna and the organizations that represented them thus continued their mobilization efforts.

On October 11, 1996, which is La Día de la Raza ("the Day of the Race" or Columbus Day), several thousand Garifuna traveled to the capital city and staged a massive protest, demanding that the government take action to produce land titles for Garifuna communities. Protesters drummed, danced the punta, and shouted slogans such as "The Earth is our mother" and "A people united can never be defeated" (Anderson 2000:231). The protest has since become known as La Primera Gran Marcha Pacífica del Pueblo Negro de Honduras (the First Great Peaceful March of Black Hondurans). Leaders of Garifuna organizations united on this day and met with President Reina and other government representatives. After only a few hours of negotiation, the Garifuna leaders emerged with a signed agreement to resolve the land problem. This was the first agreement in Honduran history between the government and Afro-Honduran communities. It established three streams of action: *titulación* (titling), *saneamiento* (regularization) and *ampliación* or *dotación* (extension). Land titling, or the legal documentation of a community's possession of lands, granted through the INA, was the first process to begin. The process of saneamiento, or the procedure to determine the legal owners of lands within the community limits, is currently under way in a number of communities. This process is long and complicated, because its goal is to determine which lands have been illegally occupied, and by whom. Unfortunately, land that was "irregularly" obtained, such as stolen lands or harvest lands that were obtained through squatter's rights but are now held under a legal title, do not fit the category of "illegally occupied land" and therefore cannot be reclaimed under the saneamiento process. However, there are many illegally held plots of land that communities can reclaim. Often, large landowners will extend their land on all sides, constructing a private gate around the periphery and stopping community members from accessing the land. This has occurred in Sambo Creek and is described in chapter 4. The process of *ampliación*, or authorizing more lands in favor of communities that require it for growth and development, has been requested by a number of communities, including Sambo Creek.

As a result of the October 11, 1996, march, the government allotted 1.7 million lempiras ($131,000) to the INA for work on the titling of Garifuna lands. On January 11, 1997, the Instituto de Antropología e Historia (the Institute of Anthropology and History) donated 200,000 more lempiras ($15,385). Since then, 38 more titles have been issued, totaling 52 Garifuna titles, including communal and cooperative landholdings. All titles have been of *domino pleno* (definitive titles of ownership) and are communal titles, which means that the land cannot be sold and can only be passed through inheritance to members of the community.

Despite what appears to be significant achievements in terms of securing land for the Garifuna, the land titles excluded ancestral territory. Land titles are seen as leading to enhanced security of land tenure, thus promoting investment and rejuvenating the land market. Formal land titles are crucial, because without security of land rights, it is difficult to attract foreign investors to enter new markets. Economists studying Honduran agricultural development argue that the disincentive to invest in land that is not securely held translates into production inefficiency, meaning that the land is not meeting its potential in terms of market output. In effect, the communal titles encouraged investment by legalizing community limits, opening up property beyond borders for private purchase. For Honduras to increase foreign capital investment in its coastal areas, it needed to rectify the coast's insecure land tenure. Alongside the communal titling programs, the government attempted to further open the land market through additional congressional amendments.

Hurricane Mitch, Tourism Development, and the Repeal of Article 107

On June 8, 1998, in an effort to spur more foreign investment in coastal lands, the Honduran government announced its plans to amend Article 107 yet again. Garifuna organizations, fearing that they would lose both their occupied and unoccupied land, were outraged. On October 12, 1998 (Columbus Day), approximately five thousand indigenous and Garifuna people protested outside of the presidential palace to block the potential amendment. They further demanded the release of imprisoned peasant activists, resolutions to a dozen murders of indigenous people reputedly killed by landowners, and their right to receive titles for their land (Griffin 1999). Police broke up the demonstration with tear gas, batons, and rubber bullets, injuring at least six. Two weeks later, Hurricane Mitch hit Honduras, wiping out entire communities, and further devastating the country's already weak economy.

Over six thousand people died in Hurricane Mitch, and 10 percent of the population was left homeless (Phillips 2011:224). Eight hundred kilometers of road were destroyed, as were 169 bridges and 171,378 homes (Morris et al. 2002), amounting to 60 percent of the country's infrastructure (Phillips 2011:224). Ninety percent of the banana crops were lost. Poor rural households lost 30–40 percent of their crop income, and poverty levels immediately increased from 69.2 percent of households to 74.6 percent (Morris et al. 2002). Garifuna communities were severely impacted by the hurricane. Six hundred homes were completely destroyed, and a thousand were partially destroyed, affecting more than fifteen thousand families. Ninety-five percent of Garifuna crops were destroyed, and the majority of coconut trees died from the lethal yellowing disease that arrived in the wake of the hurricane (Organización de Desarrollo Étnico Comunitario 2002). The economic cost to the country was $3,308,000, or 59.8 percent of the country's current gross domestic product (Gass 2002). Thus, as Honduras entered the twenty-first century, its economy remained weak, and the country still suffered from huge external debt.

Honduras turned to the International Monetary Fund and the World Bank for help. In 1999 Honduras was declared eligible to receive bilateral debt relief under the IMF's Highly Indebted Poor Countries initiative. To achieve this relief, Honduras signed the Enhanced Structural Adjustment Facility (which is now known as the Poverty Reduction and Growth Facility Agreement) with the IMF. These programs focus on reducing state spending and encouraging foreign revenue through development initiatives that would open the Honduran economy to foreign investment. The primary economic development strategies from the 1990s forward have been agro-industrial production, the expansion of export processing zones (maquiladoras), and tourism. Tourism grew 18.3 percent between 1998 and 2001 and is now the third-largest source of income after remittances and maquiladoras.

The principal zone for tourism development is the region occupied historically by the Garifuna: the north coast, the Bay Islands, and the Cayos Cochinos. Honduras's tourism opportunities are commonly advertised under three broad categories: (1) the nation's "living cultures," which include the archaeological Maya ruins and Honduras's seven indigenous and ethnic groups; (2) eco-adventure opportunities; and (3) beachfront "fun and sun." The north coast is a region in which tourists can experience a variety of Honduras's best attractions: Caribbean beaches, ecotourism in the area's mountain ranges, and Garifuna "living culture."

Apparently, some members of Congress felt that promoting tourism development along the coast could move far more swiftly if Article 107 was further reformed to open all land within 40 kilometers of the coast to foreign purchase. Government officials used the economic impact of Hurricane Mitch as the final push to lead Congress to meet in a special night session on November 30, 1998. In this night session, while the country was still in turmoil from the hurricane and living under curfew, Congress voted to reform Article 107. As would be expected, this reform was met with severe protest from the Garifuna community. On January 25, 1999, several hundred indigenous and Garifuna people traveled yet again to the capital and protested outside of Congress, declaring the reform unconstitutional. This protest received significant media attention, reaching beyond national viewers to international audiences. Garifuna organizations and supporters were able to capitalize on the international spotlight, highlighting the impact of the hurricane and linking the land struggle to global discourses on human rights and racial discrimination. Both print and Web media featured stories of the reform of Article 107 and the countermobilization.[5]

While the Garifuna were receiving significant support for their mobilization efforts, Honduran government officials were dumbfounded. Officials from the Honduran Institute of Tourism told me that they could not understand why the Garifuna felt threatened by the reform in the first place. In an interview, one official said to me: "The reform of 107 was just to make things easier, so that if you wanted to sell, you could sell immediately, with no approval process [from the Ministry of Tourism]. It [the reform] didn't obligate the Garifuna to sell. No one said they had to. Because they already have their lands, and the lands are communal, not individual. So if someone wanted their lands, they would need to get everyone to agree." The officials I spoke with at the Instituto Hondureño de Turismo (Honduran Institute of Tourism), or IHT, thought the mobilization was unnecessary. They believed that the communal titles possessed by Garifuna communities were sufficient protection against the privatization of land. Although it is true that the majority of communities held communal titles, they represented significantly less land than the communities traditionally used; ancestral harvest and cultivation lands were therefore "unprotected" or "open" to foreign purchase.

Garifuna organizations continued to mobilize through media and letter-writing campaigns. They used their position against both presidential candidates for the 2001 elections, first arguing that if Congress did not un-reform the constitution, they would influence their constituency to vote for the opposite party's candidate. Thus, on October 12, 1999, Rafael Pineda Ponce, who at the time was the Liberal Party's presidential candidate and president of Congress, fearing he would lose the 2001 election, succumbed to pressure from the Garifuna organizations and authorized Rodrigo Castillo Aguilar of the National Congress to sign an Act of Compromise with the Garifuna. This compromise declared that the proposed reforms for Article 107 would not be incorporated into the Legislative Agenda, and thus Article 107 would not be ratified. However, once the compromise was signed, Garifuna organizations did not switch their support to Ponce, arguing that there would be nothing to keep him from reforming Article 107 postelection. Throughout the presidential campaign, Ricardo Maduro, the National Party's candidate, never wavered from his stance that he would not reform Article 107 during his presidency, which signaled to the Garifuna that his administration was not backing privatization and investment in coastal lands to the extent that Ponce's administration was. Maduro was elected president on November 25, 2001, and did not go back on his promise. Maduro furthered his commitment to the Garifuna by signing an agreement with ODECO, promising to make the Garifuna land problem a major priority for his administration.

Despite Maduro's official pledge to not reform Article 107 and commitment to resolve property conflicts in Garifuna territories, his administration facilitated the passage of new property laws that would further reregulate indigenous lands to facilitate tourism development, which became a national development priority at the turn of the twenty-first century. The year 2001—the time when I was just beginning my fieldwork—was named the "Year of the Tourist." Tourism became Honduras's third-largest source of foreign exchange, beaten only by remittances and industrial production through maquiladoras. The country began advertising tourism as the key to the advancement of the nation's economy, and the government established a joint police-military force to patrol the streets in major tourist destination cities. This special police force, known as "Balam" (or Jaguar),[6] was one of President Maduro's "zero tolerance" initiatives aimed at reducing the massive crime problem that had resulted from the growing destitution of most of the population and served as a serious deterrent to attracting potential tourists. On the Ministry of Tourism's web page, President Maduro was quoted as saying:

> Tourism has become one of the world's largest industries, and the revenues it generates have grown increasingly important for the global economy. That is why my administration has made tourism a priority, believing that the industry will not only benefit the country by creating new jobs and bringing in foreign currency, but also by strengthening our national identity, increasing development and competition, and giving Hondurans a higher standard of living. Our country is privileged to have an extraordinary natural and cultural heritage . . . there are beaches of singular beauty, exuberant scenery, colonial towns and living cultures throughout the country.

The Sustainable Coastal Tourism Project, an initiative funded under the World Bank's Honduran Poverty Reduction Strategy, was approved in July 2001. The four-year program aimed at "strengthening local and municipal capacity to manage and benefit from coastal tourism" (World Bank 2001). The International Development Bank (IDB) loan provided assistance to the IHT to increase its environmental planning resources and provide technical assistance for environmental assessment and tourism destination management to north coast municipalities. Credits were also used to finance technical assistance and training in the private sector and community-based organizations to develop small and medium sustainable tourism enterprises along the north coast. The project was designed to take into account social and environmental concerns, including land security and conservation (World Bank 2001).

The project promoted a "participatory process" and local capacity building "through skills training in environmental management, tourism management, and entrepreneurship" (World Bank 2004). As the principal ethnic group living in the coastal territories slated for this tourism development project, the Garifuna theoretically should have participated heavily in the development project, in both its planning and its management, as their territories (land and sea) and their "culture" are what were being appropriated for the economic advancement of the Honduran nation. Yet the World Bank funds were provided to municipal governments, not local governing structures (i.e., *patronatos*). A municipality is essentially a city government, having its own democratically elected representative leadership. Several local communities (Garifuna, mestizo, and mixed communities) fall under the jurisdiction of each individual municipality, and the Garifuna have little voice within this level of governance. The municipality holds the right to make decisions about Garifuna territories. Therefore, if a municipality wishes to turn Garifuna-occupied land into a national park, it can do so without consulting the Garifuna population. This has in fact happened along the coast, in the controversial case of Tela Bay.

Since the early 1970s Tela had been the on-again, off-again proposed site for the famous Tela Bay project, a large-scale luxury hotel project modeled after Cancun. This $450 million construction project included eight new hotels with the capacity for 1,600 guests, 124 residences, and 100 condos to rent, through investment by Canadian, Mexican, and Honduran businesses (*Tela News* 2000).[7] According to the IHT brochures, the high point of this development scheme would be the nearby Garifuna villages, especially Miami, a quiet Garifuna fishing village with no electricity, one road, and latrines, and where children still speak mostly Garifuna.

The Tela Bay project was surrounded by controversy and conflict because the land slated for development had been secured by the government through a series of abuses of power, from reclassifying lands into national parks where the government can now enforce regulations on land use, as in the case of Miami, to amending the constitution to make it possible for city governments (i.e., municipalities) to annex community lands (as in the case of Tornabe, Triunfo de la Cruz, and San Juan).

In 1992, when Congress passed Decree 90/90, amending Article 107 to enable the reclassification of any area declared apt for tourism use an "urban area," the municipality of Tela annexed parts of Tornabe, Triunfo de la Cruz, and San Juan (despite strong protests by the Garifuna living there). Tela has since sold 220 hectares of what was once land held by these three Garifuna communities. The Committee for the Defense of Triunfo's land filed a complaint with the attorney-general for ethnic groups against Tela for abuse of authority and for selling 48 acres of their land to Inversión y Desarrollo el Triunfo, a Honduran company interested in investing in the Tela Bay project. The land reportedly sold for 60 centavos a square yard for beachfront property (much less than real value) (Griffin 1997).

In addition to the gross misuse of power to rewrite the constitution such that the Garifuna have lost significant tracts of land, the government and IHT used the Garifuna's unique culture to attempt to attract tourists and foreign investors. IHT's analysis of Tela's potential to serve as a tourist destination notes that "the presence of the Garifuna culture, with their interesting culture and traditions, is a point in favor of tourism potential in the bay area" (Instituto Hondureño de Turismo 1993). Tourist outfits also profit from the Garifuna culture. The most successful tourist outfit on the north coast is Garifuna Tours, an Italian-owned organization that runs day trips to surrounding national parks. When I asked a staff member about the role the Garifuna play in the organization and how the organization benefits from them, he replied that "it's [the name Garifuna Tours] just a label." None of its trips focus specifically on Garifuna culture or communities. Only one of its tours includes a stop in a Garifuna community, where some community members may benefit from the sale of refreshments and handicrafts to tourists.

In sum, the current neoliberal governing structure means that even if Garifuna communities wish to maintain control over development processes within their territories (and communities now hold communal titles to some of their land), they are not given the means to manage local resources. Rather, under the decentralized governance model, the coastal municipalities of Tela, Omoa, La Ceiba, and Trujillo, and the island governments of Roatan and Utila, receive funds and direction from the central government and international agencies to "develop" and "manage" the resources found within Garifuna communities. Municipalities are then able to "sell" those resources and local culture to tourists, while the community patronatos and residents receive nothing more than the possibility of low-level income generation.

These paradoxes of "participatory development" were not lost on Garifuna activists, who turned back the language of participation to contest the neoliberal programs of the World Bank. Here I draw on Mark Anderson's observations of OFRANEH activists during the July 2004 consultation meeting of the Consulting Group of the government Program to Support Indigenous and Black Communities (PAPIN) (Anderson 2009:142–171). PAPIN receives most of its funding through IDB loan money, and in addition to the various projects it funds within ethnic communities, it is responsible for creating an institutional dialogue across the state and indigenous and black communities. To this end, PAPIN composed a "consulting group" of several ethnic federations; Anderson attended the fourteenth meeting of the consulting group in the capital city. His observations come out of two of four key issues under consideration at the meeting: (1) the proposal to create a centralized office for state ethnic politics and

(2) the new property law that would accompany the Sustainable Tourism Initiative, Ley de Propiedad Decreto Número 82-2004.

Garifuna activists present at the meeting were particularly resistant to a centralized office of ethnic affairs, calling attention to the fact that the proposal was produced without input from the ethnic federations. The office was expected to serve as the central hub and platform for indigenous and black Hondurans to communicate with the government, increasing accessibility and coherence in government–ethnic group relationships. Yet the proposal emerged from the IDB-funded PAPIN, and specifically from a Miskito professional who had moved from work for the World Bank into government employment with PAPIN (PAPIN falls under the secretary of government and justice). Not only was the proposal for the office produced without consultation from federations, its structure also threatened that some ethnic federations would be prioritized over others. Whose voice would become the centralized voice? The activists' critiques echo classic critiques of "participatory development," where the individuals most affected by the proposed development are invited to participate but the parameters of participation have already been established from above (see also Cooke and Kothari 2001; Woost 1997).

In addition to resisting the centralized office of ethnic affairs, Garifuna activists were also highly critical of the government's further efforts to "modernize" land through the passage of Ley de Propiedad Decreto Número 82-2004, which went into effect in 2004. PAPIN brought in a legal expert to explain the new law, which included a chapter on the regulation of real estate for indigenous and Afro-Honduran peoples. Emphasizing the virtues of this neoliberal agrarian policy, the legal expert drew on Harvard research that demonstrated the high transaction costs and corruption associated with inefficient property regimes, arguing that the new law would create mechanisms to reduce the cost of property registration and resolve conflicts over property rights (Anderson 2009:148). Activists were outraged yet again by the incompatibility of indigenous territorial regimes and the view of land as a market commodity. The 2004 law was yet another rung in the neoliberal ladder transforming the coastline through the deregulation (reregulation) of Garifuna ancestral communal lands. These reregulatory processes, and their gendered nature, are explored at the community level in the next two chapters, following an introduction to land shortage in Sambo Creek.

THREE

Mestizo Irregularities, Garifuna Displacement, and the Emergence of a "Mixed" Garifuna Community

Introducing Sambo Creek

Sambo Creek is located on the north coast of Honduras, 20 kilometers west of La Ceiba. Sambeños trace their community's foundation to 1862. According to local narrative, the first Garifuna families arrived by boat, originating from the communities of Guadalupe and Santa Fe in the department of Colon, stopping first in the Cayos Cochinos, and then arriving in the area now known as Sambo Creek. Local folklore states that the first arrivals encountered a Miskito man (called Sambo in English) along a creek, from whom they requested permission to clear the land and remain. According to this story, the man agreed, and so the community of Sambo Creek was born. Other Garifuna followed and it is estimated that 95 percent of the Garifuna population's ancestors originated from other coastal communities, including Santa Fe, San Antonio, Trujillo, Iriona, Corozal, and Triunfo de la Cruz (Central American and Caribbean Research Council 2002). Sambo Creek appeared in government records by the 1880s, reported as having 25 *manzanas* (about 43 acres) under cultivation, and one school (Anderson 2009:51).

With its proximity to La Ceiba, and extensive transnational ties, Sambo Creek has witnessed significant changes in infrastructure, demographics, and land tenure. La Ceiba is Honduras's third-largest city and the capital of the department of Atlántida. The city's population is roughly 174,000. Today the city serves as the heart of the tourist trade, having transformed

Figure 3.1 Sambo Creek, 2006. Photo by Keri Brondo

from a banana-exporting port to a link to the popular tourist destination of the Bay Islands.

Sambo Creek's population has grown steadily over the last few decades. In 1981 Carolyn McCommon (Anderson 2000:88) reported a population of 1,196, stating that 90 percent were Garifuna and 10 percent were mestizo. According to census data from 2000, the total population was 2,720, of whom 47.87 percent were Garifuna, and 51.03 percent *"otros"* (largely mestizos) (Anderson 2009:37).[1] In 2002 Sambo Creek's population was estimated by the Central American and Caribbean Research Council to be roughly five thousand, at least 40 percent of whom were mestizo (2002). This estimate likely included both Sambo Creek residents living in country as well as those living abroad. My estimates based on household surveying placed the population in 2002 roughly between 2,500 and 3,000. In 2005 Scheerer conducted a full census and reported 607 households and a total population of 2,891 (Carey Scheerer, unpublished data).

In comparison to other Garifuna communities farther west along the coast, Sambo Creek is a "modern" community. By "modern," I refer strictly to amenities. Many of such changes occurred within the last two decades. In 1982 Carolyn McCommon (Anderson 2000:85) described Sambo

Creek as a: "traditional, rural, Black Carib village . . . there is no electricity, telegraph lines or sanitation service. Few houses have latrines or adjacent outhouses. Water is obtained from the river and hauled to homes in pans carried on individuals' heads." In 2002 community members remembered those days well, but this "traditional" "village-like" atmosphere was long gone. In the 1980s the road was paved between La Ceiba and Trujillo, and La Ceiba subsidized electricity for the community. In the early 1990s the municipality of La Ceiba built a potable-water and sanitation system. Moreover, the majority of traditional *manaca* houses (mud walls with palm-thatched roof) began to be replaced with homes constructed of *bloque* (cinderblock). These new homes were typically financed through remittances. At the time of my research, the existing infrastructure included a stone-paved street, a health center, a primary school, a middle school, two Catholic churches, seven Evangelical churches,[2] one communal center constructed with support of members of the community who live in the United States, a hotel in the urban area,[3] and three hotels in the rural areas, two of which are on the coast.

In March 2002 Barceló, a major Spanish resort chain, opened a resort location on the beaches of Roma, less than two miles from Sambo Creek and just slightly past the community's ancestral limits. The resort structure was originally built in 2001 with investment capital from wealthy Hondurans from Tegucigalpa and opened that year under the name Caribbean Sands. By 2004 the resort had undergone another change of hands and complete refurbishment and expansion. This time it was placed back into Honduran hands and opened as the Palma Real Beach Resort and Casino. Several other small tourist accommodations and private lands also opened between the mid-1990s and 2011. All these new tourism developments cater to Honduras's image as a destination to satisfy all tourist types: those looking for the three S's (sea, sand, and sun), those seeking eco-adventures, and those wishing to experience "living culture." These new developments offer beachfront accommodations; views of both the Caribbean Sea *and* the forest canopy (the north coast communities are buttressed between the sea and Pico Bonito National Park); and assistance in booking adventures in kayaking, white-water rafting, scuba diving, or ziplining; and the Garifuna are often brought in to put on "cultural productions" for the hotel guests. At the Palma Real Beach Resort and smaller local hotels, "cultural productions" were performed by a Sambeño music and dance group, which consisted of approximately ten young men and women. In 2006 I joined them to observe the show at one of the smaller hotels. The artists performed "traditional" music with drums, maracas, and conch shells, and enticed the tourists to dance along with them. Several tourists joined to display their newly acquired punta skills, laughing at themselves and their friends, as they engaged in what likely appeared to them a lewd dance (the perceived vulgarity of the dance was made apparent when one man tried to stuff dollar bills into a Garifuna dancer's skirt while he danced with her).

Despite the above infrastructure advances and influx of people, there were still communication and travel limitations in 2002. Taxis from La Ceiba did not service the community. Most community members were reliant on the bus service to get to La Ceiba or elsewhere, although there were households that had their own cars or trucks. One landline phone serviced the entire community; some people did have cell phones. Almost all households owned a television with cable. By 2005, however, Sambo Creek had regular taxi service, an internet café, a Western Union office, and several phone lines.

Gender, Labor, and Migration

As amenities have increased over the years, local economic opportunities have substantially decreased. Throughout much of the twentieth century, many of Sambo Creek's residents were employed by the Standard Fruit Company, working on its docks, railroads, and fields, and as mechanics or carpenters in its workshops. But these jobs largely disappeared after the company restructured its labor force in the 1960s and then moved its shipping facilities out of La Ceiba in the 1980s (Anderson 2009:42). While fishing and agriculture had been important local economic activities of the past, they are now on decline. A variety of factors contribute to this decline, including a growing remittance economy, lack of available land, and enforced fishing regulations in the Cayos Cochinos. The Cayos Cochinos are located four hours away by *cayuco* (dug-out canoe), and one hour by motorboat. The area historically has been an important source of subsistence and cash economy for the Garifuna of Sambo Creek. A dwindling group of older men still fish in the Cayos Cochinos, shrinking from about 30 in 2002 to only a handful by my last visit in 2011. The community retained rights (although not formal title) to Cayo Bolaño, where fishers could stay overnight. Other employment opportunities for local men included construction work, hourly wage labor in La Ceiba, or becoming wait staff in the newly constructed hotels. Income generated through hotel work was less than adequate. In 2002 the wait staff I knew earned 1,600–2,000 lempiras a month (approximately $96–121).

Figure 3.2 Fishing boats on Sambo Creek's shore. Photo by Keri Brondo

Vending had once been an important economic activity for women. They sold various products (e.g., fruits, casabe, coconut bread, coconut pastries, and drinks) out of their homes as well as on the banana plantations. Such employment opportunities have become limited with the decline in agriculture, the abandonment of the banana plantations, and, more recently, the lethal yellowing disease that followed Hurricane Mitch in 1998 and destroyed many of the coast's coconut trees.[4] These factors narrowed the products and the spaces available for women to sell.

Some women continue to vend on a small-scale basis; others work in San Pedro Sula's maquiladoras, as household help in La Ceiba, or as kitchen and cleaning help in the local hotels. Like men, women employed at local hotels make salaries less than adequate to sustain their families. In addition to facing low pay, women who become pregnant may lose their jobs. One pregnant employee of a local hotel was officially terminated for "making too many mistakes," but her past employer did tell me that "she would have had to go anyway since she was pregnant." Misunderstanding, I said, "Oh, I guess she'd have to stop working eventually to take care of her baby?" "No," the employer responded, "we cannot have a pregnant girl, because the law here is that if you employ pregnant women, you have to pay her health insurance, the cost of delivery, everything." The terminated woman did return to her employer and allegedly threatened to sue unless she received severance pay. She allegedly requested 2,000 lempiras. The employer paid her 1,500 lempiras (approximately $90), and the "problem" went away.

All in all, economic opportunities at the local level are few and far between, and the vast majority of residents either rely on remittances from their families members who have migrated abroad or migrate themselves in search of labor. While not a central focus of this book, the importance of transmigration cannot be overstated. Most households rely heavily on the money and items they receive from abroad,[5] and migration is seen as the only way to accumulate wealth and achieve upward mobility (England 2006: 123–124).

In 2002 the patronato estimated that remittances from abroad served as the only source of income for approximately 50 percent of households in Sambo Creek. Still others supplement wage labor with remittances. In 2002 some 59.57 percent of the households I interviewed were receiving money from family members who had migrated to one of Honduras's major cities (i.e., Tegucigalpa or San Pedro Sula) or to the United States. Scheerer's 2005 household census (unpublished) found that 49.9 percent of all households in Sambo Creek were receiving remittances on a regular basis, and 94.6 percent of the remittances were coming from the United States. By way of comparison, in the 1990s, 52.5 percent of England's (2006:122) sample of Garifuna from Limón (department of Colon) lived outside of the community, with a third of them in other parts of Central America and two-thirds in the United States.

In the 1940s and 1950s, men were the primary labor migrants from Garifuna communities, finding employment as merchant marines from Central American ports and the West Indies. From there opportunities opened to join the National Maritime Union, which was based in New York City. Many joined the union, enabling them to earn higher wages, benefits, and US residency, and leading to the establishment of residential Garifuna communities in New York City (England 2006:44–45). Numbers of merchant marine migrants blossomed in the 1950s after the 1954 Great Banana Strike and subsequent decline in banana plantation labor. As the number of migrants grew, transnationalism came to be a mainstay socioeconomic strategy among Garifuna communities (England 2006:44–45).

While some women did migrate within Central America for wage labor before the 1970s, they were paid significantly less than their male counterparts, so many women chose to remain in their home communities (Kerns 1983). As a result, Garifuna villages were often talked about as "nurseries and nursing homes," reflecting the fact that the majority of working-age men were outside of the community, leaving behind an elderly population and women and young children (England 2006; González 1988; Kerns 1983). In the mid-1970s, Garifuna women joined their male counterparts in nearly equal numbers as transnational migrants, finding employment in the ever-expanding feminized service sector as domestic help (England 2006:47). Women's labor migration has continued alongside that of men through to today. Although women of working age have increased their level of migration to parallel men's, Garifuna communities remain feminized to a certain degree, as women continue to fill the role of primary caregiver.

Dreams of migration and stories of family members living abroad punctuated my interactions with Sambeños, from friendly conversations to formal interviews. Marriage inquiries, offers to take daughters back with us to work as household help, pleas to petition the US embassy for a visa, and requests for accommodation if friends made their way *mojado* (illegally, literally "wet" or "damp") were commonplace. For months, my friends Kety and Lesbeth (two sisters) pleaded with me to convince my brother and his male friend who were coming to visit us for a few weeks to marry the girls so they could get to the United States. Kety was the most bold, talking with my brother openly about her proposal when he arrived. She explained to him that she was a serious student with visions *para superarse* (to better herself), that she was not at all interested in being his wife or girlfriend, and that a US education in civil engineering would far surpass what she could obtain in Honduras. Kety had been studying in Tegucigalpa, the capital city, when she became pregnant with her son; she returned to her mother's house to have the baby. My brother's refusal did not squash her dreams: within months Kety was back in Tegucigalpa, working on her bachelor's degree, paid for by her uncle in New Orleans. Her son remained in Sambo Creek, to be raised by his grandmother and aunt Lesbeth. In 2010 Kety married an American man and had a second son with him, and in 2011 the family of four was making plans to move to a major city in the US East Coast.

One cool evening, sitting out in the patio of his mother's home, Marlon, unemployed, and Edson, a waiter at a nearby restaurant, began talking about migration and the cost of living. Both wanted to "go north" for work, lamenting that they could not afford to construct a home in Sambo Creek. Not only was there no available land for them to build on, but they estimated that the construction materials alone would cost 40,000–50,000 lempiras, not to mention the cost of home furnishings. At a salary of 1,600 lempiras a month, supporting a spouse and five kids, and paying for his own continuing education in La Ceiba, it would take full-time employed Edson well over a decade to save that kind of money. Edson joked, *"Nosotros jóvenes tendrán que volver a hacer las casas de manaca (madera), porque no tenemos pisto para bloqueo!"* ("Soon we younger people will have to go back to making houses of *manaca* [wood], because we cannot afford the concrete!"). The two began to list all the requirements to get a visa for travel to the United States—house, car, bank account, land, business, and so on, and then said, "If I had those, why would I want to leave?" (*¿Si tuve estas cosas, por qué querría salir?*).

Consumer goods and brands associated with US black culture were immensely popular among youth and were status markers. Suffice to say, much of my "hanging out" times with Sambeños in my age set included them showing me the pop culture gifts they received from abroad or their combing through items in my living room (magazines, CDs, books) that my family and I had brought with us to the field. Items associated with the United States were typically a central topic of our daily conversations. For instance, a few of my female friends were particularly taken with Céline Dion and had me transcribe the lyrics to all her songs, so they could memorize them and sing along, and then translate their meaning into Spanish. My young-mother friends and I would read through children's books written in English, for the benefit of all of us—alongside their children, they would learn English, while I worked on my Spanish translation.

Had I been particularly interested in the topic of consumerism and black cosmopolitism at the time of my study, I would have had an enormous data set and captive audience for my constant questioning. Yet I was more interested in the presumed opposite: tradition and the expression of indigeneity as located in territory. In *Black and Indigenous: Garifuna Activism and Consumer Culture in Honduras*, Mark Anderson (2009:32) eloquently shows how practices of black cosmopolitanism exist alongside engagements with images of the Garifuna as a traditional subject with "deep cultural traditions that are rooted in ethnic difference." Thus, the Garifuna subject is at once modern and traditional, cosmopolitan and indigenous. Yet Garifuna organizations and activists downplay the significance of black cosmopolitanism as it is irrelevant or counterintuitive to their struggles. The image of a rooted population, who retains a nonwestern culture and cosmovision, forms the basis for Garifuna claims to political and cultural rights (Anderson 2009:199).

The history of Garifuna migration in which more men than women left natal communities has strongly influenced Garifuna society and culture, such that women play important roles in the local economy, subsistence activities, and religious practices. Women are also responsible for teaching the language and cultural practices to future generations. Although women are generally expected to remain monogamous, men frequently have sexual relations with more than one woman, and it is not unusual for a man to have children by two or more women (Anderson 2000:76). Thus, many of the Garifuna homes in Sambo Creek consist of generations of women and their children; in short, women have come to form the stable core of Garifuna homes, communities, and culture (González 1969; Kerns 1983). In 1988, González (1988:8–9) observed that among the Garifuna

> Women have become central, perhaps by default . . . if one were deliberately to set out to "feminize" an entire sociocultural system, there could be no other way than to remove the institutionalized male functions. In the seventeenth and eighteenth centuries, men alone hunted and fished, served as religious leaders, as warriors and as headmen. In the earliest days of migratory wage labor (eighteenth century) it was also a masculine endeavor, and one which led to both economic success and personal glory. But bit by bit these roles have been either removed from the Garifuna culture completely, or, as in the case of migration and religious leadership, women now participate as well. As one male informant put it in 1975—there is nothing a man can do that a woman can't do as well or better. . . . A basic feminist argument today is that the overall status of women in a society is related to the nature of the roles that they are allowed to fill. The Garifuna case is almost a mirror image of what has more often happened to women since the onset of the industrial revolution. That is, the roles assigned to men have been deleted or diluted to the point that men as a class seem somehow less important than women. The general situation which remains has struck many observers, themselves members of a different kind of social order, as being "matrifocal."

Within Honduras, Garifuna organizational leaders support González, claiming that Garifuna gender relations surpass Mestizo gender relations. In 2005 Thorne (n.d.: 10) was told by OFRANEH leadership that unlike ladino men, "Garifuna men 'respect' the views of women and work in a mutually supportive way around community issues . . . that when Garifuna women meet, men are not excluded, but are often present, playing a supporting role and encouraging women's involvement." Although it is true that women do hold a relative degree of power within the community,

Sambo Creek has yet to have a female president of patronato (although women have served in most of the other key positions, including vice president and secretary). Outside of the political sphere, women do serve as the core of the community, and children become obligated more to their mothers than to their fathers. Children develop close relationships with their mothers, maternal grandmothers, and aunts and assume responsibility for supporting them as they age. Those who migrate send money back to their female relatives, and children present in the home, permanently or visiting, will offer physical labor to aid with home and land improvements. As mothers and grandmothers age, daughters typically seek support from other relatives to care for them.

Ethnographic studies on the Garifuna diaspora and transnational linkages show that Garifuna who do migrate abroad for work retain deep attachments to their natal communities (England 2006). Like the Garifuna immigrants England (2009) met from other areas of Honduras, Sambo Creek immigrants to New York City have formed a hometown association and soccer league. It is quite common for Garifuna to spend their working years in the United States and return to their natal community upon retirement, and many elder Garifuna residents of Sambo Creek did just that.

Constant migration has fed the rapid spread of communicable disease within the community, and HIV/AIDS is affecting the population. The Garifuna population as a whole has one of the highest levels of HIV/AIDS in the Western Hemisphere. In Honduras, HIV prevalence in adults between the ages of 15 and 49 exceeds 8 percent, and the rates for adults in their twenties are twice as high (UNAIDS 2004). Honduras's Garifuna organizations cite Sambo Creek as one of the most heavily affected communities, estimating that more than one-third of the community is infected. Despite efforts to increase awareness of the disease and how it is spread, shame and denial persist in the community. The HIV/AIDS epidemic has impacts on all facets of Garifuna life, including land use and management. Its impact has yet to be thoroughly explored and is an important area for future research.

In addition to HIV/AIDS are several other serious health concerns within the community. Despite the arrival of potable water, Sambo Creek still lacks facilities to treat the water with chlorine. Thus, a significant portion of community residents suffer from health problems directly related to deficient sanitation infrastructure. And although the community has a health center, it is not a 24-hour clinic, and the closest hospital is in La Ceiba. Malaria, gastrointestinal diseases, and other infectious diseases are prevalent in the community.

Land Shortage

Prior to the 1980s Sambo Creek's settlement was restricted to a small plot of land between the beach and the railroad tracks, referred to today as Barrio Centro. The railroad was built in 1910 by the Suiza Planting Company (a subsidiary of the Standard Fruit Company) when they established banana plantations nearby. (These plantations were abandoned in the 1920s when disease destroyed the crops [Anderson 2009:52]). From initial settlement through the 1930s, the Garifuna cultivated the majority of the land immediately surrounding the community. When the banana companies withdrew in the 1930s, work as laborers on plantations and docks largely disappeared for men, and women saw reduced opportunities to sell food products and refreshments on the plantations.

A central paved road cuts from the main coastal highway down to the beach, intersecting with a dirt road that runs along the coastline wide enough for the city bus to turn around. Several roadways intersect these two main paths, not all of which are wide enough for cars to travel, and seemingly endless dirt pathways run throughout the neighborhoods, connecting the several corners of the community. Within the main settlement area, houses are packed in like sardines, with younger generations building their homes in areas that were once family backyard gardens. Many homes house ten or more people, and the local cemetery has reached its capacity. People say there is no room to bury their ancestors. With no room to expand, graves were dug so close to the sea that several coffins were once washed away during a storm (Anderson 2009:51). There is no available land to build houses, to make a new cemetery, to plant crops, or to build community infrastructure. But what is really striking is that when you walk around Sambo Creek, this land shortage is not so obvious—there seem to be plenty of empty lots. This is because so much of Sambo Creek's land has been sold as private lots or encroached upon.

Much of Sambo Creek's ancestral land is now in the hands of mestizos who came to hold it through squatter's rights or "irregular" processes. "Irregular processes" refers to encroachment by powerful and elite Hondurans who obtained land through intimidation, trickery, or outright theft at gunpoint. By 2002 many of these irregularly obtained empty plots were on the market with asking prices far beyond what a local could pay. For example, in 2002 plots that were one quarter of a manzana (or about .375 acres) in the most impoverished areas had asking prices of around $10,000; one foreign landowner was asking $100,000 for slightly more than two manzanas (or about three acres). For a community largely reliant on

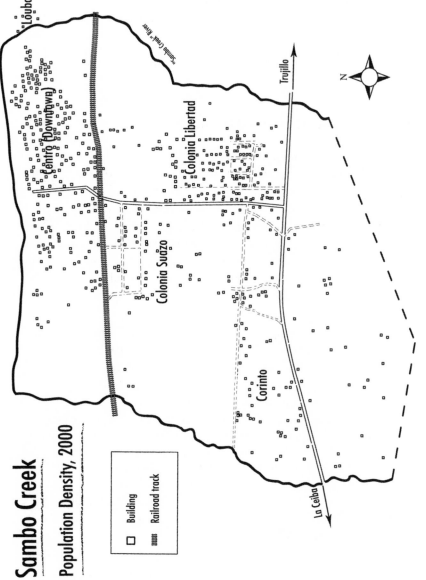

Figure 3.3 Population density of Sambo Creek neighborhoods. El Centro and Colonia Libertad are the most densely populated. Map by Juan Mejia

remittances from the United States, these prices were (and continue to be) astronomical. As noted earlier, those households that were receiving remittances in 2002 were sent about $200 a month, but remittances are irregular. Working households brought in approximately $125 a month. At this rate, it would take a lifetime just to save for a small plot. As Sambeños would say, "in order to have a home of their own, our children must wait for their grandmothers to die."

Mestizo Encroachment and Garifuna Sales

In the 1930s, when the banana companies began withdrawing from the area, wealthy mestizos started to usurp community land, including that which was once used by the Garifuna for cultivation and harvest.

According to local oral history, a mestizo associated with the National Party of the president and dictator Tiburcio Carías Andino (1933–49) appropriated a large portion of the community's cultivation lands to use as a cattle ranch (see Anderson 2000). Elders (i.e., 70 or older) recall the National Party representatives and Ceibeño police forcibly removing Garifuna farmers from these lands.

> We Garifuna have always been fighting for our land. And it is in all Garifuna communities, not just Sambo Creek. . . . In 1941, or maybe it was 1942, the government robbed us of our lands, and then many others left out of fear of the political party. People who worked in the government—not the president, but people who worked for him—these people with money—they came and took the land from us. This [the colonias] used to be full of cassava. It was all cassava. [70-year-old Garifuna man]

> This land was ours, but the powerful bosses that live in La Ceiba saw us as less than them and they came with pistols, humiliating us, and said to leave our lands. They said to us, "Here's five lempiras; don't come back." We were afraid and we left. We did not have documents, so we could not fight. [74-year-old Garifuna man]

"People with money," "powerful bosses," those with money, power, and political connections were responsible for decades of government-sanctioned racist exploitation of Garifuna territory. Lands appropriated through such activities include the *colonias* known as Colonia Libertad, Colonia Suazo, and Corinto. Much of the land remained unused throughout the years, passing through the hands of cattle ranchers and other powerful outsiders.

In the late 1970s community activists began petitioning the INA for the recuperation of their illegally seized lands. During that time Felipe Suazo, a wealthy Garifuna resident, bought a large portion of this land (i.e., what is now Colonia Suazo and Corinto) from a mestizo owner who was threatened with losing the entire plot to the community. According to McCommon (Anderson 2009:51), Suazo divided and sold this land to individuals on the condition that they build cement homes with zinc roofs. The costs imposed by this condition prevented those who most needed land from obtaining it, and as a result, the area is starkly differentiated from the rest of the community, with the large, well-built homes and gated yards of the well-off Garifuna (who are typically those who have worked for many years on cruise ships or in the United States).

Some impoverished Garifuna families lost their land to Felipe Suazo through a loan process. Several individuals told me stories of women signing over their family's cultivation plot to Suazo in exchange for food, medicine, shoes, or other necessary supplies. When they could not pay back the money they owed for the items, he took control of the land. For example, one close friend shared that his mother sold his family's land for 100 lempiras, so that she could buy his sister a pair of shoes, leaving him and his siblings without an inheritance. Wealthier mestizos supported this history in private conversations, yet they made the case that Suazo's exchanges were fair.

> People now say that they were robbed of their lands, but the truth is they weren't; they were paid the going rate. Let me give you an example of how this works. In 1991 I bought my house in La Ceiba for 90,000 lempiras, but now I could sell it for 500,000 lempiras. When I bought the house I thought it was expensive, but now it is worth much more. It is the evolution of the country—the value is increasing. . . . Nobody stole their land. Nobody was robbed by force. Some people exchanged their land for food. Others gave it to a doctor so that the doctor would cure their baby. Now they say this was stolen. But it was a fair exchange.

Wealthy mestizos were not the only ones to settle on Garifuna cultivation land. Poor inland mestizos seeking labor opportunities encroached as well. Anna's story provides an example. Anna is a 64-year-old mestizo woman who was not born in Sambo Creek but has lived in the community for as long as she can remember. Anna and her family live on contested land in Corinto. Anna's parents are both from the interior of the country, and like many other poor mestizos, they migrated to the coast in search of a better life. They settled in the center of Sambo Creek around 1940. Like many older women from the community, Anna never received any formal schooling; when she was younger she sold fruits and bread on the banana plantations. Anna was quite ill in 2002 when I came to know her, with undiagnosed heart problems, and could no longer work. She had five grown children—four lived in La Ceiba at the time, and one son and his family lived with Anna and her husband on their plot of land in Corinto. Anna's husband worked as a cattle hand on a local ranch. His modest income provided for very few luxury items in their home. Anna did have one luxury that many people in the center of the community could no longer afford because of the land shortage, and that was fruit trees. Anna had avocado, mango, lemon, apple, and coconut trees. She also kept chickens.

In 2002 Anna and her husband did not have a title for their plot, nor did they have sufficient money to obtain one. However, they both desired a private title, because they feared they might lose their land to Garifuna community members through a future land occupation. This fear was heightened when in the summer of 2002 she and her husband saw representatives from the INA on their property, measuring it. The INA official reassured her that she should "not worry about anything because her land is very little." The INA was measuring all the contested land in Sambo Creek, and Anna was legitimately worried because she obtained her plot through squatting: "I will tell the truth, because I am a woman who does not like to lie. In those times [1964] my husband and I wanted our own house. We were living in a house in Sambo Creek that was someone else's, not our own. So my husband came here and cleared this land, and we stayed here. Some people said this wasn't our land, but there was a man named Manuel that we knew nearby, and he said it was okay for us to stay. So we did." She speculated that if the land was a cultivation plot of a Garifuna family, they could not tell at the time, seeing no evidence that it was under use. It is possible that due to the Garifuna practice of shifting agriculture, Anna, her husband, and other poor mestizo immigrants mistook fallow fields as unutilized, thus transforming portions of ancestral farmland into places of residence. While Anna recalled a time when the land in Corintu was under cultivation, she said: "People here don't plant anymore because they sold their lands. This here [pointing to her land and surrounding lands] used to all be full of yuca, but the people sold the land. The Garifuna don't want to work anymore, because they have spouses who live in the US and bring money to them here."

Anna expresses some hint of frustration with the contestation over land rights. She, like many others, suggests that even if the lands were returned to the Garifuna, they would not be used for the cultivation of traditional foodstuffs. Past recuperations suggest she might be onto something.

In 1982 the community succeeded in recuperating some of its lost land, securing rights under a communal title to what is now Colonia Libertad. The land was recovered via the National Agrarian Institute after several years of community petitioning (petitioning began in the late 1970s). The patronato was given authority to divide and distribute the land among landless community members, and Garifuna and mestizo residents entered a lottery to receive individual plots. Although the land was originally envisioned to be dedicated at least in part to cultivation, it has become primarily a residential area (see also Anderson 2009:51–52). Today much of the land has been furthered divided and sold as private land.

Through the various avenues detailed above (i.e., theft, intimidation, sale, and immigration), by the turn of the new century Sambo Creek's ancestral territory had been transformed into settlements and grazing pastures. These changes brought demographic results. Based on a sampling strategy of every fifth household across the various subsections of the community,[6] my 2002 community survey revealed the extent of mestizo encroachment on ancestral cultivation lands.

The comparison of ethnicity by section of the community showed that Sambo Creek's early settlements (Barrio Centro and La Louba) were largely Garifuna. Eighty-five percent of the sample from Barrio Centro and 100 percent from La Louba were Garifuna. Areas of Sambo Creek that had historically been used for subsistence agriculture and harvest (Corinto) had become largely mestizo (i.e., 100 percent of the household interviewees in Corinto were mestizo.) Colonia Libertad, the area donated back to the community in the 1980s, appeared to be largely Garifuna (i.e., 82 percent of interviewees were Garifuna). Colonia Suazo, the area with the nicest homes, had grown into a more mixed-ethnicity neighborhood (i.e., 67 percent of interviewees were Garifuna, while 33 percent were non-Garifuna), reflecting that the area has been largely privatized and sold to individuals who can afford to pay the market price.

Although it is probably accurate to state that mestizos have taken control of the majority of Sambo Creek's ancestral cultivation and harvest land (i.e., Corinto), this does not mean that all mestizos are recent transplants from elsewhere. As my household sample showed, there are mestizo families who have generational roots in the community as well. Table 3.1 depicts the birthplace and place of socialization for all interviewees.

Table 3.1 Place of Birth and Socialization for Household Interviewees by Ethnicity

Ethnicity	Born and Raised in Community	Born outside but Raised in Community	Born and Raised outside of Community	Total
Garifuna	81% (n = 34)	2% (n = 1)	17% (n = 7)	100% (n = 42)
Mestizo	30% (n = 3)	40% (n = 4)	30% (n = 3)	100% (n = 10)
Other	67% (n = 2)	0% (n = 0)	33% (n = 1)	100% (n = 3)
Total	(n = 39)	(n = 5)	(n = 11)	(n = 55)

Of the ten mestizo participants, three were born and raised in the community, and four were born elsewhere but grew up in the community. Thus, 70 percent of the mestizos from the household sample knew no other home than Sambo Creek. How did the mestizos who participated in my household sample obtain the land they called home? Table 3.2 reports these data, showing the processes through which interviewees obtained their land and the price (if any) they paid for the plot on which they lived.

The table shows that the largest number of interviewees received land through inheritance. All eighteen respondents who lived on inherited land noted that the land was passed matrilineally (either from their mother or from their spouse's mother). Moreover, all eighteen of these individuals were Garifuna.

While the data set is limited, comparisons of the average purchase price for land reveal some interesting patterns. First, Garifuna individuals who sold land during the same time period as Suazo set their prices lower than he (50 lempiras vs. 304 or 600 lempiras), which suggests class distinctions within the community. Next, Suazo sold land to Garifuna who were native to Sambo Creek at half the cost he did to a mestizo from Sambo Creek and a Garifuna from outside the community (304 lempiras vs. 600 lempiras). In an interview with a mestizo landowner (whose data are not included in the household sample), I learned that Suazo sold him his plot in Colonia Libertad (i.e., the land recuperated in 1982) for 50,000 lempiras (approximately $3,570). These observations support what Garifuna community members told me about Suazo's sales: that he "looked after the Garifuna community" by buying their ancestral lands back from the mestizos who claimed them and then selling it back to the Garifuna community at a low cost. Suazo's sale prices also reflect Garifuna cultural expectations

Table 3.2 How Households Obtained Their Parcel of Residence (n = 55)

Means of Land Acquisition	Count	Average Cost (in lempiras and dollars*)	Time of Sale
Inheritance	18 (33%)	0	N/A
Donated (Colonia Libertad)	9 (16%)	0	N/A
Encroachment	2 (4%)	0	N/A
Sold by Suazo to mestizo or Garifuna from other communities	2 (4%)	L 3,000 ($600)	1982–83
Sold by Suazo to Garifuna native to Sambo Creek	6 (11%)	L 1,522 ($304)	1978–82
Sold by Garifuna (excluding Suazo) to Garifuna	3 (5%)	L 100 ($50)	1960–85
Sold by mestizos (non-natives to Sambo)	5 (9%)	L 19,375 ($2668)	1995–97
Unknown (includes 5 renters)	10 (18%)	0	N/A
Total	55 (100%)		

*The cost in dollars was calculated using information about changes to the official exchange rate of the lempira, which was determined to be US$1 = L2 since 1918. In 1990, under President Callejas, the lempira was adjusted to US$1 = L4, and in December 1993 it fell to US$1 = L7.26. Thus, for sales that took place in the 1980s, I applied the exchange rate of US$1 = L2, and US$1 = L7.26 to sales that took place between 1995 and 1997. The lempira has steadily devalued since all the sales reported here, dropping, for instance, from US$1 = L14.839 in 2000, to US$1 = L16.433 in 2002, to $ US1 = L18.882 in 2010.

Sources: Photius, www.photius.com/countries/honduras/economy/honduras_economy_monetary_ and_exchange~8536.html, accessed January 10, 2006, and Exchange Rates, http://www.exchange-rates.org/Rate/USD/HNL, accessed August 20, 2010.

regarding "fair pricing": Garifuna who charge one another beyond what is considered fair are socially stigmatized (England 2006:48). Finally, we see that mestizos from outside the community are the only people who sold land in the last decade to the people I surveyed. In addition to regular market growth, land prices were also affected in the 1980s and 1990s by the devaluation of the lempira.

In Sambo Creek, the process of territorialization (i.e., marking territories "within states for the purposes of controlling people and resources" [Igoe and Brockington 2007:437]) has been overtly gendered. The next chapter explores how as the Honduran state moved to "control peoples and resources" by delineating territorial boundaries through the privatization of communal land and distribution of collective land titles, women's rights became increasingly restricted.

FOUR

Gendered Rights and Responsibilities

Privatization and Women's Land Loss in Sambo Creek

The processes of territorialization are often gendered. Not only are new (attractive) values assigned to previously untradable goods, thus bringing in new market-oriented actors to the coast, but women are assigned different values in their own communities. In Sambo Creek, the reregulation of land has meant that women's responsibilities and relationships to territory are redefined by neoliberal discourse and practice, further disenfranchising them within their households and communities.

Communal Title, Private Lands

On August 27, 1997, Sambo Creek received a communal title of domino pleno (the highest level of land ownership) for 184.23 hectares. The only other title issued to the community had been a title of occupation that protected just 41 hectares, issued by the INA in 1979. ODECO, who assisted in processing the legal paperwork for the 1997 title, worked for it to protect Sambo Creek's residents from the potential threat of outsiders purchasing their untitled land for investment projects. ODECO leadership frequently reiterated that before the 1997 title was issued *all* land in the community was not legally protected. However, the residents of Sambo Creek issued serious complaints over the limits established by the title. Their disapproval of the title led the community patronato and the Committee for Defense of the Land to issue a statement to the INA indicating that ODECO should henceforth not be granted the authority to represent Sambo Creek in any further land issues.

Like most of the titles granted to Garifuna communities, the 1997 land title did not include ancestral territory, which is estimated to extend beyond 1,000 hectares, nearly ten times what was granted in 1997 (Central American and Caribbean Research Council 2002). Some areas of the community that have been occupied for well over a century, and perhaps even since the community's foundation (e.g., La Louba or *el otro lado*, or "over there") were completely left out of the title. About 50 Garifuna individuals in nine houses live in La Louba, all descendants of an 86-year-old Garifuna woman who inherited the land from her mother and now holds a private title. The families that live in this area reported to me that the municipality of Jutiapa is now asking them to pay taxes (whereas in the past they were considered part of Sambo Creek and under the jurisdiction of La Ceiba's municipality).

While traditional landholding in Sambo Creek is communal, with the patronato having the ultimate authority regarding its distribution and use rights, and many of the Garifuna I knew stated they preferred communal holding and use rights, the rules of communal holding apply only to land that *was not previously privately titled*. Unfortunately, much of the land had already been privatized prior to 1997. The majority (75 percent) of households I surveyed reported that their land was private land, including households located in Colonia Libertad (i.e., the donated area of the community), and homes constructed on land obtained through encroachment. By 2002 many people had already gone through the legal process to obtain a private title. Even those who had yet to begin the legal procedure to privatize their holdings still stated a preference for private land titling over communal land titling. When I asked, inevitably I was told it is "because private titles are more secure" and "no one can take your land if you have a title." One mestizo respondent reported that the reason he got a private title was that "the *negritos* wanted to take our land." The two mestizos who reported obtaining land through encroachment desired a private title, fearing that under the current land struggle they might lose their land to Garifuna residents.

In general there is a shared sense among local mestizos and Garifuna that private property is a more secure form of property ownership, even in light of state-sanctioned communal lands. Collective land titles appear ambiguous—exactly which members of the community have rights to the land, and how are communal plots managed on a day-to-day and long-term basis? The ambiguity in the meaning behind collective land titles combines with the rising value of private property to form an imperative among local people to prioritize individual, private landholding.

Matrifocality, Privatization, and Women's Land Loss

As mentioned earlier, Garifuna homes typically consist of generations of women and their children, and women form the stable core of Garifuna communities. Children thus become more obligated to their mothers than to their fathers. In Anderson's (2000:76) description of gender relations in Sambo Creek, he notes,

> When husbands are present, women still maintain their own spheres of social and economic power, particularly when their children become working adults. Children (male and female) typically develop close relationships to their mothers, maternal grandmothers and aunts and acquire obligations to support them through financial or practical means (i.e., helping build or repair a house, clearing a garden plot). They almost always speak in terms of sending money to their mother or building a house for their mother rather than for their parents, or, certainly, their father.

Anderson's observations are in line with the property history data presented here, which were collected five years later. In property history narratives, Garifuna spoke almost exclusively of their mothers and grandmothers as primary landowners and homeowners. Yet the trend toward privatization has significantly disadvantaged Garifuna women. Two sets of evidence suggest these gendered inequalities: homeownership data and oral histories.

Survey data on homeownership and inheritance patterns reveal that Garifuna women were more likely to control use rights to both household settlement plots and cultivation plots. In 2002 women were reported more often than men to be homeowners.

Of the 55 households for which homeownership data were collected, 30 (60 percent) were reported to be female-owned (all but two female owners were Garifuna), 12 (24 percent) were reported to be male-owned, and eight (16 percent) were reported to be jointly owned. Of the 26 Garifuna female interviewees, 15 (58 percent) reported living on land they inherited matrilineally. The other 11 women lived on purchased land in Colonia Suazo or donated land in Colonia Libertad, but prior to obtaining their own plots, they all reported living in the homes of female relatives, supporting a trend of female homeownership.

The means by which male homeowners acquired plots further supports the tradition of matrilineal inheritance and that men were largely responsible for the private land sales of cultivation plots. Three of the men who were reported as homeowners bought their homes from women, two lived on donated land (Colonia Libertad), and two others bought their land from Suazo and Fernandez (the latter is a central figure of land-loss stories introduced in the coming pages).

The second set of evidence that supports the gendered nature of privatization is oral stories surrounding loss of cultivation plots. When I began to explore the forces behind the transition from communal landholding to growing privatization and a limited (limiting) communal title, the stories of women were the most salient. Berta's account is illustrative of women's testimonies.

> When I was told [of the land limits set by the 1997 title], I immediately reacted. I said, "I do not agree with what is happening!" It [the community limits according to the title] appears to be from this side of the river to this area over here. And what happened to the rest of the community? Because I remember. Me, with my mother—when I was 18 years old, my mother and I went until there, until Rio Ramirez for firewood. My mother brought me to the other side, to Rio Pierda, to get wood and yuca. And I went to the line of the mountain. When I went there the other month, I didn't need to rest. Why? Because I know it! The mountain line, all of this, I went with my mom to bring yuca, to bring wood. For this, I am not in agreement with what is happening. I know my community very well.

Berta's body knows the terrain of her ancestors so well that she did not tire when, as a member of Sambo Creek's patronato, she accompanied the INA and OFRANEH activists to the mountains to measure the limits of their ancestral territories. Other Sambeño women shared similar memories of accompanying their mother and/or grandmother to the mountain or to the Corinto area to tend to or harvest crops and fruits. While it is true that men also participated and continue to participate in agriculture, female ancestors were mentioned most often in stories of land loss (74 percent of formal interviews and surveyed households).

I remember very well going to the mountain with my grandmother. We'd go early, while it was still dark. We would cross the road and go through the woods to get to our plot. One day we got there and a man was there saying that it was his. He said that Valentin [a member of the patronato] sold it to him for 70 *lemps!* I was so mad, but I couldn't do anything, because I was little. And my mom didn't do anything, and neither did my aunt. I was so angry! For 70 lempiras! [25-year-old Garifuna woman]

My grandma said that all that is here . . . all of these haciendas and where the hotels are now . . . it was all cassava. My grandmother planted yuca there during her lifetime. But people came and threatened them, telling them that they had to leave or sell...they were scared and didn't know how to defend themselves. [Garifuna woman, age 32]

After listening to such comments, I often followed with direct queries for concrete examples of stolen lands. This 46-year-old Garifuna woman provided an example.

When I was a girl, we worked the land with my mother. This was a long time ago. We would get up at 4:00 or 5:00 in the morning and go to the other side of the road to collect the cassava, plantains, *guineo*. . . . When I was around 39, I stopped planting. We had to stop because people moved in on the land and robbed us of the land. Sampson, for example. He was a teacher here in our school. [Therefore] we trusted him. He went around to all the parents of the school and collected our signatures, about five hundred or so, asking us all for 10 lempiras so that we could get [potable] water. We all agreed and we trusted him. But he ended up stealing the land from the people.

The story of Mr. Foráneos Caso Sampson tricking the community by alleging that community members were signing a petition to bring in external aid for local development projects was well known. Most of those whom I interviewed recalled this petition, saying Sampson went around to the mothers of school-age children, claiming that he would bring potable water to the community. Later, Sampson returned with documentation citing his ownership over a significant tract of land in Corinto. This land is now private.

In 2002 the most contentious conflict was over the lands of Castillo, a politically connected mestizo who had illegally extended his holdings with private gates and hired a watchman to guard the land. Community members were prohibited from crossing the land to access the sea or river. Many stories circulated in the community regarding how Castillo obtained the land. Abuse of power and authority, exploitation of Garifuna poverty, and racial discrimination were central themes in these stories. Marta, a 35-year-old Garifuna woman had heard the story from her grandmother.

> In the land of Castillo there was a Garifuna woman that was the original owner of this land. A neighbor's pig came into her lands and was destroying the land, eating her yuca. She hit the pig, but then the neighbor got mad at her and she became frightened, and ended up abandoning her lands out of fear. Afterward, this neighbor took the woman's lands and passed the land to their kids and then to their grandkids. Eventually the land was lost. [Author's translation from Spanish]

Notice that the original owner was cited as a woman. Women were the central victims even in stories told by men. The following is an example.

> Consesa Buity was the original owner. She did not have any money, and she did not sell the lands. What happened was that her husband died, and she didn't have money to pay for his coffin. At that time a coffin cost 7.50 lempiras. Miguel Fernandez bought the coffin on loan for her land. But then Consesa died and her daughter was afraid of Fernandez, so she did not recuperate the lands. So after a time Fernandez sold the land to Castillo, about 25 years ago. Flores was a lawyer and so he worked on the papers to do this process.[1]

Stories such as these circulated within the community as to how Fernandez and then later Castillo came to own the land in Corinto. According to a report from the CCARC (2002), the land passed first to Suazo, the local store owner and money lender who later sold it to Fernandez.

Beachfront land, as one would imagine, is highly desired by outsiders with resources and is quickly becoming monopolized by well-off mestizos and foreigners. Maricela's story is typical of the deals brokered with poorer Sambeños.

Maricela, a 53-year-old mulatto woman, was born in the center of Sambo Creek to a longtime resident but does not identify as Garifuna. She spent most of her adult life struggling to care for her 10 children; her husband immigrated to the United States with plans to send her remittances but has since married in the United States and stopped sending support for his family in Honduras. The three youngest children still live with her, and the others rent in other places in the community. In 2002 Maricela entered into a contract with Flora and Amilcar, the owners of a local business on the beachfront, who were looking to expand their operations.

Flora is a Honduran-born mestiza who married a foreign immigrant in the 1990s. With her husband's money, the couple bought a plot of beachfront land to build a restaurant. Over the years it had become very successful, with people from La Ceiba regularly traveling to Sambo Creek just to eat at the restaurant. Although the money to purchase the land may have come from her foreign spouse, the land title was put in Flora's name because under Article 107 only Hondurans can own beachfront land. The couple eventually acquired more and more land within the community, and it all was registered under Flora's name (again, Article 107). After some time, Flora left her husband for Amilcar, a mestizo who was working for Flora and her husband as a watchman.

At first, Flora and Amilcar approached the Garifuna man who owned the plot of land next to their restaurant with a proposal to trade his beach plot for a house in Colonia Libertad on land that was owned by a mestizo who lived in La Ceiba. The Garifuna man refused the offer, because he did not want to leave the beach for the Colonia.

Not to be deterred from their goal, Flora and Amilcar approached Maricela, who lived on the main road, two plots inland. Maricela's house was in extremely poor condition. The roof leaked in numerous spots, so much so that the entire house was always wet and had developed a mold problem. She needed a home for her children and thus agreed to move to the house in Colonia Libertad in exchange for her land close to the beach. Maricela's house was demolished in order to build a new home on that land for the Garifuna man who did not want to leave the beach. The contract stipulated that the Garifuna man would exchange his beachfront plot for Maricela's plot and a newly constructed house, and Flora would purchase the land and house in Colonial Libertad for Maricela's family.

Dire situations like Maricela's (i.e., substandard living quarters and no income to feed one's children) serve(d) as common impetus for Sambeños to turn their land over to wealthier entrepreneurs. The above stories and the accounts of Suazo's land ownership and subsequent sales to outsiders reveal that what has taken place in Sambo Creek is more complicated than mestizos exploiting Garifuna through physical threat and political sway. Although it is true that much of the community's ancestral lands is now in the hands of mestizos and foreigners, Suazo, a Garifuna man, facilitated some of this transition. Sambeños of other ethnicities are also threatened by land speculation. One consistent pattern, however, is gendered inequality.

Stories of land loss center around women, because land loss, whether to a mestizo or to another Garifuna (like Felipe Suazo) is a process by which women have lost resources to men.

Gendered Environmental Rights and Responsibilities

Land is capital, and the reregulation of community land into private land encourages capital growth by increasing its potential for productivity. Ownership of land thus creates opportunities for wealth through its productive capacity. Land ownership also provides further means to increase capital and wealth, as property title deeds are the main way to secure loans and credit (Lee-Smith and Trujillo 2006:163–164). In addition to its potential for economic capital, land is a form of social and symbolic capital, and ownership is a sign of status.

Why are women's property rights so crucial? There is a direct, positive correlation between a woman's ownership of productive resources and her risk of poverty (Deere and Leon 2001a:331). Land ownership provides the best guarantee that a woman will be able to contribute to the household's food requirements (Deere and Leon 2001a:331). This is critical in the largely matrifocal households found in Garifuna communities. Land ownership is also associated positively with increased productivity, as it mediates access to credit and other services. Moreover, women property owners have more bargaining power within relationships, higher levels of decision making within households, and a greater range of marital options (Deere and Leon 2001a:331).

While the data are limited, much of what we know about the gendered distribution of property confirms the existence of inequalities. Most countries do not collect property ownership data by gender, but for those that do, the percentage of women owning property is a distinct minority. In many countries, women live under customary or religious laws that do not provide them with the legal rights to own or inherit property (Lee-Smith and Trujillo 2006:164), and women's access to land is often regulated by the men who have authority over them (Derman, Odgaard, and Sjaastad 2007:11). Moreover, the majority of land programs are "gender-blind." Not considering gender is the near-equivalent of discriminating against women in land projects, as in many countries women and men have different levels of education, networks, and cultural norms (Giovarelli and Lastarria-Cornhiel 2006:14). While the Garifuna had traditionally contradicted gendered patterns that privileged male land ownership by passing use rights matrilineally, once the value of coastal land grew, Garifuna women became seriously disadvantaged as competitors in the global marketplace.

The accounts in this chapter reveal that the decades-long processes of privatization have moved land from a largely Garifuna women's resource to that of mestizo and foreign men. The "gender-blind" neoliberal land policies of the 1990s served to expand land displacement and gender inequality, especially in the tourism boom on Honduras's coastline.

Neoliberalism in the agrarian sector is based on the notion of enhancing security of land tenure for producers in order to turn an investment on the land, increasing productivity and production (Deere and Leon 2001c:440). Land titling programs enable this productivity, making the land market more efficient, as land becomes easier to sell and purchase (Deere and Leon 2001c:440). Nearly all Latin American countries undertook land titling programs in the 1990s, most of them funded through the World Bank and Inter-American Development Bank (Deere and Leon 2001c:440). Honduras was no exception (e.g., the LMA, reviewed in chapter 2). But how did women fare as a result of these modernization and titling programs? What about Garifuna women?

Deere and Leon (2001b:42) offer a gender comparison of beneficiaries of land titling since neoliberal agrarian reform in Honduras (the authors analyze data from 1995 to 1997), showing that women received only 25 percent of the titles granted. When compared to other Latin American nations, this number is quite low. This is because Honduras's neoliberal agrarian legislation does not have mandatory mechanisms of inclusion. Countries that do, such as Chile and Ecuador, saw a more even distribution of titles by gender (43 percent to women in Chile, 49 percent in Ecuador), a result of inclusionary mechanisms such as an explicit priority to titling poor peasant households headed by women. Because Honduras's law is gender-blind, a smaller percentage of women benefited from land titling. However, Deere and Leon (2001b:44) point out that while these numbers are low in comparison with other countries, they are still markedly higher than in past reform periods when women represented only 3.7 percent of beneficiaries, perhaps a reflection of the international feminist agenda tricking down.

While Honduran women in general are making some headway in terms of receiving private land titles in their names, Garifuna women's land loss has accelerated under neoliberal land titling programs. Honduran legislation recognizes women as producers, but the laws are aimed at modernization, globalization, and the privatization of the economy. Legislation thus focuses on the issuance of private land titles as opposed to communal land titles with matrilineally based use rights. Garifuna women lack the conditions necessary to benefit from these laws—specifically, education, experience in a market system, access to credit, and investment capital. As a result, the ways in which environmental rights and responsibilities are restructured within neoliberal contexts are alarmingly gendered, both in terms of the division of resources and the division of power (Rocheleau, Thomas-Slayter, and Wangari 1996:4–5). Who owns and manages land (i.e., the division of resources) and who becomes legally sanctioned to preserve or protect it, or to make decisions that will affect the actions of others (i.e., the division of power), are now largely men. As the above data from Sambo Creek show, for decades the drive to privatize land has fundamentally disempowered women, and neoliberal land policies have contributed to their increased land displacement. With Garifuna women not holding legal title to matrilineally inherited use rights for specific plots of communal land, ancestral property has been transformed from a woman's resource to a man's.

Changing Livelihoods

Today very few families cultivate the land in Garifuna villages that border major coastal cities, like Sambo Creek. Such communities have suffered significant land loss in the face of new housing developments associated with urban sprawl and the emerging tourism economy. In addition to land shortages, the increasing remittance economy and youth interests contribute to the decline in agriculture. A comparison of data regarding labor choices and opinions about the decline in agriculture within Sambo Creek is illustrative.

In 2002 very few people worked in "traditional" economic activities, such as fishing, agriculture, vending, or craft production. Those engaged in traditional labor were all older than age 50, with the exception of one young man involved in craft production (this business expanded in later years; featured in photo at right).

Only one woman in Sambo Creek mentioned agriculture as her primary occupation, and she noted that she cultivated for supplemental subsistence, not income. I did follow questions about current occupations with direct questions about whether members of the household cultivated yuca. While some households had banana, plantain, coconut, and other fruit trees on their land, only two of the households I spoke with reported

Figure 4.1 Local artisans producing traditional drums for tourism economy, Sambo Creek. Photo by Keri Brondo

Table 4.1 Primary Occupations for Household Sample in Sambo Creek, 2002

Reported Primary Occupation	# Women	# Men	Total
Agriculture	1	0	1
Fishing	0	1	1
Vending/Craft production	1	1	2
Small business owner	1	1	2
Domestic labor in La Ceiba	4	0	4
Hotel staff	2	1	3
Religious work	0	1	1
Construction/metalworking	0	2	2
Seamstress	1	0	1
University student	1	0	1
Homemaker	13	0	13
None/Reliant on remittances	2	4	6
Retired	0	5	5
Total	26	16	42

having an additional plot of land where they grew cassava. Younger men and women reported work as wage laborers or small business owners, or they were reliant on remittances. Table 4.2 shows past occupations for the 32 Garifuna individuals old enough to have changed jobs or to have spouses who changed jobs.

The transition in livelihood strategies is clear. Before the 1950s, many residents were engaged in the banana industry as plantation workers or vendors. As bananas declined, the search for work began to take people out of the community. Men sought employment on cruise ships and commercial fishing boats or migrated to Honduras's larger cities to work as wage laborers, while women typically stayed in the area (although in recent decades many young women migrate as well). The trend of men leaving the community in somewhat higher numbers continues, with 73 percent of the Garifuna women (19 of 26) I interviewed stating they had a male spouse or partner who was not currently living in their home. Two of the nineteen women reported that their partners lived with them when they

Table 4.2 Reported Past Occupations for Household Sample in Sambo Creek

Reported past occupation for self and spouse	# Women	# Men
Plantation work for Standard Fruit	0	6
Vending traditional food products (on plantations or in La Ceiba)	9	1
Work on cruise ship	0	4
Domestic labor in La Ceiba	2	0
Local fishing	0	2
Commercial fishing boat	0	2
Construction	0	4
Wage labor in Tegucigalpa or San Pedro Sula	2	3
Nursing	1	1
Total	14	23

were in the country. Of the seven who had men in their homes, three noted that they became permanent residents in the house only upon retirement from cruise ships.

Notably, not one person reported agriculture as a past occupation. However, when asked directly if they ever *participated* in agriculture, all 42 of the Garifuna interviewees responded that they did. All respondents (men and women) further noted that they cultivated with their female relatives (mothers or grandmothers). Table 4.3 details the reasons people in the household interviews believed there was a decline in agriculture.

Garifuna interviewees cited the loss of their ancestral land as the primary reason for the decline in agriculture. Non-Garifuna offered different reasons for the decline, including lack of water and the growing remittance economy. Both Garifuna and non-Garifuna recognized that contemporary youth are not interested in agriculture. Despite the near-disappearance of agriculture in Sambo Creek, the majority of Garifuna individuals (69 percent) that I surveyed said they would plant crops if sufficient land were made available.

As is explored in the next chapter, at the organizational level the Garifuna struggle to reclaim ancestral territories is often articulated in a way

Table 4.3 Household Interviewee Reasons for Decline in Agriculture

Question: Why do people in the community no longer plant crops? (n = 55)

Response	# Garifuna	# Non-Garifuna	Total
Land was stolen/lost to immigrants	31	1	32
Youth are not interested	6	3	9
People sold the land	5	3	8
Crop theft/Animals killed crops	7	1	8
People do not need to because they receive remittances from the US	3	4	7
Lack of water (not lack of land)	0	2	2
Total	52	14	66*

* The total is greater than the sample size because some individuals mentioned more than one reason for the decline in agriculture.

that highlights cultural traditions such as fishing or agriculture. Yet fewer and fewer young people engage in these activities. Only a handful of the young women I knew in Sambo Creek made casabe; they may have helped their mothers when they were young, but today they are more interested in wage labor and education. The following excerpt is from an interview with a 19-year-old activist who was studying in La Ceiba. I followed this young man's political growth over three years (from the summer of 2000 until November of 2002), watching him go from a strong OFRANEH affiliation to an ODECO supporter. We were talking about his hometown community, which is near Trujillo, and the shifts in the number of people who devote their time to agriculture. He told me that his grandmother and mother still planted, but that few others were doing it today. Victor's comments are illustrative of many Garifuna youth, including those who live in Sambo Creek.

> KERI: Do the youth in XXX [his hometown] still plant?
> VICTOR: The youth don't want to plant. For example, me, I go to XXX and I will be a community leader. I don't want to go to XXX to work the land. I want an office. I want a computer. And there are many more youth like me.

KERI: And in your experience with ODECO, they think that the youth want to plant?

VICTOR: They know that the youth don't want to plant.

KERI: Then what is the alternative in the eyes of ODECO?

VICTOR: For ODECO? Supposedly to motivate the youth.

KERI: To plant?

VICTOR: To have projects to motivate them to plant.

KERI: And fish?

VICTOR: And fish. We were talking in this past meeting last year about projects to do this year. I said, "I don't think I will go to my community to plant. I think I will go to work with my community. But not in the mountain! I think I will go to create businesses."

KERI: And is OFRANEH the same? Do they want to motivate the youth to plant?

VICTOR: OFRANEH in this moment looks to develop projects for adults, so that they can have crops.

KERI: Why do you think the organizations focus on motivating people in this way—in cultivation and in fishing, and not in other types of jobs?

VICTOR: . . . Because they always think in traditions and not in reality. Because the reality is we do not want this. We in the communities need more practical things, and we [the youth] are going to fight so that they [the organizations] are in agreement with the demands and the necessities of the population. Why do they fight for the lands? I am going to fight for what is mine, yes—to have what is mine, and to be able to negotiate it. But I am not going to fight for things that I am not going to occupy. . . . These things [fishing and agriculture] are not what the priorities are now. These are what were years ago, when the majority of Garifuna communities were like this. Agriculture and fishing. But today is a different reality. Our reality is to have a better education. Our reality is a new technology.

Later on, we began to talk about the land struggle and the benefits of communal versus private land.

VICTOR: Ah, Keri. It's very interesting to talk about land tenure. In these times it is very difficult for a variety of reasons. We Garifuna are fighting for the land, and it looks good to me, and we have the right to recuperate them. But what happened? Now we don't want to work the Garifuna land. I proposed in a meeting with Celeo Álvarez, with

ODECO, that the Garifuna land should be sold to investors for business, to people that would invest in the community.

KERI: And what was the reaction?

VICTOR: Of Celeo? He nearly died. He answered me very strongly, very angrily. He said, "How could we trust the lands to unknown people in these departments [states of Honduras] ?!" But we don't work the lands!

KERI: Your proposal was to sell to investors?

VICTOR: Not to sell, but to negotiate.

KERI: To people from outside or from within the country?

VICTOR: To whoever invests first. But he doesn't want this.

KERI: Why do you think that is?

VICTOR: I don't know. It would be good to find out. We have this problem. We lack education. Why? Because the people in Garifuna communities do not have access to a high school. Why? Because we do not have money. Infrastructure. Bad infrastructure. . . . I am going to talk specifically about my pueblo—Trujillo. Now we have a North American company that wants to bring a project, called Ciudad Flotante. It's a floating city.

KERI: Yes, I've heard of it.

VICTOR: Oh you have? OK, good. So, they want to invest, but it seems they also want to use a part of the communal land to have access to it. They asked to use the land that belongs to the community, and the community said they want it, but ODECO is against it. . . . Why don't they negotiate? You put in the capital; I'll put up the land. And of the earnings, we'll get this percentage. Don't you think this is the most logical?

I wish to compare Victor's comments to those of Dilcia, a 25-year-old woman from Sambo Creek who was studying engineering in Tegucigalpa. While she also told me that she represented the majority of youth in her community in that she has no interest in agriculture, she had very different opinions on land investment and development initiatives.

Dilcia described a visit from World Bank representatives in which, she explained, the representatives tried to "sell" the community on the privatization of social services (schools, water, health services, etc.). According to Dilcia, the representatives promised the arrival of *maquila* factories that would pay workers forty cents an hour. She recalled the World Bank representatives saying they were supportive of the Garifuna land struggle and wanted to assist them to resolve the land claims and administer land titles.

When I asked her opinion of the meeting, she told me that she thought the "real reason" the World Bank wanted to help with the land struggle was that they wanted to "take over" the community's land, privatizing it in order to facilitate the entrance of maquilas, not because they wanted to aid the community in gaining autonomy over their territories.

Dilcia said she believed the World Bank was trying to "trick" the people of Sambo Creek into supporting World Bank programs and the Plan Pueblo Panama, and that they were using the residents' lack of education and desperate need for employment against them. She feared the privatization of community services, saying "How can we pay for schools and water if we are making just 40 cents an hour? Our kids will not be able to get an education!"

While neither Dilcia nor Victor envisioned a future in fishing and agriculture, both expressed a shared concern with the ability of the Garifuna to control decisions about land use, and to choose the type of livelihood strategy that they find most suitable to their needs. Victor's position demonstrates a commitment to a development model based on progress, economic development, and foreign investment. In contrast, Dilcia is more supportive of communal resources and skeptical of international development programs. With caution I note the gendered distinction in their views on development, with Victor embracing a westernized, masculine model of development, while Dilcia reflects feminist critiques of modernity. I take this risk of oversimplification and generalization as it foreshadows the discussion in the next chapter.

FIVE

Representing the Garifuna

Development, Territory, Indigeneity, and Gendered Activism

Indigenous rights is arguably the most valuable rights-based discourse in the Garifuna struggle for territories. Yet, curiously, while an assertion of indigenous rights increases the ability of ethnic activists to influence state and international policies, only one of the two principal Garifuna organizations embraces these rights discourses. This chapter takes up the differences between the ethnopolitics of La Organización Fraternal Negro Hondureño (OFRANEH) and La Organización de Desarrollo Etnico Comunitario (ODECO), and their approaches to development, beginning with an overview of the relationship between indigeneity and territory.

Indigenous Rights and Land-Rootedness

Indigenous activism is based on the articulation of a specific meaningful relationship of indigenous peoples to their territories, behind which lies the ultimate political goal of the right to self-determination. The struggle for territory goes beyond land reform to include the right to communal land, environmental protection, and control over development. The link between indigenous identity and control of territory has been credited to the UN-commissioned study the "Problem of Discrimination against Indigenous Populations." The study began in 1972 and was completed in 1986, resulting in the multivolume work compiled by special rapporteur José Martínez Cobo that has become a standard reference for discussion of indigenous peoples within the United Nations system (United Nations 2004). The Cobo report identified land-rootedness as the principal marker of indigenous identity (Lâm 2004).

> Indigenous communities, peoples and nations are those which, having a historical continuity with preinvasion and precolonial societies that developed on their territories, consider themselves distinct from other sections of societies once prevailing in those territories or parts of them. They form at present nondominant sectors of society and are determined to preserve, develop and transmit to future generations their ancestral territories, and their ethnic identity, as the basis of their continued existence as peoples, in accordance with their own cultural patterns, social institutions and legal systems. [Cobo 1983]

With this definition of indigenous communities, international bodies officially recognized that the ability of indigenous people to survive is inextricably tied to their right to occupy their traditional territories and control local resources.

Around the same time, in 1982, the United Nations Working Group on Indigenous Populations was convened to begin discussions of what later became the draft Universal Declaration of the Rights of Indigenous Peoples. This declaration, which was first issued in 1989 and expanded in 1990, raised international consciousness of the issues indigenous communities faced, by advocating the right of indigenous groups to

> develop their own ethnic and cultural characteristics; to protect their cultural practices and ceremonial, historical, and archaeological sites; to practice their own spiritual traditions; to promote their own languages; to name themselves and their communities; to have a voice in legal and administrative proceedings . . . ; to control their own schools; to have access to the mass media; to gain recognition of their customary laws and land tenure systems; to receive restitution or compensation for lands that have been usurped; to enact a wide range of environmental protection; to actively participate in their own social and economic improvement with state support; to have autonomy in internal and local affairs . . . ; to gain direct representation in the political affairs of the state; and to exercise autonomy in international and local affairs. [Warren 1998:7]

The rights outlined in this declaration have been confirmed through additional international declarations and conventions that have come out in the last 20 years. These include: the United Nations Educational, Scientific, and Cultural Organization's (UNESCO) Declaration of San José, and the International Labour Organization's (ILO) Convention concerning Indigenous and Tribal Peoples in Independent Countries (commonly referred to as ILO 169), and most recently the UN Declaration on the Rights of Indigenous Peoples. These passages made the link between previously ratified international conventions on genocide and racial discrimination (e.g., the 1948 Convention on the Prevention and Punishment of the Crime of Genocide, the 1966 International Convention on the Elimination of All Forms of Racial Discrimination) and the necessity of territorial and resource control, claiming that the infringement of this right is both a violation of human rights and ethnocide. Moreover, these declarations note that cultural ethnocide is effectively equivalent to genocide (Lâm 2004). Honduras ratified all of the conventions listed above, providing a legal structure through which indigenous groups can make their claims.

ILO 169—which was discussed at length in chapter 2—was the most significant international achievement and critical document in support of Garifuna territorial rights at the time of my field research on the subject (spanning 2000–2006). ILO 169 was adopted in 1989 after years of discussions on revising the ILO's 1959 Indigenous and Tribal Convention 107. Indigenous peoples, human rights advocates, and international jurists widely condemned ILO 107 as an assimilationist and racist document, and in serious need of revision (Niezen 2003:36–40). The revision of ILO 107 marked a conceptual transformation on the part of nation-states, moving from a view of indigenous populations as temporary societies that were doomed to disappear through acculturation to recognition that they are permanent societies deserving of status equal to other nationalities within a country. Hence, ILO 169 is an instrument of inclusion (or the recognition that people have the right to different ways of living), as opposed to the integration instrument that was ILO 107 (Deere and León 2001b:59). ILO 169 therefore shifted the focus of Convention 107 from an integrationist perspective to something more in line with indigenous people's needs and aspirations, recognizing their rights to self-determination. Cultural autonomy and difference were now protected as human rights.

While ILO 169 was the most concrete manifestation of increasing international responsiveness to indigenous demands at the time of my field research, since then the United Nations has adopted the Declaration on the Rights of Indigenous Peoples, burgeoning support for indigenous claims to territory. The UN Declaration on the Rights of Indigenous Peoples was approved on September 13, 2007, by the 61st General Assembly after more than two decades of negotiations. The declaration "establishes a universal framework of minimum standards for the survival, dignity, well-being and rights of the world's indigenous peoples." It addresses both individual and collective rights and ensures the right of indigenous peoples "to remain distinct and to pursue their own priorities in economic, social and cultural development" (Office of the UN High Commissioner for Human Rights 2007). Importantly, within the declaration itself, "indigeneity" and "indigenous peoples" remain undefined, indicating an international recognition that self-identification is the most fundamental piece to recognizing a peoples as indigenous. The open-ended nature of the definition of "indigenous peoples" encourages the expanding identification of Garifuna activists and intellectuals with the global indigenous movement and increases their ability to influence the actions of international and state entities (French 2011). What this has meant was that "blacks" could also be indigenous.[1]

OFRANEH activists were part of this growing movement to expand international understandings of indigeneity. In my first interview with a core leader of OFRANEH in 2000, before beginning our discussion the female activist asked to look over my set of interview questions. After reading the two pages of questions, she said she would like to begin with a question listed under the subcategory "other," nearly three-quarters into the interview schedule.

> This question interests me a lot—"*Como identifican los Garifunas? Como indígenas, autóconos, ó los dos?*" I believe it is hard to define *indigenous*. You must see this in your work as well. The Garifuna are not indigenous to Central America, but we do identify as indigenous as an *autoidentificación* (self-identification). I think this is important—that we choose to identify ourselves in this way. In 1992 [*sic*], when the Year of the Indigenous was celebrated, there was a lot of debate over how *indigenous* is defined and what it was that makes a people indigenous. If you ask a Garifuna person if they are indigenous, they would say, "No; I'm *negro.*" But they are culturally indigenous because they share the cultural traits of the indigenous Arawaks in this hemisphere. Our language is indigenous. We have the pigment of indigenous peoples. Therefore, to say we are indigenous is a self-identification, and this is what is important. We are the only *negros* in Central America with our own language. [Author's translation from Spanish]

By beginning our meeting with the contemporaneous debate over the meaning of indigeneity, this activist establishes the centrality of self-identification in Garifuna ethnopolitics. Her comments reflected debates over scale of place in tracing indigeneity. Like the place-making strategies of the Maya in Belize that Medina (1998) discusses (i.e., that they argue for indigenous rights based on being indigenous to the region, not just to the territorial boundaries of Belize), Honduran Garifuna can make similar arguments to their indigenous heritage. As the Garifuna leader points out, the Garifuna share "cultural traits" with the Arawakans of the Western Hemisphere.

Another advancement in the Garifuna struggle for territorial rights is UNESCO's 2003 recognition of the Garifuna's "intangible cultural heritage." According to the United Nations Convention for the Safeguarding of the Intangible Cultural Heritage, an intangible cultural heritage refers to

> the practices, representations, expressions, as well as the knowledge and skills, that communities, groups and, in some cases, individuals recognise as part of their cultural heritage. It is sometimes called living cultural heritage, and is manifested inter alia in the following domains: (i) oral traditions and expressions, including language as a vehicle of the intangible cultural heritage; (ii) performing arts; (iii) social practices, rituals and festive events; (iv) knowledge and practices concerning nature and the universe; (v) traditional craftsmanship. The intangible cultural heritage is transmitted from generation to generation, and is constantly recreated by communities and groups, in response to their environment, their interaction with nature, and their historical conditions of existence. It provides people with a sense of identity and continuity, and its safeguarding promotes, sustains, and develops cultural diversity and human creativity (United Nations 2005).

The international declaration that people who identify as "Garifuna" possess a cultural heritage that is in danger of disappearance and should be preserved legitimizes Garifuna claims to resources if they can demonstrate that cultural survival is incumbent upon continued access to those resources. While UNESCO recognizes that there are aspects of "culture" that exist beyond geographic space, they also note that "culture" is shaped through historical relationships to the environment. Like ILO 169 and the Cobo report, the Convention for the Safeguarding of the Intangible Cultural Heritage affirms that maintenance of cultural identity is tied to one's surroundings. Thus, in the early to mid-2000s, the ability of Honduran Garifuna to demonstrate that their unique cultural heritage was derived from a historical relationship to nature increased support for their land claims. By the end of the decade, with the emergence of the 2007

UN Declaration on the Rights of Indigenous Peoples, the link between culture and territory was critical. The UN declaration moved away from definitions of indigenous peoples that necessitate an historical connection to precolonial territories, enabling the flexibility of inclusion for displaced and diasporic indigenous peoples (French 2011:247).

Garifuna Organizational Stances on Development and Land Rights

Resolving land conflicts in Garifuna communities is complicated by the existence of two principal Garifuna organizations, each with a distinct vision for the future of Garifuna landholding and development projects on ancestral territories. OFRANEH is a grassroots support organization that was formed in 1977 and received official recognition in 1980. While it was formed to represent "Afro-Hondurans," a category that includes English-speaking blacks and the Garifuna, it has since transformed into an organization that focuses exclusively on Garifuna representation, with an emphasis on self-determination, autonomy, and protection of Garifuna territory and culture. Today, women dominate leadership positions in this organization. ODECO is an NGO that serves as an intermediary between international aid agencies and Garifuna communities. ODECO was formed in 1992 (and received official recognition in 1994) by a group of ex-OFRANEH members who left the organization due to "differences in philosophies" (common phrasing for the split by leadership in both organizations). The organization's founding president, Celeo Álvarez, had been a member of OFRANEH in the 1980s and was the former head of the largest medical union in Honduras. Álvarez continues to lead the organization through today.

Based on interviews with leading Honduran black activists, historian Dario Euraque (2004) provides a history of black politics among the Garifuna on the north coast of Honduras. Euraque explores how the political situation, population demographics of blacks in coastal departments, and individuals' educational and vocational backgrounds combined to influence the discourses and approaches of ODECO and OFRANEH. Euraque reminds us that the context in which Celeo Álvarez (1959–) came of age was quite different from that of founders of OFRANEH Dr. Alfonso Lacayo (1926–1985) and Basilio Arriola García (1930–). During the time Álvarez was completing his primary education in La Ceiba, in 1972, the unique racial identity of the Garifuna culture was being recognized and valorized, revealed by the presence of Garifuna dances at the 1972 Feria Patronal de San Isidro (Euraque 2004:165, 169). This was a time when the vindication of "Africanness" and blackness as an autonomous ethnic identity was powerful, and it shaped the organizational outlook and discourse for ODECO when it emerged in the early 1990s. The founders of OFRANEH, in contrast, were children of the 1950s labor movement, with strong ties to the Liberal Party at its most radical points, and these factors influenced the foundational ethnopolitics of OFRANEH (Euraque 2004:171).

The two organizations articulate quite differently with the meaning of "development," and the philosophy and reality of neoliberalism. Content analysis of platform statements and communiqués issued by ODECO and OFRANEH reveals that while ODECO positions itself as a collaborator alongside central government to combat racism *within* development initiatives, OFRANEH's approach is reflective of a larger indigenous rights critique that sees globalization and neoliberalism as attempting to enforce a separation of humanity from the environment. I utilize documents from the time period of my most intensive fieldwork on land rights (2002–5), as these reflect the discourse of Garifuna organizations at the time that I was talking with Sambeños about land loss and reclamation processes. In years since, the two organizations have issued several other statements reflective of their ethnic politics and positions on national development models; the contemporary moment is explored in the penultimate chapter.

In 2002 ODECO gave me the following document summarizing the Garifuna land struggle.

THE LAND PROBLEM IN GARIFUNA COMMUNITIES, STEP BY STEP

1. Until 1992, all Honduran Garifuna communities with the exception of Trujillo, had titles of occupation for the land in which they were based.

2. In 1992, the national government passed the LAW FOR MODERNIZATION AND DEVELOPMENT OF THE AGRICULTURAL SECTOR, under Decree 31-92; this action legalized the privatization of lands for investment, principally favoring foreign investment.

3. Due to the lack of definitive land titles, the Garifuna were harassed by national and international businessmen, military, and politicians, who wanted their lands, and strategically declared them zones for tourism development.

4. Between 1993 and 1995, 14 Garifuna communities received definitive titles, with the disadvantage being that these "titles" did not include

the historical land of the communities, which is to say, the community lands were reduced drastically. Moreover, all of the urban parts of town or places where houses are constructed that were not included in the title are considered exclusive areas for tourism and therefore property of the state.

5. On October 11, 1996, the Coordinadora Nacional de Organizaciones Negras de Honduras held LA PRIMERA GRAN MARCHA PACIFICA DEL PUEBLO NEGRO DE HONDURAS in Tegucigalpa, the capital of the republic, leading to the signing of an AGREEMENT for the first time in history where the government promised to resolve the problem of titling [documenting the legal possession of land through the National Agrarian Institute], Saneamiento [the legal procedure that determines who are the legal owners of land and who have obtained land through irregular procedures], and Ampliación or Dotación [authorizing more land in favor of communities that require it for their growth and development].

6. The October 11th march achieved 1.7 million lempiras ($131,000), authorized to the National Agrarian Institute ("INA") on December 20, 1996. On January 11, 1997, the Honduran Institute of Anthropology and History donated 200,000 lempiras more, also for the process of titling the lands of Garifuna communities.

7. One of the people who has hoarded the lands in Garifuna communities is the businessman MIGUEL FACUSSE, who on June 26, 1997, received a WORLD BANK loan for 55 MILLION DOLLARS, to strengthen his investments in a project called the GRAN PROYECTO DE TRANSFORMACION "GPTN" [Great Project of National Transformation]. This project received unconditional support from the government, private business, and other privileged sectors of the country. This signifies that each day that passes is a day working against the Afro-Honduran community's goal to achieve their legitimate right to land.

8. The Law for Modernization and Development of the Agricultural Sector declares that after three years of squatting without interruption, any Honduran over 16 years can claim it as their legitimate property. We ask, why then after 204 years, isn't the Garifuna community's right to their historical lands recognized?

9. Tourism investment in Honduras is already a reality, and an activity that we do not oppose, as long as the Afro-Honduran communities participate at all levels as strategic partners in the process. We wish that the communities are the owners of their lands and the projects that are developed on their lands; the fight is just and if we are united, we can win.

10. This adverse situation impels us to conduct forceful battles, including the promotion of a strong campaign of denunciation and international solidarity to pressure the Government to fulfill the Agreements to Title, Adjust, and Extend the territories of the Garifuna and black communities. On this particular issue, the President of the Republic, Ricardo Maduro, subscribed to a campaign commitment with the Afro-Honduran Communities, through ODECO.

In 1797, the English exiled the Garifunas of St. Vincent from the land, and 204 years later, the main problem that faces us is the land; nevertheless the fight begins . . . we do not have to surrender.

Additionally, Hurricane Mitch caused severe material damage and human losses in Afro-Honduran Communities . . . 95 percent of crops were destroyed; the coconut palms are now prone to die, being attacked by the disease called AMARILLAMIENTO LETHAL. Some of these communities . . . lost many houses, as well as lost part of the equipment they need for fishing, one of the traditional income-generating businesses . . .

The AfroHonduran community is at a true crossroads. On the one hand, it is dealing with reconstruction after the damage caused by Hurricane Mitch, and on the other, it is fighting for the legalization of its land, while the Government attempts, through the National Congress, to reform Article 107 of the constitution to give away more of their rightful patrimony, LA TIERRA . . .

In this challenge, the egalitarian application and practice of inalienable human rights, and national and international solidarity play a predominant role.

Celeo Álvarez Casildo
President of ODECO
"BUSCAMOS VOCES QUE ACALLEN EL SILENCIO"
["We Seek Voices that Quiet the Silence"]

In this document, we see ODECO linking the passage of the LMA with the loss of land in Garifuna communities (LMA is the 1992 law that enabled cooperative members to sell their plots as private lands). Álvarez makes a case for titling Garifuna communal lands, noting that powerful interest groups harassed the Garifuna because they lacked institutionally recognized land rights. Álvarez highlights Garifuna mobilization, especially that spearheaded by ODECO (see point 10), as leading to a governmental commitment to resolve the land problems faced by Garifuna communities. He notes the irony and contradictions inherent in the LMA (point 8), which recognizes squatter's rights for Hondurans after three years, but not the Garifuna's centuries-long use of coastal territory. Further, Álvarez admonishes the government's endorsement of Honduras's business elite who have "hoarded" Garifuna territory and accelerated the expansion of nontraditional exports and tourism through the GPTN (point 7).

Following these statements, however, Álvarez's remarks about tourism investment (point 9) suggest that ODECO is not against the privatization of land or the country's neoliberal development policies that rely on privatization and foreign investment, as long as the Garifuna have ownership over their own land and are equal participants in the development process. In the closing statement, Álvarez notes that Hurricane Mitch damaged the traditional economic activity of Garifuna communities, but he never links these activities to indigenous rights and cultural survival. The international discourse that is evoked is human rights. Álvarez reiterates the Garifuna's positioning as Afro-Hondurans, illustrating ODECO's emphasis on the fight for racial equality. This position and representation of the Garifuna is quite different than OFRANEH's.

Below are two 2002 statements from OFRANEH leadership to national powers, the first to President Ricardo Maduro, and the second to the National Congress. These are prime examples of how OFRANEH calls upon the global discourse of indigenous rights, indigenous ecological knowledge, and international bodies such as the United Nations to articulate its stance on the land struggle, and its view of development policy.

EXPOSITION BEFORE THE PRESIDENT OF THE REPUBLIC RICARDO MADURO

November 13, 2002

INTRODUCTION

In spite of having occupied the north coast of Honduras for more than 205 years, we, the Honduran Garifuna, lack official territorial recognition, which jeopardizes our nutritional security and the legal support that we need to guarantee our survival as a distinct people.

Of the 48 communities in which you'll find our population located along the north coast, 28 of them are within protected areas or tropical zones. This is a clear signal of the role that we have played in the conservation of natural resources and how our traditional knowledge is essential in the management of coastal and marine ecosystems.

Unfortunately, the lack or our territorial and ecological recognition has resulted in agricultural colonization, which is devouring our forest resources, leading to the destruction of our river basins and increasing our vulnerability to disasters caused by global warming.

Our people were severely affected by Hurricane Mitch and the tropical storms Catherine and Michelle, demonstrated by the degree of erosion to our channels, rivers, and tropics. And still to this day, effective measures have not been taken to solve the deforestation, the drying up of the river basins, and the disappearance of forest cover vegetation.

The erosion of biodiversity and the destruction of ecosystems affect the development of the tourist industry, as it depends in great measure on the supply of this country's environmental and cultural wealth.

To date, Garifuna communities have preserved the traditional culture of our people, which was declared last year by UNESCO as "the cultural patrimony of humanity." At the same time that we have one of the lowest crime rates, we are a society that struggles against insecurity.

In order to be able to preserve our culture and the peace in which we live, it is essential that processes for territorial recognition be put in place, that we stop the sacking of marine resources, that we recover the coconut plantations, and further, that we confront the AIDS epidemic in an effective manner.

In the rich social fabric of our country, we can play an essential role in strengthening the processes of nature conservation and implementing new ways of obtaining currency, such as tourism. For these reasons, it is highly appropriate that the executive authority offer support to guarantee conflict resolution, thus improving the relationship between the Garifuna society and the Honduran State.

Given this situation, it is urgent that the following demands of our communities are addressed:

DEMANDS

1. Solve the land problem in Sambo Creek: return the land seized by the Castillo family; they currently occupy 12 manzanas. This is a clear example of the desperation and grave overcrowding in which they live.

2. Return the lands seized by Mr. Jaime Rosenthal in San Juan Tela. This is a case that was tried in the courts before in the city of Tela, and some of the leaders of this community have been jailed.

3. Solve the usurpation of 22 manzanas by the mayor of Tela in the community of Triunfo de la Cruz.

4. Provide the approval of funds from the National Congress for the saneamiento of the community of Punta Piedras.

5. Register the property titles of the cays of Chachahuate, Bolaños, and the community of East End in Cayos Cochinos.

6. Solve the problem of 30 Garifuna nurses, who a year and a half ago completed their studies and are still waiting for their titles from the Ministry of Health, and wish to be paid for social service as nurses in Batalla and Tocamacho.

7. Help initiate community tourism, based on a proposal from OFRANEH that was developed through consultation and discussion with the communities. Right now we are on the verge of inaugurating the first tourist footpath with financing by la Cooperación Española, AECI. [Author's translation from Spanish]

The next selection from a statement to the Honduran Congress builds on the previous. Analysis of the two documents follows.

PLAN BEFORE THE NATIONAL CONGRESS

The Black Fraternal Organization, OFRANEH, and the Garifuna communities of San Juan, Triunfo de la Cruz, Sambo Creek, Punta Piedra, Batalla, Tornabe, present the following to the National Congress.

Considering, that the Garifuna have been declared by UNESCO as possessing an Intangible Heritage, in recognition of its culture (language, dance, oral tradition, architecture, cosmovision, spirituality, etc.)

Considering, that the Honduran government has undertaken the development of a poverty reduction program. And we recognize that the guarantee of land to the most vulnerable sectors of Honduran society is fundamental for the alleviation of poverty.

Considering, that the Honduran state has executed a political strategy to develop the tourist industry, as a means to generate foreign investment and revenue, and that the potentially rich zones for tourism development are the areas where the Garifuna communities are located, since one of the fundamental principles of the tourist industry is to guarantee the psychological and physical security of visitors.

Declaring, that for indigenous peoples, the concept of conservation and sustainable use of biological biodiversity is not an empty concept. . . . These concepts, for native peoples, are intimately related to their spirituality and respect for Mother Earth. Life, territory, knowledge, and collective rights are inseparable. Article 8j of the Convention on Biodiversity recognizes this fundamental principle.

Considering, that the Honduran state ratified ILO 169 in May 1994, an international legal instrument that recognizes the collective rights of indigenous and tribal peoples worldwide.

Considering, that the community of Punta Piedra has been facing a land possession conflict for 10 years, which originated because a group of people from outside of the community took possession of the community's productive lands. [Author's translation from Spanish]

OFRANEH's approach is to begin their statements by highlighting the distinct cultural heritage of the Garifuna people, who exist in a special relationship to the environment. They point out how the environment has deteriorated since the Garifuna lost territorial control. In the first statement, OFRANEH makes a series of specific demands to the government, including the resolution of outstanding unresolved land conflicts, the registration of Garifuna territories not yet titled, and governmental support for ecologically and culturally sustainable community tourism initiatives, such as low-impact footpaths, that OFRANEH designed in conjunction with heavy local-level participation.

In both documents we see OFRANEH reminding the Honduran nation that the success of the tourism industry "depends in great measure on the supply of this country's environmental and cultural wealth," and that tourism relies on areas where visitors feel physically safe and psychologically fulfilled (Garifuna communities are presumed to provide this type of feeling). OFRANEH notes "to date, Garifuna communities have preserved the traditional culture of our people," pointing out the international recognition (by UNESCO) of the Garifuna's "intangible heritage" and "cultural survival." They use the significance of culture to impel the government to listen to their demands, asserting that the proposals for economic advancement are possible only with the "survival" of Garifuna traditions. They further note that "in order to be able to preserve our culture . . . it is essential that processes for territorial recognition be put in place." Territorial control, conservation, and cultural survival are inextricably linked, an argument articulated in the language of indigenous rights. OFRANEH's leaders make clear that for the Garifuna "the concept of conservation and sustainable use of biological diversity is not an empty concept . . . these concepts, for native peoples [like the Garifuna] are intimately related to their spirituality and respect for Mother Earth."

Here and elsewhere, OFRANEH activists articulate an "indigenous place" in the world as a conceptual tool in their political mobilization.

Drawing on Escobar (1992), Muehlebach (2001:425) described this form of ethnopolitics as a "politics of morality."

> The politics of morality continues as part of a larger global trend in which social movements are forming "not only [against a specific type of] politics and democracy, but [against] a whole civilizational design based on modern reason" (Escobar 1992:41). . . . indigenous "place-making" has fundamentally challenged this design. Attaching "the nucleus of all civilizing rationality," namely the "denial of man that he is part of nature" (1992:54), indigenous "place-making" at the U.N. has made visible the multitudinous relations said to exist between indigenous "subjects" and a meaningful entity—nature. Thus indigenous delegates have since their emergence on the global political scene insisted on the inseparability of two seemingly separable realms—ecology and ethnicity.

Comparing the above statements of OFRANEH and ODECO brings to light OFRANEH's participation in the international indigenous leadership's critique of a civilizational design based on neoclassical free-market development ideals. Invested in place-making through the articulation of Garifuna indigeneity, OFRANEH evokes the image of the Garifuna as a distinct people, drawing upon indigenous rights discourses that link indigenous identity to the environment, rooting the Garifuna—as indigenous peoples—to the land that has been and continues to be taken from them. They are fighting alongside other indigenous groups for the right to self-determination and the control over their own destinies. This form of ethnopolitics differs from ODECO's emphasis on racial equality and integration, and is arguably linked to the way in which each organization approaches "development."

OFRANEH's senior leadership is quite suspicious of development as a concept and as a process. In our first encounter in 2000, I asked one of their leading activists how she defined development.

> Development is difficult to define. It can, and most often does, destroy culture, customs, folklore, and spirit. I cannot give you a concrete definition. It is a complex concept. The popular definition is to change sustainably for the better, but the reality is that development can cause destruction. You have no way of knowing if it will be for the better. For example, many people think putting latrines in pueblos is development. It isn't enough. The communities need sustainability, education, food,

etc. Some people think that the Garifuna communities that do not have electricity need to have it for development. But I disagree. Electricity isn't automatically development. Our communities have certain traditions because we do not have electricity. Women all gather together at night to talk beneath the moon. If you bring electricity to their community, they will stop, and this will destroy their traditions. [Author's translation from Spanish]

These comments echo those shared by other OFRANEH affiliates who saw development as a direct threat to Garifuna identity and "tradition." Unlike OFRANEH, ODECO's board of directors did not engage in theoretical discussions over the meaning of development. Rather, they take development as a point of departure, naming their organization a *development* organization (the Organization for Ethnic Community Development). ODECO has assumed a place within the current neoliberal development conditions and partners with the state system to integrate Garifuna voices into development planning, or as they say, "transform the Garifuna from development objects to development subjects." A look at their stated goals illustrates this point.

What are ODECO's Principal Objectives?

To provide for the *integral development* of the black community in Honduras (Garifuna and non-Garifuna).

To conduct actions aimed at the rescue, conservation, and strengthening of the national culture values, as manifested by the Garifuna and other ethnically Black Hondurans.

To plan, execute, direct, and evaluate work, actions, projects, programs, and plans, with the goal of increasing the social, economic, and political level of the Black Honduran community, through the help of national and international institutions and organizations.

To establish *cooperative relations* between communities and national and international organizations.

To *train and organize* members of small, self-managing businesses to combat unemployment, poor quality of life, massive emigration, and the abandonment of natal communities.

To *train and organize* women so they can be successfully *incorporated as a force in national development.*

To conduct preventative activities that protect children from malnutrition, abandonment, drug addiction, alcoholism, prostitution, and illiteracy.

To fight for the *respect of Human Rights*, conforming to the Universal Declaration of Human Rights and the Republic's Constitution.

To help members in cases of catastrophe, in accordance with the stipulations presented in the Statutes and Rules.

To promote the *creation and development* of cooperatives, loans, and friendly help, to schools, libraries, technical training institutes, collaborative offices in hospitals, experimental fields, or sports and other organizations dedicated to the professional and cultural aims of solidarity and welfare (provision).

To work for the rescue and conservation of the ecological equilibrium that benefits life. [Organización de Desarrollo Étnico Comunitario 2002, author's translation from Spanish, emphasis added].

ODECO maintains its position as a nongovernmental agency working to integrate the Garifuna as *partners* in development projects. Anderson (2009) describes their political orientation based on a discourse of "Afro-visibility," one which demands affirmative action and anti-racist policies to address the specific conditions of inequality faced by Afro-Hondurans. OFRANEH, in contrast, is more radically confrontational in its ethnopolitics, which emerge from a quest for self-determination. OFRANEH argues for the Garifuna ability to fully *control*—from design to implementation— projects within their own communities.

There is a danger in framing the Garifuna struggle solely in terms of human rights and racial equality. This danger is associated with what Bram Büscher describes as a "discursive blur," something Büscher notes surrounds conservation social scientists and biologists in the current era. During his participation in the Society for Conservation Biology's 2007 Annual Meeting, Büscher (2008) observed a tendency for participants to talk about the potential for neoliberal "win-win scenarios," even in spite of growing evidence that such approaches do not often benefit local people and their environment. Büscher (2008:229–230) found that conference participants often used "nice-sounding yet often empty words" (e.g., *participation, ownership, good governance, better policies*) and seemed to always attempt to speak positively. ODECO's interaction with development policy also runs the risk of suffering from such a discursive blur. Its focus on integration, incorporation, cooperation, training, and involvement has the look and feel of participation and equality, but it blurs the abuses associated with the underlying structural systemic causes of poverty.

ODECO's tolerance of neoliberalism transcends national politics. In addition to heading up ODECO, Celeo Álvarez serves as the president of

La Organización Negra Centroamericana (the Central American Black Organization [CABO]), or ONECA, an alliance of 16 black organizations from across the Americas.[2] Emerging from their 2002 annual summit in San Jose, Costa Rica, was a formal commitment of support for the region's neoliberal development agenda. Excerpts include:

> We, the AfroCentralAmerican organizations that belong to the Central American Black Organization . . . met in San Isidro de Coronado, San José, Costa Rica in order to reaffirm our determination and true conviction that *we must be actors in our development processes; it is our right* as citizens of various countries in the region and in the African diaspora.
>
> Therefore we decided:
>
> To *ensure the highest level of participation* for Afrocentroamerican communities in the *Mesoamerican Biological Corridor Initiative* . . .
>
> To *support* the implementation of the *World Bank project to "Develop the Institutional Capacity* for Central American Afro-descendant Organizations," which is *financed by the World Bank* through the Central American Commission of Environment and Development (La Comisión Centroamericana de Ambiente y Desarrollo, or CCAD), and in which *ONECA will be the executor*. . . .
>
> To guarantee that *our communities participate as important actors in the development models* of the Plan Puebla Panama, the Free Trade of the Americas Agreement, and affirm that the communities' rights are protected and respected. . . .
>
> To conclude the writing process for the *Master Plans of Development* for Afrodescendant Communities, and continue to pressure our governments so that these plans are incorporated into their programs and strategies of poverty reduction in Central American countries...
>
> To conclude the execution of the World Bank's Project to Map the Afrocentroamerican organizations . . . [ONECA 2002, author's translation from Spanish].

Through ONECA, ODECO formally endorsed the neoliberal development model and associated projects in 2002. Comparatively, beginning in 2005, OFRANEH's communiqués have almost exclusively been framed as strident critiques of neoliberal development policies and their negative impact on indigenous cultural survival. The organization's written discourse has escalated in line with heightening violence against Garifuna activists since the mid-2000s. Following is one of the first of several examples, written after police raided the home of a key leader of OFRANEH.

March 28, 2005

PERSECUTION OF GARIFUNAS

OFRANEH denounces the raid of the home of Miriam Miranda. This is a *clear case of persecution of the defenders of the ancestral lands of indigenous and black peoples.*

The break-in took place on Friday March 25 (Good Friday), between two and three in the afternoon. Eight officers of the DGIC (Criminal Investigative Division), some of whom were wearing hoods, broke into Miranda's home, with orders to search for stolen articles and weapons.

Miriam Miranda has a long history of involvement in the struggle for the defense of the rights of indigenous and black peoples, especially the rights of the Garifuna people and the defense of their land and culture. We therefore presume that *this raid was a form of pressure to intimidate Miranda and tie the hands of OFRANEH, so that it becomes nothing more than one more NGO carrying out projects, like other NGOs involved with World Bank projects.*

OFRANEH believes we are *living in a very important historical period.* The ratification of the Free Trade Agreement with the United States will *speed up the process of economic globalization and lead to increased poverty,* given the enormous gap that exists between our country and the North American Empire. As well, the *traditional agricultural economies of our country will be undermined* and there will be a huge increase in the number of campesinos who have no choice but to join the migration to the North.

The raid of Miranda's home does not augur well, given that Miranda was not involved in any of the alleged activities named by the authorities. On the contrary, she has been recognized both nationally and internationally for her hard work and dedication to the defense of the rights of indigenous and black peoples.

Law enforcement in Honduras is suffering a regression. In fact, it has turned into a witch hunt, much like it was in the eighties. *With open warfare against the so-called maras (gangs)—the children of neoliberalism—we are very close to returning to the persecution of the popular movement that we saw in the past.*

The Empire's attempt at economic globalization is a total failure and the situation will only get worse with the implementation of projects such as the Free Trade Agreement with the United States, the Plan Puebla Panamá, the Mesoamerican Biological Corridor and the PATH (Land Administration Project of Honduras), all of which directly affect the future of the lands of our peoples.

Financial institutions such as the World Bank and the InterAmerican Development Bank are attempting to implement these projects. At the same time, wherever possible, *they try to sow seeds of division in popular movements and buy their leaders.*

The break-in at Miranda's home happens at a time when there is an attempt to divide our organization, financed by the office of the *Nuestras Raíces Programme,*[3] which comes under the FHIS (*Fondo Hondureño de Inversion Social*) which, in turn, is financed by the World Bank. In 2002, the programme was given the task of dividing the CONPAH (Confederation of the Native People of Honduras) and financing the now-defunct CINH, also administered by the *Nuestras Raíces Programme.*

At the same time, the state of Honduras, along with the PATH, has begun to *put pressure on the Garifuna communities, through a project whose aim is to break up ancestral lands.* Teresa Reyes, of Triunfo de la Cruz, was sentenced to preventative custody for the crime of defending a piece of land that has belonged to her family for years.

We hereby alert the public to the direct and indirect pressure to which the members of our organization are being subjected. We also denounce the deliberate attempt to divide us by a state organ financed by the World Bank.

This division could destroy our people's resistance movement and lead to the break-up and loss of our ancestral communities. [Author's translation from Spanish]

Issued in La Ceiba (Honduras), March 28, 2005.

Gregoria Flores

OFRANEH[OFRANEH 2005]

This communiqué draws out the connection between structural violence and real violence, as street-level crime and youth gangs emerge out of the inequalities produced in the wake of neoliberalism's economic model. The "children of neoliberalism" then face state-led violence as the administrations of the new millennium attempt to crack down on the rising crime associated with gangs and drug trafficking. The interdependency of actual violence and structural inequities can be made apparent only through an approach that starts from a critical stance on development. As one can see from the above, Flores is clear that in OFRANEH's opinion economic development plans, such as the Central American Free Trade Agreement and Plan Puebla Panamá, and the establishment of the Mesoamerican Biological Corridor (a project to map and monitor land cover and ecological balance within the framework of sustainable economic development) are direct threats to the rights of Garifuna people. Moreover, she calls attention to the divisions in Garifuna leadership, denouncing, without explicitly naming, ODECO's history of working with international institutions to carry out local development projects.[4] OFRANEH sees its role as an organization that speaks out against injustices caused by economic globalization, situating itself as part of a broader movement against neoliberalism.

Gendered Activism

OFRANEH's approach to development closely mirrors feminist critiques of development. Some feminist approaches to development have been deemed too essentializing, such as Shiva's (1989) ecofeminism that depicted women as possessing a "natural" relationship with the environment. When it comes to the ways in which indigenous groups articulate their relationship to nature, similar critiques of essentialism pop up. However, other feminist scholars who study the relationship between gender, environment, and development draw on political ecology to argue that differences in experiences of nature and environmental responsibility derive not from biology but from social constructions of gender that vary by class, race, and place (Peet 1999:189). Women's environmental activism thus emerges not out of a "natural" connection to the earth but because women experience more negative fallout from environmental destruction or, in this case, reregulatory measures.

In 2007 I argued that the gendered dimensions of the land struggle had been hidden from Garifuna mobilization as they organized along indigenous terms (Brondo 2007). In the early 2000s, feminist scholars (Deere and Leon 2001; Richards 2005) drew attention to the implication of broadened spaces of mobilization — gender can get lost, or gender issues become subordinated or downplayed in order to advance other, more universal goals of a particular movement. Warren and Jackson (2002:29) discussed this as a collision between international development discourse and local expectations where indigenous groups must repackage their concerns and identities in order to access wider audiences and resources. At the time, it seemed as though unifying as indigenous peoples first and foremost meant that the differences in how Garifuna women and men experienced land loss and privatization went unrecognized (in the sense that they were not often explicitly written about in the media or in academic literature).

While it is true that there was not much scholarly attention to the gendered nature of the Garifuna land struggle or discussion of Garifuna

women's activism (Safa 2005 and Thorne 2005 are two important excep-
tions), a careful review of media coverage from the last decade shows
women activists standing at the forefront of the land struggle and, sadly,
often suffering physical attacks by public and private security forces for
their participation in resistance movements that counter land privatization (Thompson 2011). For instance, on May 30, 2005, Gregoria Flores
of OFRANEH was shot and wounded in La Ceiba on her way to collect
testimony to present before the Inter-American Commission on Human
Rights (IACHR). A few months prior to this incident, the home of Miriam
Miranda was searched by masked agents of Honduras's Criminal Investigative Division (the incident referenced in the statement by Gregoria
Flores). The authorities, claiming to be searching for weapons and stolen
goods, showed a search warrant that was signed by a judge but not directed
at any particular individual. After the act of intimidation was publicized,
the judge who signed the warrant explained it was an "intelligence error"
(Human Rights First 2006). On June 22, 2006, Jessica García, a leader
from the Garifuna community San Juan Tela, had been threatened at
gunpoint to sign over community land to a real estate company linked to
the "Tela Bay" tourism development project. Initially she refused, but after
an unidentified man threatened her and her children's lives, she signed
the document stating that community land belonged to the owner of a
real estate company. García remained concerned that further threats on
community members would ensue as the company attempted to extend its
landholdings (Amnistía Internacional 2006). On August 6, 2006, another
woman from San Juan Tela was allegedly targeted for her landholdings.
Nineteen-year-old Mirna Isabel Santos Thomas was forced out of her
home by a group of masked men armed with AK-47s; she was found dead
alongside a road outside of town the next morning.

Garifuna women's traditional cultural activities connect them to community territory (land or sea) in a number of important ways. The gendered
division of labor is such that women sow the land, care for and harvest
crops, prepare food, and sell traditional food products. Arguably, access
to land and sea are required for women to prepare traditional foodstuffs,
such as *ereba* (cassava bread made from yuca), *machuca* (mashed green
plantains served with a seafood and coconut-based soup), *pan de coco*
(coconut bread), and other dishes. Foods are important in multiple contexts, including secular celebrations, everyday nourishment, and religious
ritual (González 1988:98).

Women are also connected to the land and sea through their ancestral
religion, *Dügü*. There are various rituals that require access to the earth

Figure 5.1 Woman resting on *cayuco*. Photo by Monica Kar

Figure 5.2 Communal cooking in Rio Esteban. Photo by Monica Kar

and sea in order to fulfill the requests of ancestors. The three main ancestral rites that are practiced are the *Amuyadahani* (bathing the spirit of the dead), the *Chugu* (feeding the dead), and the *Dügü* (feasting the dead), which all require feeding the ancestors traditional foodstuffs (Cayetano and Cayetano 1997). Reenactment ceremonies marking the Garifuna settlement require access to land and sea, because ancestors arrive from land (Amerindians) and sea (Africans). Women play key roles in these ceremonies, preparing foods, singing, and performing gender-specific dances for the ancestors. The core organizer and primary financial sponsor of a wake (*novenario*) is the eldest female descendant of the deceased; the organizer's sisters and their grown children are also expected to contribute financially to the event (England 2006:93). Women can also fill the role of a *buyei* (shaman) who leads the various ceremonies.

While men's activities also connect them to the land and sea, and women's participation in traditional activities has been on the decline as their participation in transnational migration continues to rise, it is still women who are cited as the responsible parties for teaching traditions to children. England (2006:91) argues that the fact that women still continue to engage in "traditional" activities in spite of increasing migration is acknowledged by Garifuna villagers as "proof of the resilience of Garifuna culture and strength of women." In fact, growing migration enables women to financially support the continuation of traditional culture through remittance support sent to remaining female kin, enabling a woman to fulfill her role as a "good daughter" who supports her mother, and as a "good mother" who supports her children (England 2006:91–92).

When gender becomes subordinated within indigenous mobilizations, there is a risk that when gender does appear, it is in ways that essentialize indigenous women. Indigenous women are valorized for their role in the reproduction of indigenous culture and as the main agent of socialization (Moya 1987). From this perspective, communiqués from OFRANEH can be read as reducing women into archetypes, ignoring difference and reproducing stereotypes of Garifuna culture. *Or* we could read the statements produced by Garifuna *women* activists as essential (even if essentializing), because they are critical interventions in building a case for women's continued access to ancestral territories.

For example, when the activist I quoted earlier spoke with me about development in 2000, she contrasted development with cultural survival. She emphasized women's traditions, such as sharing stories with their children under the moonlight, as playing a key role in teaching Garifuna culture to future generations. These arguments adopt international indigenous rights discourse, which tends to essentialize women as bearers of culture and as responsible for the survival of the Garifuna people, and they pit development (read: modernity) against a static indigenous community (read: tradition). Represented this way, women's traditions—such as talking beneath the moonlight, the making of ereba or machuca, dancing punta, or enacting the Dügü—are implicitly assumed to be the transmitters of "culture." Through their communiqués, OFRANEH's female leadership signals to the nation-state that Garifuna women's knowledge is central to Honduras's successful development of cultural and ecotourism initiatives, and points toward the international resolutions (e.g., ILO 169, UNESCO's recognition of the Garifuna "intangible cultural heritage") that validate this relationship. Women's traditions are implicit in the activist's demand for territorial recognition, as they are tied to "cultural survival." The ethnopolitics embraced by OFRANEH became a cornerstone in grounded territorial claims within Sambo Creek between 2001 and 2005.

Grassroots Activism: Sambo Creek's Struggle to Recuperate Ancestral Lands

In June 2001 Luis Fernandez (known locally as "Rasta"), a young, charismatic man who had spent the last 13 years of his life in Belize, returned to his natal community of Sambo Creek and organized the Comité Pro-Defensa de la Tierra (the Land Defense Committee) to head an effort to recover the community's ancestral territory. Based on their ancestral right, the group began a series of land occupations on what they believed were irregularly or illegally obtained and unutilized private lands. Several small-scale occupations occurred in August 2001. None of these early attempts resulted in reclaimed land, because either the landowner produced a title or another community member testified to the group on behalf of the "foreign" landowner.

The largest and most serious case was that of Miguel Castillo, mentioned in chapter 4. In mid-August 2001 community members occupied his land, constructing approximately 80 temporary dwellings in an effort to reclaim the land. Others soon joined the group, and according to a CCARC (2002) report, nearly the entire community, including women and children, turned out to protest.[5] At the demonstration the group burned the national flag, symbolizing the territorial right of the Garifuna to the land. Castillo's watchman notified the owner, and in less than 24 hours (and on the weekend) a judge heard the case and ruled for an arrest of the demonstration leaders.[6] The police used tear gas and force to pacify the group, arresting and detaining seven members of the community (six men and one woman). Several people (mostly women) were injured, and one pregnant woman lost her baby as a result of police force. The detained community members called upon both ODECO and OFRANEH to aid in their defense; OFRANEH responded positively to their call. Drawing on an existing accord between the Supreme Court of Justice and the indigenous and Afro-Honduran populations that states that no indigenous or Garifuna person can be detained for land conflicts, OFRANEH was able to assist the community members in gaining their freedom.[7] The seven detained community members were released from prison within 24 hours. Yet the charges of usurpation remained against Rasta, and OFRANEH continued its involvement in the case.

While Sambo Creek was awarded the 8.89 manzanas of illegally gated ancestral lands, unfortunately, as Anderson (2009:222) notes, this success should not be taken as evidence of a vindication of collective territorial rights or as precedent for future state interventions to return ancestral territories. Indeed, the community reclaimed only one-third of the land occupied during the land occupation of 2001, significantly less than the amount illegally occupied by the Castillo family. Moreover, by paying the Castillo family a reported $10,000 for land they originally purchased for 425 lempiras ($212.50) in 1987, the state sent a clear signal that it recognized the private property rights of this elite family, rewarding them rather handsomely for their land speculation (Anderson 2009:222). Furthermore, INA officials reported to Anderson (2009:222) that the state did not have funds available for future land purchases, nor was there much interest from multilateral lending institutions (e.g., the World Bank or IDB) to finance the same. In the end, their efforts and success did little to destabilize the power differentials within the region.

SIX

Roots, Rights, and Belonging in Sambo Creek

Identity formation involves the creation of subjects through discourse. *Discourse* refers to the practices that create the conceptual frameworks that inform people's thoughts, words, and actions. The production of discourse happens through systems of control and rules of exclusion and inclusion (Foucault 1973). Chapter 1 revealed how coastal and foreign elites had historically excluded the Garifuna from a "native status" through particular nation-building discourses. Yet within the last two decades, the Garifuna successfully created and deployed a new subject identity as indigenous peoples. Riding home from an interview with a leading member of OFRANEH in 2002, my friend Zita, who had asked to accompany me to the interview, thanked me for bringing her along, reflecting, "*Ella es tan inteligente. Aprendí bastante de ella*" (She is so intelligent; I learned so much from her). "Really? That's great," I said. "What did you learn?" "*Que somos indígenas. Yo nunca lo habría dicho antes, pero ahora tengo sentido*" (That we are indigenous. I never would have said it before, but now it makes sense). And in that moment I saw the making of indigeneity. Zita would bring back her newfound identity and share it with her fellow Sambeños. Having just recently rotated onto the patronato, she was also now well positioned to raise consciousness within the community over their shared history and identity, and its connections to local resources. But while Zita may become involved in indigeneity making, other Sambeños are drawn into their own identity projects to undermine Garifuna rights and maintain an ethnic hierarchy where Indo-Hispanics maintain power and control over local resources.

In 2002, at the height of Sambo Creek's land occupations, I visited with a friend of the Castillo family. Maria, a well-to-do mestiza, had interacted with OFRANEH activists in the past. Responding to Sambeños' claim that significant portions of their historical territory had been usurped by more powerful interest groups, Maria exploded.

> They say this is their ancestral land?! This is not their ancestral land—their ancestors are from Africa! If they want to recuperate land, go to Africa! This country's ancestors are *indios*, not Africans! The only people with any right to land here are *indios*. That woman I spoke to at OFRANEH, she said they are indigenous; that they are fighting for their ancestors' lands. But she had the hair and dress of an African! . . . What are they thinking—dressed as Africans and saying this is their land? And Vincente—he has long, dreadlocked hair, and green eyes—the indios here don't have green eyes! I don't have green eyes—look! [widening her eyes]

I was intrigued by her use of the label "indio," often applied colloquially to, and sometimes among, mestizos of lower status, but I had yet to hear a mestiza woman of status self-identify as indio. I interrupted her to clarify: "Are you using the word *indio* like I do *mestizo* or *ladino?*"

"Yes, mestizo. We are mestizo—pure Indians don't exist anymore. We have mixed; first with the Spanish and then with other races. But *we* are the ones with rights, those with *my* skin [showing me her arm], not moreno skin. We are [the ones] with ancestors here, not the Garifuna. Their ancestors are in Africa. I have a right to this land!"

Maria's reaction to Garifuna indigeneity and territorial rights points toward the ways in which notions of race, culture, history, and "roots" are caught up in claims to local resources within Sambo Creek. As we saw in the past chapters, the recasting of the Garifuna from Negro, Afro-Honduran, or autochthonous—all past identities ascribed to and/or assumed by the Garifuna (Euraque 1998, 2003)—to indigenous (Anderson 2007, 2009; Brondo 2006, 2010) has given Garifuna communities international avenues of recourse for asserting their cultural rights. Yet the successful production of Garifuna indigeneity has also set in motion new expressions of localized racism and questions about which "types" of Hondurans have the right to coastal territory under a growing tourism economy.

Place-Making in Sambo Creek: Race, Class, and Indigeneity

A countereffect of the land reclamation process in Sambo Creek has been heightened local racism as historical power holders work to maintain their positions within the class and ethnic hierarchy. Faced with the internation-alization of Garifuna indigeneity and national legislation that opened spaces for mobilizations based on Garifuna cultural rights, mestizos at the local level are (re)constructing their own ethnic identities in response to a shift in recognition of Garifuna rights under neoliberal multicultural projects. Those with historical power hark back to forms of mestizaje that protected their place within the racial hierarchy and denied Garifuna rights as Hondurans.

Malkki (1997:56) argued that people often think of themselves as being "rooted" in a particular place and as having derived their identity from that "rootedness." As a result, identity becomes "spatialized" (Gupta and Ferguson 1997:3) and associated with particular territories. The processes of cultural territorialization (Gupta and Ferguson 1997) are essential in transforming a geographic space into a place associated with a particular people. Thus, "place-making" involves actions to territorialize geographic space (Malkki 1997; Medina 1998).

Understandings about land, place, and cultural identity are derived from individual experiences, such that a geographic space acts as a bridge between one's experience of identity and traditions, which are tied to rituals and occur in specific locales (see also Occhipinti 2003). Byron Foster's (1987) analysis of the *Dügü* ritual provides an example of Garifuna place-making, in that he argues that what the ritual is really about is establishing rights to these territories.

> Now, this symbolic emphasis on the earth was particularly appropriate for the emerging Garifuna society, for whom a homeland was absolutely the prime consideration. Land for maroon communities was the source of their fertility; it had been taken from them—or they from it—by slave traders. The Garifuna had won it back in another hemisphere. Without it, maroon societies like the Garifuna could not have existed as autonomous entities. And this source of their fertility was continually threatened by the European colonial powers . . . by constructing a ritual which portrayed the earth as the place of the dead the Garifuna were able to emphasize St. Vin-cent as the land of their ancestors and hence as *their* land. The Garifuna thus made the earth both a ritual symbol and a political one, for in "stating" that the land was theirs, the *dügü* rite generated an ideology counterpoised to that of the colonizers, whose intention was to take that land in the name of their source of fertility—the British crown (Foster 1987:6).

The *Dügü* ritual has been transferred with the Garifuna from St. Vin-cent to their mainland communities. The ritual can still be understood as a means to claim Garifuna rights to land. In Honduras, as in St. Vincent, the political and economic elite are attempting to take Garifuna land—land that they had "won back" when they were exiled from St. Vincent. Foster (1987) also makes note of the dual arrival of Garifuna ancestors in the *Dügü* ritual. Recent ancestors who have been buried in the earth are brought out through traditional dancing, and more distant ancestors (from St. Vincent) arrive by boat from the sea. This ritual symbolizes Garifuna indigeneity, demonstrating their Caribbean and Arawakan roots. Through the ritual, Garifuna place-make by expressing a right to territory based on the fact that they descend from a particular region, not just the territorial boundary of Honduras, which to them is an artificial boundary set up by the European descendants who founded the nation-state.

Medina (1998) describes a similar case for the Maya, who base their indigenous status in Belize on being indigenous to the Central American region, not to the area that falls within the Belizean nation-state boundaries. Moreover, during the *Dügü* ceremony, food products from the land (cassava) and sea (fish) are also given as offerings for the ancestral spirits. The performance of the *Dügü* therefore also demonstrates that the Garifuna need a particular place to enact their culture. ILO 169 and UNESCO's Convention for the Safeguarding of the Intangible Cultural Heritage affirm that right.

The processes of place-making are intertwined and overlapping with those of history making in the Garifuna land struggle. As Medina (1998: 126) notes, "the identity of people with territory is reinforced through constructions of history which account for and produce both people and place simultaneously." The construction of history therefore becomes central in legitimizing a people's rooted identity. This implies attributing and assigning particular cultural practices to a given geographic space. "History making" (Brown 2002), then, plays a role in reinforcing the link between territory, identity, culture, and a particular group of people. *History making* refers to the creation and re-creation of history, which is "an ongoing process of interpretation and reinterpretation in which historical accounts are constantly assembled and reassembled. 'Facts' may be added, dropped, reinterpreted, or forgotten; old themes may change or continue in new relationships in the contemporary setting" (Brown 2002:107). Therefore, even though many Garifuna are now born in the United States or live significant portions of their adult lives outside of their natal community, they can still trace their ancestors to a "rooted" place where their cultural traditions were once enacted. History-making thus plays a key role in local land reclamations, as the Garifuna imbue territorial space with historical accounts of access, use, and conservation. People "make place" by recalling and reciting accounts of traditional practices and, in so doing, legitimize their course of action. By telling stories about abuses of power by mestizo immigrants who settled on cultivation plots, Garifuna people are at once (1) place-making by linking particular cultural practices to geographic space, (2) demonstrating historical processes of exploitation and structural violence in which ownership and rights are usurped, and (3) legitimizing their actions—from local land occupations to international court proceedings—to reclaim lost Garifuna land. These stories need not have been lived by the storyteller—descendants can recount the stories, or the stories could even be tales of abuse from as far back as the Carib wars on St. Vincent. Moreover, the storyteller need not be Garifuna. Mestizos too can place-make to support—or *contest*—the reclamation of what was once Garifuna communal territory.

The 2001 land occupations led by "the children of the community" were efforts to reclaim ancestral land seized by *extranjeros* (foreigners, outsiders). The term *extranjero* was used within Sambo Creek to mean people of a foreign origin. In practice that could mean a number of things, including (1) people who were born outside of Honduras, (2) wealthier mestizos who were born outside (or even within) Sambo Creek but had used their power to usurp Garifuna lands, (3) people who were born in Sambo Creek but married foreign-born individuals, and (4) people who were born in Sambo Creek, accumulated wealth while living in another country, and then returned to invest in local property. *Extranjero* was never a label applied to Garifuna.

Long-term residents of Sambo Creek (both Garifuna and mestizo) frequently cited *extranjeros* for privatizing and guarding what was once communal land, for disallowing passage to access water or harvest fruit, and for restricting women from selling bread or other products to tourists who visit the beach in front of their privatized land (despite the fact that under Honduran law, *all* beaches are public). *Extranjeros* not only were criticized for introducing new forms of land tenure, but they were also charged with bringing violence to the area as a means to protect landholdings (employing armed guards and shooting trespassers).

According to a public bulletin from Honduras's National Human Rights Commission that described police offenses committed against the Garifuna involved in recuperation efforts, the land occupations commenced with an attempt to recuperate land from Maria (whose quote opened this chapter). In that document, the detained activists described their attempts to recuperate land held by a foreigner. Within the passage Maria is labeled

Canadian and said to have appropriated lands irregularly through (or with) a group of French.

A light-skinned mestiza, Maria was born in Sambo Creek. Her father, like other community men, worked on the docks for Standard Fruit (when the banana industry dominated the coastal economy). She spent most of her childhood in La Ceiba, and later lived in Canada, where she met her husband. Maria told of community members sending a letter to OFRANEH declaring that a *francesa* (Frenchwoman) moved illegally onto community land; she was upset that she was labeled a "foreigner," "Frenchwoman," or "Canadian" because she married a French Canadian man. While she was raised in La Ceiba, she professed a right to live in Sambo Creek because her parents had lived there when she was born, and her father worked alongside many Garifuna men on the *muelle* (on the Standard Fruit docks).

Vincente, a Garifuna man in his thirties and a key figure in the Land Defense Committee, claimed to be the original owner of this particular plot. After some years outside of the country, Vincente returned to Sambo Creek to occupy his familial landholdings (presumed inheritance), a plot that was about two *manzanas* (approximately three acres). Vincente intended to share the land with other community members who did not have homes of their own. As they were clearing the land, he and his associates were approached and told that it had been sold. He argued that despite living elsewhere for a number of years, he was born in Sambo Creek and therefore had a right to reclaim his inheritance. Vincente explained that Maria was able to produce a title, and his group peacefully retired from clearing the land.

In this debate, both Maria and Vincente acknowledge the significance of historical roots as a prerequisite to claim rights to community land. The difference between their two positions is that Vincente felt that Maria, like many other wealthier mestizos, had taken advantage of Garifuna residents' ignorance of the increasing market value of their communal landholdings. Maria, on the other hand, countered that such were fair exchanges. In addition to her position that the privatization of Sambo Creek's land resulted from "fair exchanges" in a market economy—ignoring the historical abuses of power within the region and unequal access to resources—Maria also believed Garifuna claims to historical territory were unsubstantiated because: the Garifuna were not "truly" indigenous, and because indigenous systems were not recognized by the state. Introduced at the start of this chapter, here is the extended response from Maria:

Vincente—he has long, *blanco* [dreadlocked] hair, and green eyes—
the indios here don't have green eyes! I don't have green eyes—look!
[widening her eyes] . . . They speak of African traditions—that's where
their ancestors are. But they don't think like this. . . . They want to
impose socialism like the Indians in Canada. . . . But this system for
the Indians in Canada was established many years ago in Canada—not
recently. . . . The indios are going to revolt, [and] I am not the only one
who thinks like this. We will revolt! They did it in Guatemala—the civil
war. I just need a few others to listen to me. Just like Vincente—it only
takes one person to start something like this. He was in front, and then
others followed.

Claiming an affinity with the Maya uprising in Guatemala, Maria's
comments could be interpreted as an attempt to place-make in a manner akin to Garifuna place-making: the Garifuna identify with indigenous
Arawakan roots, whereas Maria identifies with her historical ancestors who
may have intermixed with coastal Miskitu.[1] Following this logic, mestizos have deeper roots in the country—stemming from Honduras's "truly
indigenous" groups, those who were present pre-Columbus—while the
Garifuna have much shallower roots, with only a little more than 205 years
(at the time of the research) in the country. The Garifuna's "true roots" are
in Africa. Maria points toward eye color, hairstyle, and the celebration of
African ancestry as evidence of this connection. On other occasions, Maria
would call upon Vincente's physical appearance, time out of the country,
and command of the English language to his "place" in Belize, *not* Honduras. Ironically, the same argument could be constructed about Maria:
she speaks French fluently, spent a significant portion of her adult life in
Canada, and has effectively "whitened" through the process of mestizaje.
Blanqueamiento (whitening), a common thread of mestizaje discourses
and practices throughout Latin America, asserted the superiority of white
European culture over indigenous and black culture. Afro-indigeneity
challenges white norms by proclaiming their own cultural autonomy (Safa
2005:308). Maria's discourse emerges in response to this challenge, and she
attempts to reassert the Indo-Hispanic national mestizaje identity discourse
that dominated Honduras until its recent transition to multiculturalism.

While attempting to place-make as a rooted Indio-Hispanic mestiza,
Maria negates Vincente's claims through the curious adoption of the term
blanco to describe his dreadlocked hair. *Blanco*, in racial terms, means
"white." Within Honduras it can be used to refer to people of European

descent, to mestizos of economic means, or, at times, to mestizos as an entire ethnic class. By describing Vincente as embodying whiteness, Maria equates his relative power and "native status" with that of the historical power holders of the nation-state, separating him out from native Sambeños, while unifying herself with locals through the proud self-reference as an indio.

The Indo-Hispanic mestizaje that Maria is appropriating was created and deployed in the 1920s to eliminate class boundaries between mestizos and to support the mobilization of poor, jobless mestizos against coastal blacks (Euraque 1998). Such a discourse privileges the "Indian" and excludes blackness, glorifying an indigenous past while projecting the white/European side of background into the future. Yet such discourse is losing its efficacy in the context of Honduras's newfound commitment to multiculturalism. That there might be a movement of *mestizo-"indios"* to reclaim land is an absurd pronouncement. There is no collectively identified Miskitu or other indigenous group beyond the Garifuna in the Sambo Creek area, nor is there any impetus for collective mobilization of "indios" (read: mestizos). Maria's discourse therefore should not be read at face value, but rather understood in its context as a reaction against Honduras's newfound commitment to multicultural rights, under which the indigenous systems that Maria argues the Garifuna are attempting to impose are officially recognized by the Honduran state (even if not recognized in practice). Maria's use of the label "indio" in this passage is not an actual claim to be "Indian"; rather, she is claiming place in Sambo Creek based upon an Indo-Hispanic national mestizaje identity discourse.

In Honduran discourse, the term *indio* is used by both Garifuna and mestizos. The image of the violent indio (a common stereotype of mestizos) sits in contrast to the tranquilo Garifuna and reflects the broader racial hierarchy within Honduras, and associated fears of the dominant racial order (Anderson 2001:154–155). Garifuna communities are often described as refuges of urban degradation, which are claimed to have resulted from indio (mestizo) activity, not from Garifuna or black crime. At the community level, the image of the violent indio is often evoked during accounts of past mestizo abuses of Garifuna, especially with regard to stories of property loss. Maria's self-identification as indio in this passage does not suggest an indigenous self-identity, nor is she associating herself with the negative connotations associated with the *indio* label (violence, abuse). Rather, she is appropriating the pejorative epithet to reassert her place—as a successfully whitened mestizo—at the top of the racial hierarchy, while at the same time attempting to mask her wealthier mestizo identity. The continued use of *indio* at the local level, and its associated stereotypes, sheds important light on power relations, control over property, and rights to land (which do not correlate evenly with access and control of ancestral territory). Maria's discourse invokes this historical relationship. With her discourse surrounding Garifuna appearance and cultural characteristics, Maria is attempting to delegitimize afro-indigeneity and its associated rights.

Other historical power holders within the region are similarly reactionary. Some business owners who employ Sambeños regret what they perceive to have been past charitable behavior to their employees. Tulio, a friend and past employee of a coastal business shared:

> Let me tell you a story about Claudia. I asked Mark [Claudia's husband] if I could buy a plot of his land for 10,000 lempiras and build a house. He said yes and we measured it out and everything, and I was going to pay him over two years. Well, then he talked to Claudia, and she said no."

> KERI: I don't know Claudia very well, but it seems to me that they have two different ways of looking at things—

> TULIO [interrupting]: Yes, she is a rich Honduran, and he is a poor foreigner. Mark believes that when he does well, he wants to share it with others and help others. Claudia is used to the hierarchy here in Honduras and thinks that she should remain on the top.

Claudia, on the other hand, thought she was using her class position to "help" the people of Sambo Creek and nearby communities. But since the efforts to recuperate land owned by her mestizo and foreign peers began, she became increasingly frustrated with the community.

> Let me tell you something—we were some of the first to build here. Before we came, it was ugly. There wasn't anything—no hotels, no restaurants. We made it beautiful. . . . I hire from Sambo Creek. I helped these people. Before they didn't know how to use a stove or toaster, didn't have a refrigerator. I taught them. Now they have them in their own homes. I helped them. I give to the community. This is what I do for the community. I also wanted to build houses for my employees, because there are many people without houses—[names her employees]—they don't have homes. They have to live with relatives. I was going to let them build houses on my land and pay it off at a low price. I wanted to do many things for the community, but now, no! After these problems, now? No. I was looking into bringing a police station here, allowing them use

of my land. I began talking with [a] doctor [friend] and other people to construct a small hospital, but now no. Now I don't want to do anything. No. It's like this: say your husband cheats on you. You say, OK, I forgive you. But it's always there in your mind and you're always watching—you never forget. Now, whenever I see a moreno, I wonder if they are going to try and take my land.

Claudia felt scorned by her Sambeño employees, none of whom actually participated in the land occupations. Yet because they too were morenos (like those she had heard "invaded" other foreign- and elite-owned private property), she no longer trusted her employees.[2]

Based on a shared perception that the land reclamations emerged as a result of activists from Garifuna organizations and were populated by the local Garifuna population, Claudia now reports distrust of all morenos, and Maria questions the legitimacy of Garifuna claims to local resources. Non-elite mestizo Sambeños expressed similar concerns. Because Sambo Creek's 1997 communal land title is a "Garifuna title," some less-advantaged mestizo and English-speaking blacks felt as though they have come under undue skepticism about their place in the community.

Anna, a poor mestiza immigrant who had lived in Sambo Creek since she was two years old, obtained her current plot through encroachment on Garifuna ancestral territory. She worried that her land would be usurped and redistributed to Garifuna residents. Margo, an English-speaking black, had been waiting nearly two years (and was still waiting at the close of the research) for a statement from the patronato that she was the rightful occupant of her lands. She suspected that her affinity with an alleged "foreigner" (a Honduran native living in the United States and holding beachfront property for retirement) whose land was also targeted for recuperation by the Land Defense Committee in 2001 had placed her in a precarious position. Ema, a 57-year-old mestiza widow with a family history of at least a hundred years in the community articulated feelings of exclusion.

> Supposedly, the patronato represents everyone. [But] if a mestizo wants them to do anything for them, they have to pay them. If you're not Garifuna, to measure your land and authenticate it, you must pay the president of patronato. [And so] I never talk to the patronato. Yes, I'm not Garifuna, but I was born here. My dad was born here. I never attend meetings, because I attended a meeting once and I didn't understand anything because it was all in Garifuna. When I want to go, I can't, because they speak in Garifuna, and I don't understand what they are saying.

Holding meetings in a language that not all community members understand or speak can be interpreted as a form of place-making, as a signal
that "true" members of the community are Garifuna. Elsa, another woman
with long-standing roots in Sambo Creek, echoed Ema's remarks about
the patronato, stating that she did not attend patronato meetings because
"they are closed, between them." [continuing] "When they meet, they do
not take us into account." Consesa, a top officer in the patronato in 2002,
articulated their concerns in response to my questioning whether there
were any negative feelings among mestizo residents that the patronato was
comprised solely of Garifuna residents.

> Yes . . . in the beginning some ladinos [were upset by the all-Garifuna
> patronato]. But a few talked to me, and I said to them, "Don't let this
> bother you." Because we find that our community of Sambo Creek
> has always been mixed, and all ladinos who were born here—who are
> native to the community—there is nothing against them. Eh, the only
> thing that I don't agree with regarding relations with the ladinos is that
> normally the ladinos who come to the community bring harm to us and
> do not typically agree with us. And more than just not agreeing with
> us [with our cultural outlook/lifeways], they also harm us . . . we need
> their collaboration, because the work is for the good of the community.
> [Author's translation]

In response to a line of questioning about Elsa's knowledge and participation in the local land struggle, she expanded on her confusion about
being excluded from local politics, saying, "I don't know if I am india, Garifuna, or mestiza. I've lived here forever. I think I am Garifuna." Despite
feeling as though she were Garifuna, which signaled her sense that she
truly "belonged" in the community, Elsa stated that the only reason she
knew anything about the land struggle was that she witnessed it by living
in the community, seeing it on television, and hearing it on the radio, not
because she was invited to participate.

All four women have familial roots in the community; Ema and Elsa
were able to trace their ancestors' occupancy on their plots for over a hundred years. None of the women come from wealth, nor have they received
regular remittances. Anna was unemployed and married to a cattle hand
at a nearby ranch; Margo, a single mother of six, worked temporary labor
at a maquila (alternating work and child-care responsibilities with her
daughter); Elsa is a widowed cook at a local restaurant; and Ema maintained a snack stand at a community school. None of the women associated

with the more powerful mestizo landowners in the area. The relationships they had with wealthier mestizos were hierarchical working relationships, as were most relationships between Sambo Creek's residents and wealthy mestizos (who typically keep residences *outside* of Sambo Creek). Yet each woman expressed that she felt excluded from local politics and feared she would become a target for land recuperation by Garifuna residents.

Apart from—and more important than—some shared phenotypic and cultural traits, what these women all held in common was their occupancy of prime real estate. Two women held private title to the most expensive real estate locations in Sambo Creek: Elsa held beachfront property, and Ema underdeveloped land near the highway (i.e., where new housing subdivisions were being constructed). The two other women held unsecured land (i.e., they were each waiting on the patronato to officiate their land). Anna's land was located on the very outskirts of Sambo Creek and was quite expansive by comparison to residents in the center of the community. Margo's plot was on the outskirts of community, near the beach, and cater-cornered to the private plot she watched over for a transmigrant living in the United States. The combination of their landholdings, lack of participation in local politics, and affinity with wealthier mestizos who have "brought harm" to residents placed them in a precarious position. Similar to my family's affinity with certain well-positioned mestizos, these women's intentions were questioned, which led them to question their own belonging (and identity) within Sambo Creek. The experiences that these four women, and those of the elite mestizas cited above (Maria and Claudia), have had with Garifuna indigeneity and multicultural rights stand in contrast to other mestizo residents who participated in local politics and were allied with Garifuna organizations in the struggle to recuperate land.

Carla is a 27-year-old mestiza who was born on Roatan (an island off the coast of Honduras) but grew up in Sambo Creek. She and her mother moved in with her grandmother, who was living in a house in the center of the community when her mother and father split up. In contrast to the mestizas featured in the last section, Carla was active in local politics, working closely with the Land Defense Committee. While she understood "some, but not all Garifuna," she did not express feeling excluded from dialogue on community issues or by Garifuna residents' conversational code-switching. In describing the history of the land struggle, Carla shared: "We believe that we are poor now because we don't have *cocos* (coconuts), and we don't have land, and we don't have any room to grow. You see the center here [pointing toward the center of the community]—how the houses are so close together. This is why we have so much illness in our community. This is why we are fighting for extension (ampliación), so that our kids can have a better future." While Carla, like all residents I spoke to, told me that the recuperated land would be used to construct homes for families living with their relatives, she also thought some might be used for cultivation: "OFRANEH gave us a *charla* [informal lecture] about starting a cooperative there—to form a group of women who would work together on a plot of land. Everyone would be able to plant whatever they like—yuca, cocos, platanos, and so on—and then everyone will benefit."

I inquire, "Would women sell the produce?"

"No. Everyone in the community could eat. Triunfo de la Cruz [another Garifuna community] has this. I went there and it is beautiful. They have crops and food, and they don't have to buy their yuca, or cassava bread, or plantains. Not like here, where we have to buy everything. There—maybe meat, but nothing more."

As Carla and I discussed her hopes for the future of her community, she dreamed aloud of a romanticized past.

> I would like it to be like it was before—when we could find land if we needed it. Because now it is very expensive, and there is no place to buy here. If they [foreigners] want our land, they should go elsewhere. . . . Another thing we are fighting for now is more order in the community. We want to put posts up to register everyone who comes and goes from the community. And if someone comes to visit, we want to have a person responsible for his or her behavior. For instance, if I want to go see Rene, the person at the post will bring me to his house and he will sign off for me. . . . We are also fighting for the rivers and for green spaces. We used to be able to walk the rivers; now they are all gated. And the shoreline of our beaches. The same thing has happened there.

Later on Carla shared how she appreciated the Garifuna culture—"it is beautiful because they have their own style of life, their own system of living, their own rhythm, and their own beliefs." Carla's comments—and the use of the collective "we"—suggest that she and her Garifuna counterparts share a common vision for the future—a future reminiscent of the past when the community held communal land, and relationships were characterized by reciprocity.

The proposal to put guard posts into the community—which had also been mentioned to me by several members of the patronato and Land Defense Committee—suggests that the debate over belonging in Sambo Creek is not a debate about whether mestizos belong, but about which *types* of mestizos belong. The Land Defense Committee sought land to redistribute among the "children of the community," a category that included long-term mestizo residents who had clearly expressed their alliance with the Garifuna (such as Carla).

Anderson (2009:223–226) discusses the centrality that local understandings and expressions of sociality played in Sambo Creek's land struggle. The land shortage and recuperation efforts were not only responses to economic inequalities and exploitation but also emerged due to the importance Sambeños place on sociality. In an increasingly dense settlement, Sambeños were concerned with how their household business affected their neighbors and were seeking dignity and enhanced privacy through the land recuperations. Mestizo residents who suffered the same degree of limited privacy due to condensed housing options emerged alongside Garifuna to reclaim land, further evidence of the importance of sociality in evaluating "belonging" among "children of the community."

The stories in this chapter reveal how local landed mestizos react through identity construction. Faced with the internationalization of Garifuna indigeneity and national legislation that opened spaces for mobilizations based on Garifuna cultural rights, mestizos at the local level are (re)constructing their own ethnic identities in response to a shift in recognition of Garifuna rights under neoliberal multicultural projects. Those with historical power hark back to forms of mestizaje that protected their place within the racial hierarchy and denied Garifuna rights as Hondurans. Others become active participants in the land struggle, allied in discourse and practice with the movement to reclaim land based on cultural rights. Still others are caught at points in-between. These individual identity positions emerge (1) as a result of the neoliberal economic reforms that have transformed their once undesirable land into a coveted global commodity, and (2) as an effort to assert their "rights" as historical inhabitants or historical power holders.

SEVEN

"Businessmen Disguised as Environmentalists"

Neoliberal Conservation in Garifuna Territory

In the 1990s, the trend was to convert the management of our territories in protected areas to private enterprises. The first silent expulsion of Garifuna communities occurred in Cuero y Salado, and then the strategy was replicated in the Cayos Cochinos. Meanwhile, businessmen disguised as environmentalists were taking over strategic *locations from Punta Sal to Capiro y Calentura [which span the north coast in historical Garifuna territory], places within plans for this century's tourism projects."* [OFRANEH 2011a, translation by author, emphasis added]

In OFRANEH's communiqués from the summer and fall of 2011, activists called attention to the global spread of protected areas, hybrid environmental governance (management by NGOs), links between protected area growth and the tourism economy, and the expulsion/displacement of local populations in the wake of these movements. As OFRANEH indicates, Garifuna communities are situated at the heart of the country's finest natural areas, making them particularly vulnerable to the social impacts of the protected-area management policies and protected-area tourism.

Sitting in the offices of OFRANEH on a June afternoon in 2011, don Buelto appears, a 76-year-old Garifuna man from Chachahuate-Nueva Armenia. It had been five years since I had last seen him, and while his vision and hearing were worsening, he looked just as he did back in 2006 and was equally, or more, troubled. I first met don Buelto, along with several of his fisher colleagues, in Chachahuate, during an impassioned focus group to discuss the effects of the 2004–9 Cayos Cochinos Marine Protected Area management plan on Garifuna livelihood strategies. Operating as Operation Wallacea's lead social scientists, my colleague Natalie Bown and I were responsible for overseeing 17 students working on their senior honors and master's theses on the effects of the CCMPA's management plan on the Garifuna culture, as well as the potential for ecotourism to replace fishing as a livelihood strategy. Natalie and I also interacted with the approximately 100–200 research volunteers who traveled through the Cayos Cochinos on their summer "expeditions." Opwall is the private conservation and scientific research organization mentioned in the book's introductory vignette. Opwall began its expeditions to Honduras in 2004, under a 10-year research clearance contract with the Honduran Coral Reef Fund, the nonprofit organization that currently oversees all activity within the CCMPA.

One afternoon in July 2005 I helped arrange for a large group of Opwall expedition students to travel from Cayo Menor to Chachahuate. While the student tourists enjoyed their visit—having their hair plaited, purchasing shell necklaces, and lounging on the beach drinking refreshments—the social science students and I visited with one of the families who had grown increasingly dependent on the tourism industry after the introduction of the first management plan. Alonso and Rosa were busy at work, spread out on a small wooden plank outside their small house. They did not make an effort to go to the tourist students—this is a job typically assumed by island children. Rosa sat smoothing over shells while Alonso worked to fashion earrings out of black coral. As they labored, Alonso shared a familiar narrative—he said that "the Foundation" wanted to remove the Garifuna from Chachahuate, sending them back to Nueva Armenia. He spoke of all the restrictions being put on fishers, and how they were no longer able to capture lobster during specific seasons, even if their families were hungry. While Alonso identified first as a fisher, he had turned to jewelry production to help supplement the household income. He sold necklaces, bracelets, and earrings for $5 each.

Soon some of the Opwall students found us; they were interested in seeing the jewelry that Alonso and Rosa had available for purchase, especially items unlike the typical shell necklaces that the kids were pushing along the beachfront. Alonso presented turtle shell, black coral, and conch shell jewelry (all illegal to obtain from the sea), which he sells for higher prices (around $10) due to their rarity. Alonso was careful to point out that he purchased these products in La Ceiba from a man who acquired them from Colombia. Exhibiting conch shells he sells to tourists as souvenirs, Alonso reminded us that these were dead when they washed up on shore. Rosa corrected him, saying "No, they don't wash up. You need to dive for them." And then she pointed with her lips to the areas where they could be found. Alonso repeated that they do not dive for conch—it is illegal—they only gather dead conch. Rosa insisted again that this isn't true, that they obtain them from diving. The truth is unimportant. What is salient is that life in the Cayos Cochinos has changed drastically under the CCMPA management plan, and Garifuna are no longer permitted access to specific sea products that carry cultural meaning (discussed later).

The majority of fishers that Natalie and I encountered over those early years of the management plan (2005–7) echoed Alonso's discontent with the CCMPA regulations, yet few had as successfully replaced lost fishing income with tourism. Most fishers sounded like the man I quote below, who was responding to a question about the benefits of the management plan.

> There are no positives. The only positives are for the Foundation [the HCRF]. They take the bread right out of our mouths! The Garifuna have lived here for over two hundred years, [and] we do not appreciate the Foundation trying to teach us things. We think this is unfair. We have more knowledge than them about the area and waters. It appears that the Foundation is trying to stop us from our ancestral activities. [And] they want everyone to get off the island, [but] it is *our* island!

When asked what he suggested the Foundation do differently to improve their relationship with the community, he responded: "We would like the Foundation to be more understanding of our position. I understand that lobster is prohibited, but they must realize that we need it to feed our kids. If they catch us, they take our boats and equipment. They need to stop being prejudiced towards our community. If one of us gets sick, we will catch lobster to pay for help on the mainland; that is our life."

Just how did "the Foundation" come to manage the Cayos Cochinos territory, especially given the Garifuna's historical inhabitation of the natural area? To what extent was it trying to prohibit the Garifuna from engaging in cultural traditions? And how did Opwall and its students enter into the evaluation of the effects of the CCMPA management plan on the Garifuna community?

The case of Cayos Cochinos allows us to further explore the dynamics of roots, rights, and belonging in a neoliberal era, through on-the-ground practices of conservation and tourism. As in the case of Sambo Creek, Garifuna within the Cayos Cochinos have seen their once-isolated territory converted into a coveted global commodity, this time through the guise of protected area management. The question of who "belongs" in the archipelago is most easily answered with an exploration of money and power. Those who can purchase "rights" either to the land masses, to a stake in the resource management structure, or as a tourist visitor to the protected area have come to outcompete those who claim ancestral rights as original resource managers.

Creating the CCMPA in Garifuna Territory, and its Governance Structure

The Cayos Cochinos are a set of two main islands and thirteen smaller cays located 15 kilometers off the Caribbean coast of Honduras, forming extensive coral reefs at the southernmost part of the Mesoamerican Barrier Reef System (Harborne et al. 2001). The habitats within the Cayos Cochinos archipelago include coral reefs, seagrasses, corals, sand, algae, and mangroves, which are home to fish and crustaceans of commercial value (including the Caribbean spiny lobster, *Panulirus argus*), reef fish species, the endangered queen conch (*Strombus gigas*), and sea turtle species. The CCMPA terrestrial habitats include several bird species that hold special significance for reef ecology, and two endangered reptile species, the pink boa constrictor (*Constrictor imperator*) and the black-chested ctenosaur (*Ctenosaura melanosterna*) (Bown 2010:103; Reed et al. 2007).

Six Garifuna communities fall within the Cayos Cochinos sphere of influence: two permanent settlements (Chachahuate and East End), and four mainland communities (Rio Esteban, Nueva Armenia, Sambo Creek, and Corozal). Each of the mainland communities is connected to CCMPA territory through familial ties. While Sambo Creek has a small cay with temporary dwellings for fishermen to overnight (Cayo Bolaños), families from Nueva Armenia and Rio Esteban created permanent settlements on Chachahuate and East End, respectively. Traditionally, all Garifuna communities incorporated reliance on marine resources, including the extraction of red snappers (*Lutjanus*) and groupers (*Serranidae*), white fish grunts (*Haemulidae*), and spiny Caribbean lobster (*Panulirus argus*). Red and white finfish and lobster were fished for small-scale market sales throughout the year (finfish, January–June; and lobster June–December), while white finfish were extracted throughout the year for subsistence-level consumption (Bown 2010).

Chachahuate occupies the largest of the cays in CCMPA. There are approximately 20 residents across 43 households when the cay is fully occupied during the peak fishing season (April–September); the average

Figure 7.1 Chachahuate, Cayos Cochinos. Photo by Keri Brondo

permanent resident population is 90 individuals. The vast majority of households (80 percent) rely on fishing as their central source of household income, although they supplement income with tourism activities (vending or craft production) or other forms of piecemeal labor (Brondo and Bown 2011). East End is a small settlement of 19 houses located on the north side of Cayo Mayor (the largest island). There are 22 permanent residents in this settlement, but the community can swell to around 90 during peak fishing season.

The degree to which mainland communities are reliant on the CCMPA's marine and terrestrial resources is highly variable. Sambo Creek and Corozal are closest to La Ceiba and have moved away from the traditional livelihood strategies of fishing and agriculture to a much greater degree than Rio Esteban and Nueva Armenia. These communities not only lack agricultural land but also have increased labor opportunities due to their proximity to La Ceiba and growing tourism in the area. The picture looks slightly different in Rio Esteban and Nueva Armenia, where households are much more likely to rely on fishing and/or small-scale agriculture for subsistence or supplemental income. This is especially so for Rio Esteban, located farthest from La Ceiba; Rio Esteban is particularly difficult to get

Figure 7.2 East End, Cayos Cochinos. Photo by Monica Kar

to during the wet season when the riverbed floods and cuts off the entrance to the community. However, Rio Esteban is just 12 nautical miles from the CCMPA, and so a substantial number of households had been engaged in scuba fishing for Caribbean spiny lobster (*Panulirus argus*) until its ban in 2004. Today a handful of community members are still illegally involved in this trade.

In addition to the Garifuna settlements, there are two original land-owning families within the CCMPA, who have leased or sold portions of the islands to other parties, resulting in newer occupants in the MPA. These parties include the HCRF, which currently owns Cayo Menor (with infrastructure limited to a research station and accommodations), wealthy nationals and foreigners who use smaller cays for vacation spots, and a dive resort located on Cayo Mayor that is owned by US citizens.

The Cayos Cochinos achieved protected status in 1993 through the lobbying efforts of a group of elite businessmen and politicians from Tegucigalpa ("businessmen disguised as environmentalists") who created the Society for Ecological Investments (SIEC) in conjunction with the AVINA Foundation. AVINA, a Swiss organization, was founded in 1994 to create sustainable development alliances between business and philanthropic organizations (AVINA 2011). SIEC's purpose was to fund the acquisition of the land masses within the Cayos Cochinos as well as the Honduran Coral Reef Fund, which would be tasked with managing a scientific station and developing conservation measures for the protected area (Andraka, Bouroncle, and García-Saez 2004:31). One of the effects of the global dominance of neoliberalism is the increasing acceptance of—or even a perceived need—for private-sector involvement in biodiversity conservation (Büscher and Whande 2007:31). Combining business interests with biodiversity conservation is dangerous in the sense that when parks and protected areas become run as businesses, biodiversity protection, not to mention the overall well-being of the people living within the park, can become secondary to increasing revenue sources and controlling costs. Establishing the CCMPA with a business model at its foundation has had reverberating effects on Garifuna access and control over the area's natural resources.

While the HCRF was created in June 1994 with initial funding from the SIEC, it became tasked with generating its own funding for conservation projects. One of its first arrangements was with the Smithsonian Tropical Research Institute (STRI), which signed an agreement to conduct an assessment of the biological diversity within the CCMPA and to suggest measures to preserve the health of the ecosystem. The STRI, with support from the AVINA Foundation, private owners of protected area land, and the Honduran government, built the research station on Cayo Menor that the HCRF's research tourists (including Opwall researchers) continue to use today. The STRI also took the first years of MPA resource management (1994–97). STRI's findings regarding the extent of the ecosystem damage created from overfishing by industrial boats led them to suggest a command-and-control approach to resource management: total ban of all extractive activities of marine species, full-time patrolling, and controlled development (Bown 2010:105). When the HCRF took over full management of the area in 1998, they drew upon the Smithsonian's model and available research to develop a management plan for the CCMPA in conjunction with the World Wildlife Fund (WWF) and AVINA. This plan is discussed below.

The HCRF operates under the governance structure of the Honduran Corporation for Forest Development (COHDEFOR). COHDEFOR was created in 1974 to manage the nationalized forests. In 1993 all natural resources—terrestrial, freshwater, and marine—were moved under COHDEFOR's purview. The consolidation of natural resource management under COHDEFOR coincided with the creation of Honduras's National System of Protected Areas (SINAPH) and the Department for Protected Areas and Wildlife (DAPVS); this was a time when protected areas were rapidly expanding on a global scale (Brockington, Duffy, and Igoe 2008:1–2). The 1990s also saw tourism taking center stage as an important development strategy in Honduras (as discussed in chapter 2). SINAPH and DAPVS began to receive consultation and advice from the Honduran Institute of Tourism on issues of tourist visitation to protected areas (Vreugdenhil et al. 2002), clearly a message that the Honduran government saw conservation and development as two sides of the same coin. Tourism, then, could become an income generator for protected area management. Opportunities to develop conservation research tourism were some of the first business partnerships that the HCRF sought out.

When DAPVS was assigned institutional responsibility for the management of protected areas (and their natural and cultural resources) in 1993, its governance model was grounded—on paper—in a sustainable development framework and included legislation that supported the continued practice of traditional human activities within the buffer zone, comanagement practices, and methods to coordinate and encourage community participation in the management of protected areas alongside NGO partners (Brondo and Bown 2011; Vreugdenhil et al. 2002). In theory this decentralized model of governance looked promising.

Decentralized, neoliberal conservation governance models emerged in the 1980s, a time when states were increasingly unable to effectively manage their own economies (Lemos and Agrawal 2006:302). Proponents of such models suggested that dismantling restrictive state structures and practices could lead to increased democracy and participation, by shifting the responsibility for environmental governance toward local communities and institutions (Lemos and Agrawal 2006:319). "Hybrid environmental governance structures," or public–private partnerships, where states, businesses, NGOs, and communities all come together to share responsibility for conservation efforts, would fill in the capacity gaps of state institutions, leading to social sustainability through an emphasis on democracy and equity (Lemos and Agrawal 2006). Yet, in practice, such promises rarely hold water. The DAPVS lacked the personnel and fiscal resources to successfully manage their enlarged responsibility, and so the management of protected areas, and their resources, was bid out to private enterprises and NGOs. Local communities were required to produce a development program for land acquisition but did not have the expertise necessary to create such proposals. The net effect was that the protected area resources and their management were diverted away from local communities and into the hands of elite and foreign interests, under the organizational structure of the HCRF. Traditional user rights of the de facto inhabitants of agricultural and coastal lands were ignored, overruled, or altered without notice (Brondo and Bown 2011).

Two legislative acts were of particular consequence to the Cayos Cochinos settlements. First, the cays were rezoned as urban land in 1992 under Decree 90/90, which reclassified all areas that the Ministry of Tourism felt had tourism potential as urban land. As described in chapter 2, Decree 90/90 opened up to foreign purchase land previously protected under Article 107; much of this land was located in ancestral Garifuna territory. Second, while the Cayos Cochinos settlements Chachahuate and East End received communal titles from the INA in 2001, as did Sambo Creek and other mainland settlements in the late 1990s, the MPA territory had been privatized *before* the issuance of the communal titles (Brondo and Woods 2007). The original landowning families had made a verbal agreement with the Garifuna communities, permitting them to remain on Chachahuate and Cayo Menor in East End as long as they did not extend their settlements. In 2001, when East End, Chachahuate and Bolaños (Sambo Creek's fishing cay) were granted communal land titles, the original landowners spent five years in court contesting the titles. The landowning family made the case that since the Cayos Cochinos had been rezoned as urban land in 1992 under Decree 90/90, the INA no longer had jurisdiction of the area (as the INA's jurisdiction is limited to rural land). Garifuna activists from OFRANEH brought the case to the Inter-American Commission on Human Rights, and in 2006, the Honduran Supreme Court ruled in favor of the Garifuna communities, upholding the communal title (Brondo and Woods 2007:7–9). Even so, the register of property at the municipality level neglected to inscribe and send the title to the community, because the alleged property owner continued to contest the legality of the title. The reregulation of Garifuna ancestral territory through privatization created a foundation of extreme distrust and tension between the Garifuna population and Honduran mainlanders and foreign newcomers to the CCMPA, including the HCRF staff and future business partners (e.g., Opwall).

When Cayo Menor was sold to the HCRF in 1993, the Smithsonian negotiated a five-year contract to access the area and engage in conservation research. During this time, a moratorium was placed on the removal of any form of marine life in an area extending five miles in all directions from the central cay, and a 24-hour navy patrol and watch towers were established to enforce it. The Garifuna were implicitly, and at times explicitly, blamed for the environmental destruction that had been caused by the long history of industrial fishing in the region (Anderson 2000:225–226). In 1992 shrimp and lobster exports accounted for 12 percent of export earnings in Honduras, totaling $97 million, an increase of 33 percent from the prior year and linked to a rise in the number of commercial vessels registered to Honduras (Manor 1999). Small-scale fishing, on the other hand, generated only around $555,000, two hundred times less than industrial fishing (Bown 2010: 38). While the moratorium on fishing activities may have responded to the real threat to biodiversity that industrial fishing provided, it also severely endangered the livelihoods of the Garifuna population, who relied heavily on fishing as a supplemental (or in some cases, primary) source of income and subsistence.

Garifuna organizations and residents of the affected communities formed committees in opposition to the moratorium (i.e., the Comité Prodefensa de los Intereses Garífunas de los Cayos Cochinos and the Sociedad de Pescadores de Chachahuate). When local resistance was not met with action, activists reached out to the Food First Information and Action Network (FIAN International), an international human rights organization that focuses on fighting hunger with human rights. In June 1994 FIAN wrote a letter to the Honduran government denouncing the moratorium as unconstitutional and in violation of international treaties signed by Honduras (Anderson 2000:222). The presidential decree violated international law because (1) no provisions were made to include the participation of Garifuna fishermen in the implementation of the project, and (2) the moratorium on fishing and diving prohibited the Garifuna access to their means of subsistence and essentially forced them to abandon their "cultural patrimony" (a right protected under the ILO 169 [Anderson 2000:222–223]). Responding to the activism, the government incorporated *one* Garifuna representative into the commission in charge of formulating the regulations and procedures for the reserve (the individual appointed to the commission was the president of one of the national Garifuna organizations). Furthermore, the government modified the moratorium on fishing in 1999 to permit "subsistence fishing" by inhabitants of the reserve and fishermen from the mainland, but only by hand-held lines. Diving prohibitions remained and the Garifuna were prohibited from cutting any trees or palms to build or repair their homes (Anderson 2000:225–226).

The 2004–9 CCMPA Management Plan

In 2003 the legislative decree 114-2003 redesignated the Cayos Cochinos as the only statutory marine protected area in Honduras. It was at this time that management responsibility for the area was granted to the HCRF for 10 years (2004–14). An initial management plan was developed by the HCRF with assistance from the World Wildlife Fund for 2004–9. When the plan was originally drafted, the majority of the 20 individuals consulted from the MPA-reliant communities had a self-interest in the development of tourism (i.e., they were tour operators already or had motorboats that could be used to transport tourists to the CCMPA). There had been little to no engagement with the local community to develop measures for the sustainable use of local resources.

Management under the 2004–9 plan was clearly hierarchical, top-down for preservationist purposes, and conservation-driven, and only paid lip service to the participatory, democratically driven comanagement strategies that are advocated with hybrid environmental governance models. Rather than meeting the principles of good governance and promoting participation, accountability, and legitimacy, the state was absolved of responsibility for the creation of the CCMPA management plan and did not monitor the participative capacity of the decision-making process to ensure representation from local users (see also Bown 2010:194).

The regulations with which the Garifuna population was forced to comply under the 2004–9 management plan were only a few steps improved from the 1993 moratorium. The plan banned diving for lobster and other marine species, a practice that many engaged in for sale and subsistence. Only traditional lobster traps (*nasas*) could be used, and only from June to December; juvenile and pregnant female lobsters had to be returned to the sea. Moreover, the collection of conch became prohibited. Like lobster, conch is a key ingredient in traditional Garifuna recipes. Several "no-take" areas were established, many of them in proximity to Garifuna MPA settlements, which forced fishers to travel to more distant fishing grounds for catch.

Figure 7.3 Diving for lobster, Chachahuate. Photo by Natalie Bown

Restrictions on the extraction of marine life have serious implications for the preparation and consumption of traditional foods and performance of ancestral rites. Several religious rituals call for the provision of specific sea products as offerings to ancestral spirits, and many traditional foods are fish-based. Several recipes contain conch, which the Garifuna are now prohibited from capturing. Moreover, conch shell horns historically had a wide range of uses, including calling community members to the beach to purchase fresh fish after the fishermen arrived or signaling to community members when it was time to thatch a roof (López 2000). Today conch shell horns continue to be used widely in Garifuna music production.

Figure 7.4 Traditional lobster traps stacked on Chachahuate. Photo by Keri Brondo

Enforcement and Inequality

Under the management plan, artisanal fishers were permitted within the CCMPA only if they held a license. Licenses are issued, for free, by the HCRF. However, to qualify for this license, fishers must register with the Honduran Department of Fisheries and Aquaculture (Dirección General de Pesca, or DIGEPESCA); a municipal license costs 40 lempiras (approximately $2.22), and a boat captain's license costs 1,000 lempiras (around $55). Most fishers do not register with DIGEPESCA, meaning that they are at risk of prosecution every time they enter the CCMPA.

Drawing on personal connections between the private landowners within the CCMPA and members of Congress, the HCRF was able to secure the presence of navy personnel to work with HCRF resource guards to patrol the area and ensure compliance with the regulations. The navy began a routine patrol in daytime hours, and foot patrols were added in the cay communities in 2006. Fishers caught breaking the rules were (and continue to be) subject to having their boats and equipment seized, and themselves incarcerated on the island of Roatan (where the capital of the Bay Islands is located).

While on the one hand the navy's presence has served as a deterrent to industrial trawlers and narcotics trafficking, Garifuna fishers have also suffered persecution. A petition to IACHR in 2003 detailed the human rights abuses inflicted on the Garifuna community in conjunction with the CCMPA's establishment, including the disappearance of one fisher, the shooting of another, and the abandoning of two people at high sea (Inter-American Commission on Human Rights 2007). Accounts of abuse by navy officers and HCRF guards continued through the 2000s. Several fishermen shared stories of mistreatment with Natalie and me during our summer field seasons. "Last year they [the navy] came wearing masks during the day. They put masks on their faces and threatened two or three people to leave the island. We reported it but we feel like it came from the Foundation. Sixteen people came over! The Foundation is trying to destroy us!" Those most regularly targeted were individual fishers, people who did not belong to the fishing cooperatives that the HCRF helped start in the late 1990s. In 1998 DIGEPESCA announced a Japanese-funded project to invest in artisanal fishery along the north coast. The program, called MODAPESCA, was open only to communities located within the department of Atlántida. The HCRF helped community groups develop proposals to the MODAPESCA program that would provide funding to develop fishing cooperatives. Successful groups would receive 25-foot motorized boats and fishing equipment to launch their cooperative; no capacity training (i.e., the strengthening of skills, competencies, or abilities of people in communities or groups) was provided. Previously, while Garifuna might have gone out on fishing excursions with family members or companions, they did not work together in cooperatives. When the project was announced, the HCRF did what most young NGOs working with communities do—they spoke to community elites through the local patronato. Information on the application process did not extend beyond the patronato's immediate circle of families with higher wealth and social status, thus disadvantaging the majority of less well-off families, most of whom were reliant to some degree on fishing for their livelihoods. The establishment of these cooperatives created increased disparities within communities, as well as higher status of cooperative members with the HCRF (and therefore increased opportunities to benefit from HCRF opportunities).

Cooperative members generally report favorable relationships with the HCRF and the navy, who they feel recognize them in the waters as "belonging." In fact, fear of persecution has altered fishing behavior such that many individual fishers now prefer to fish outside of the CCMPA in order to avoid patrol guards (Bown 2010:208). Others fish at night in an attempt to hide from patrols and "avoid being shot."

Grossly inadequate participation was the case from the earliest stages of the CCMPA's creation through knowledge dissemination and implementation of regulations. Even the government agency COHDEFOR contested the participation process. While COHDEFOR has legislative responsibility over the resources within the CCMPA, it was not consulted to approve the management plan. Rather, HCRF board members drew upon their political connections to take the plan directly to Congress, bypassing COHDEFOR, and defying state regulation, to produce a legally recognized yet illegitimate management plan that excluded local stakeholders and their knowledge (Bown 2010:194).

Two individuals from each of the five MPA-reliant communities were selected as representatives during the implementation stages of the management plan. While each community has its own local governing system (i.e., the patronato) in place to represent community interests, the HCRF handpicked community representatives from the fishing cooperatives that they had helped establish in the late 1990s. These individuals were conceptualized as conduits of information between the HCRF and the local communities. The exchange of information was top-down, focusing solely on regulations and enforcement procedures, excluding information about the conservation objectives and socioeconomic implications of the plan's regulations. Mutual exchange and participation in decision making was entirely absent (Bown 2010:196). Other community members felt excluded and uninformed.

> Not many people have any relationship with the Foundation. When decisions are made concerning the fishers, the only contact is between the foundation and Celeo [a pseudonym for the head of their fisher cooperative]. The rest of the fishers are rarely consulted when decisions are made. The Foundation only deals with Celeo as the fishermen are working for their own interests and do not see the need to get the *patronato* involved, even though my position is higher than don Celeo (Brondo and Bown 2011:100).

Only *los milionarios* (the millionaires) of Nueva Armenia are involved in meetings. They benefit from having a salary from the Foundation. They get paid to call on their radios and tell them when we leave and where we're heading. They use private radios so we don't know (Bown 2010:198).

Figure 7.5 Individual fisher preparing fish in East End, Cayos Cochinos. Photo by Keri Brondo

Exacerbating the tension created by feelings of exclusion from the development of CCMPA regulations, followed by perceived abusive enforcement monitoring and compliance, were the growing income disparities as cooperative members and their families continued to benefit most from tourism developments. Because cooperative members had been identified by the HCRF early on as those most dependent on the CCMPA for income, they received focused attention to reduce the impacts of the management plan. Funding for tourism initiatives—meant to replace income lost from fishing—was diverted, both intentionally and unintentionally, to members of fishing cooperatives.

One of the management plan's objectives was to seek funds to encourage the Garifuna population to explore livelihood alternatives, such as moving income-generating activities from fishing to tourism. In 2007 the HCRF secured funding from the WWF to build a hotel on Chachahuate to house overnight visitors. The WWF and USAID also funded the refurbishment of existing community infrastructure into a communal restaurant, cabanas to house overnight visitors, and a tourism center on East End in 2008. These tourism initiatives are now being run as community cooperatives, yet some individual fishers accuse them of benefiting former fishing cooperative members more than other households. The uneven internal distribution of the income generated through these developments among community members reflects power hierarchies growing within each CCMPA community. In Nueva Armenia, these men have become known as *"los milionarios"* (the millionaires, mentioned in the quote above).

Unintentionally, fishing cooperative members were given a leg up to move into tourism-related activities when they received the donated motorized boats through the MODAPESCA program. Most of these cooperative members have moved from fishing into occupations as tour guides, using their MODAPESCA boat to transport tourists from the coast to the CCMPA. Earning approximately $150 round-trip, these families have come to surpass the average household income of their community peers. Because they are better off financially, these families are also the ones able to offer homestay accommodations for Opwall tourists, who have specific accommodation standards that end up disqualifying the poorest families from participation. Opwall provides homestay opportunities for 100–200 people each week during their eight-week summer research season. These volunteer tourists stay overnight in a Garifuna community on the mainland before they transfer to the Cayos Cochinos. Opwall homestays supported the tourism industry in Nueva Armenia in 2006 and 2007, and were moved to Rio Esteban during 2008–2011.

Turning back to OFRANEH's office in June 2011, where this chapter began, don Buelto was there to draft a letter regarding the recent infrastructure development supported by Garifuna organizations and NGOs that he felt further fractured the community, widening the gulf between winners and losers. Writing to the *Fiscalía de las Etnias*, the HCRF, ODECO, and OFRANEH, Buelto says: "I remember 50 years ago when the original fishermen on the cay were selfless and caring. I remember being in the fight together when attempts were made to resettle us in 1994 and then again in 1999. I remember in 2000 going with a group of fisherman and being trained in 'leadership,' yet it now appears that the small groups of leaders are acting for their own benefit more than for the community they claim to represent" (author's translation). Don Buelto was referring to the accommodations built on Chachahuate, intended, he says, to benefit "the original fishermen," but which have come to benefit only a few. In his letter, Buelto explains he was denied a key to the structure, and that now the hotel rests in the hands of the "messengers of the Foundation." Don Buelto accuses those in charge of hiding information and profit from the broader community. He positions emerging individualism and class distinctions against traditional communitarian attitudes, suggesting that these new forms of "freedom" or "being" in the world have developed out of the global expansion of neoliberal philosophy.

The Business of Conservation

In addition to the abuses of power to push through a protectionist management plan without community participation, weak stakeholder involvement, and poor communication channels between the HCRF and Garifuna communities, there has also been a serious lack of financial transparency from the HCRF to the MPA communities. The first incident that sparked distrust of the HCRF was the introduction of entrance fees for visitors to the MPA.

According to the meeting minutes and legislation proceedings, the entrance tax was intended to be used to improve tourism opportunities both for the tourists (by ensuring conservation of the area) and for those who live within the MPA. The minutes from the October 14, 2004, meeting at the Secretaria de Estado en los Despachos de Recursos stated:

> It is very important for the success of the MPA that the communities that live within it and the influenced zones receive benefits from the conservation of the MPA. Promoting tourism as an economic alternative for the communities is a good opportunity to share with local communities in the management and conservation of the MPA. With the proposal to promote community tourism initiatives, the foreign tourists that visit the MPA through tour operators from the communities within the MPA and its zone of influence pay a reduced rate. [Secretaria de Estado en los Despachos de Recursos 2004, author's translation from Spanish]

According to the documents detailing the development of this tax, the group considered a number of items, including: (1) the importance of Legislative Decree 114-2003, which assured the operating capacity and maintenance of the marine protected area; (2) protecting and developing the tourism sector in agreement with the management plan; (3) promoting tourism opportunities for local communities; (4) managing and controlling the impact of tourism; (5) facilitating access to the MPA by the national community with education and recreation fines; (6) implementing the success of the tariff with a support base; and (7) promoting self-sufficiency in the management of the MPA and the local economy (Secretaria de Estado en los Despachos de Recursos 2004). The same document made note of the actors present at this meeting. Not one individual present represented the Garifuna community. Without Garifuna consultation, the tourist tax was passed and the collection of entrance fees began in January 2005. The tariffs apply to both visitors to the MPA and boats that enter the water within the limits. The amount of the fee varies by amount of time the tourist remains in the park (i.e., visitors who stay a year pay less), and foreign tourists pay five times more than Honduran nationals.

The following two quotes are from a top official from the HCRF, responding to the same question about how the entrance fees were established and how the money would be spent—posed to him once in 2005 and then again in 2006.

> It should help guarantee the sustainability of the area. And *it should also be used to help develop the communities, and by law it has to. . . . Due to the 2003 law, the money we collected cannot be touched until a national committee makes a decision as to where to invest it,* assuring conservation of the area. *We will present a list of projects and their associated budgets to the government,* as to how we think the money should be used. [2005, emphasis added, author's translation]

> In 2003, a new law for protected areas was passed . . . creating an entrance fee that would be used for the conservation of the protected area. . . . *The law states that the HCRF would collect the money and use it for conservation. Community development was not part of the law.* The money was to be spent on fuel costs, food for the demarcation of the protected area . . . navy patrol, maintenance of the buoy for the mooring sites. [2006, emphasis added, author's translation]

In 2005 the HCRF staff member discusses the value of the fees to the communities, which appeared in written documentation leading to their establishment. Yet by 2006 he simply notes that the HCRF is unable to use the money for community development, suggesting that it would if it could, but that the 2003 law forbids this. The HCRF's lobbying for the 2003 legislation goes unrecognized.

In 2005 I reviewed boat records from the HCRF for January–March 2005, and the Opwall season (June 29–August 31). Some 1,648 visitors were recorded as entering the MPA in the 4.5 months of data reviewed. The primary nations represented by visitors were England (n = 820) and

Honduras (n = 250), followed by Canada (n = 212) and the United States (n = 184). The income derived for the management of the MPA would have been between $11,645 and $14,480.[1] While the figures are dated, visitor numbers likely remained the same, or were higher from 2006 until the 2009 coup d'état (when tourist visitation dropped across Honduras). The tourist tax has been a constant source of tension, because the communities believed they would receive a percentage of the revenue. Rene, a 29-year-old fisher from Chachahuate reflected:

> The foundation collects $10 from each tourist. Where does it go? They seem to take money and show the tourists Cayo Menor (location of HCRF research station) and Cayo Mayor (location of foreign-owned Plantation Beach Resort), but not Chachahuate. It would be far better if we collected the $10 from the tourists when they arrive on the island, instead of the foundation taking it on behalf of us. . . If the foundation gave us the money, we would plant trees on the island, and build a communal kitchen, and buy rakes to clean the beaches. But the foundation does not contact us. [Author's translation]

Residents of the MPA communities felt that the intended uses of entrance fee money were not clearly communicated to them; therefore, the majority of community members perceived the HCRF personnel as dishonest and to be "lining their own pockets."

The fallout of neoliberal conservation, or the reliance on profit generation to protect endangered resources, is that NGOs may end up agreeing to terms that prove unsustainable for the habitat and for society. This is even more a possibility for young protected areas, early in their management strategies and without sufficient data on carrying capacity or ecological and social impacts.

In the early years of the Opwall–HCRF research contract, research tourists were arriving at an unsustainable rate. On several occasions the island ran out of water, reflecting an overabundance of people and raising questions about the damage high numbers of tourists could bring to the MPA's fragile marine and terrestrial ecosystems. We asked one of the lead HCRF staff members at the CCMPA research station whether he agreed with the organization's contract decisions. He shared: "Last week we had 215 people, and that was far too many for the island's ideal capacity of 90. . . . The other main problem is that *they are damaging the reef, and dives are taking place in areas which are designated as no-fishing zones for communities*. The extra people that are diving could affect the number of juvenile fish, and *this could lead to further resentment from the communities"* [emphasis added]. We then asked for him to explain the reasons for going over the ideal capacity, to which he responded: "This is not official, but I think it is because *the foundation is trying to become more self-sufficient and self-sustainable*. So the more money we receive from organizations, the closer we get to meeting this objective" [emphasis added].

In its pursuit of financial independence, the HCRF negotiated an extremely controversial contract with Magnolia Productions to allow the filming of a popular Italian reality show, *L'Isola dei famosi* (The Island of the Famous) in the CCMPA. Modeled after the hit CBS show *Survivor*, contestants were "stranded" on Cayo Paloma throughout the months of September and October. MPA conservation regulations for harvesting fish and shellfish—with which the Garifuna must comply—did not apply to game show contestants, who were afforded fishing rights within the reserve. Bait collection areas of the CCMPA were closed to the Garifuna throughout the show's tenure during live transmissions. During the first year of filming, the local fishing population saw no tangible benefits or compensation for lost income, or sufficient transparency of the financial gains from Magnolia paid to the HCRF, which were suggested to be around $560,000 per year.

The discontent over this in the MPA-reliant communities led to residents protesting outside the home of the head of a local fishing cooperative in July 2007. While I was not present, my colleague Natalie Bown was, and she shared her field notes. During this gathering, Garifuna fishers drafted a *carta de negociación* (letter of negotiation) demanding compensation from the HCRF for the impacts that filming the reality show had on their lives. The meeting was dominated by two women, one from a traditional lobster fishing family in Rio Esteban, and the other a nonfisher activist from Nueva Armenia. Both of these women presented the reasons that the filming of the reality show was unacceptable for all communities, and the women instigated the majority of the demands written in the letter, although consensual agreement of the contents of the letter was reached among all present (see also Brondo and Bown 2011:101).

The *carta de negociación* reminded the HCRF that the Garifuna are the "owners of the local resources, and the Foundation is only the manager of them." The authors called out the blatant violation of CCMPA regulations in the Magnolia contract, which permitted the show's contestants to fish within the reserve. These local activists demanded that the HCRF:

(1) make the contract between the HCRF and the reality show fully transparent; (2) invest in tourism-related training and infrastructure; (3) create a small loan program to encourage local entrepreneurship; (4) ensure co-ownership of MPA tourism developments; (5) employ locals for services provided to the reality show; (6) demonstrate respect for human rights; (7) replace the existing reality show negotiating committee with one that included members of the local community; and (8) assure that the environmental impact caused by the reality show be minimal (see also Brondo and Bown 2011:101).

Then, in 2008, don Buelto authored a call for action against the HCRF. The call circulated on FIAN, the international human rights organization. Buelto's letter, entitled "The Right to Food and the Lie of Conservation," condemned the HCRF for its privileging of elite foreign interests and capital gain to the detriment of Garifuna fishing community, pointing out the ironies of protected area management that enables some actors to enjoy and potentially damage local resources, while prohibiting others. Buelto writes:

> On February 7, 2008, I was forbidden from entering the area around Cayo Paloma by the Honduran navy officers and the rangers from the HCRF, who noted that it would interrupt the recording of a TV reality show. This is not the first time that the Garifuna from Chachahuate were forbidden to approach Cayo Paloma; meanwhile the Foundation continues to do business with foreign companies [permitting foreigners] in this place. For 14 years the Garifuna have not been allowed to approach Cayo Paloma, a place where we have traditionally obtained *la frai* [bait]. However, in the last two years the Cayos Cochinos Foundation [the HCRF] has permitted the presence of groups of foreigners for three-week periods, which has shocked the turtle that supposedly come to that place to spawn. The Cayos Cochinos Foundation, with the WWF and AVINA, has developed a management plan for the area that creates hunger for our people. While global warming and sedimentation is killing the coral reef, the Foundation believes that banning fishing in certain places is going to save the corals.

Buelto's letter points to the contradictions inherent in the HCRF's protected area management strategy, which are inescapable under neoliberal conservation, where nonprofits seek financial stability through market-driven approaches. The intrinsic nature of neoliberal conservation produces an operational logic that encourages nonprofits to sell "rights to nature" to foreign parties, producing new relationships between people and nature. These new relationships may in fact lead to further environmental degradation of the exact resources they are meant to protect. Cayo Paloma not only is a traditional bait collection area for the Garifuna fishing community but is also in the area where sea turtles breed during the months of June and July,[2] the same months that the HCRF permitted the filming of the reality show. While there is reason for concern about the potential harm to local ecology and cultural traditions as foreign interests are prioritized because of the wealth they generate, biological data collected by Opwall scientists and Reef Check demonstrate some species-specific positive outcomes, especially with spiny lobster (Bown 2010:242).

Between the 2008 FIAN call for action and the 2011 letter that opened this chapter, little has changed . . . yet much has changed. Little has changed in the form of conservation, and the fallouts of neoliberal conservation. Little has changed in terms of overall winners and losers. Yet a lot has changed in don Buelto's lifetime. The decentralization of natural resource management relieved the Honduran state from the considerable financial burden of managing its natural assets, leaving NGOs with the task of filling in the gaps left by state withdrawal. The neoliberal climate produced NGOs comprised of business interests, operating under a market logic ("businessmen disguised as environmentalists"). Without continued financial support by the SIEC, the HCRF immediately faced the need to ensure financial sustainability in order to carry forward its conservation agenda. This sense of urgency—coupled with their foundational market logic—moved the HCRF into some controversial partnership choices with foreign parties (especially the reality show).

Neoliberal economic theory predicts that if the product (in this case, the protected area and its resources) is unable to produce a clientele (a market), it will "disappear or be replaced by a more popular competing product" (Büscher and Whande 2007:30). Thus, the Cayos Cochinos natural area and biodiversity must ensure a demand for their continued existence. Research tourism focused on biodiversity and conservation guarantees a market for ecotourist arrivals and volunteer research tourists, further justifying the existence of conservation research tourism and coming full circle to reproduce the business model of organizations like Opwall. *However,* once a product becomes commercialized, the intrinsic, qualitative "use value" of resources, services, and people lose their relative importance as they become overshadowed by their quantitative "exchange value" or monetary worth (Büscher and Whande 2007:28; McDonald and Ruiters 2005:21).

Within the Cayos Cochinos, once "protecting" nature through conservation becomes commercialized, and the value of the service in protection is sold to tourists and researchers, the Garifuna population and their relationship to local resources begin to get in the way of profit. "Fences and fines" (Brockington 2002) are instituted under this preservationist protected-area business model. "Fences" appear through the prohibition of Garifuna on Cayo Menor when Opwall tourists are present or fishing around Cayo Paloma when the reality show was being filmed; and the Garifuna are fined for noncompliance with CCMPA management plan regulations. But as discussed in the next chapter, even the social science surrounding the effects of protected area management has been reduced or eliminated.

EIGHT

Research Voluntourism as Rights-Based Conservation

Could It Work?

In 2010, when Natalie Bown and I were working on our article "Neoliberal Conservation, Garifuna Territorial Rights and Resource Management in the Cayos Cochinos Marine Protected Area" (Brondo and Bown 2011), we reported that the social activism of Garifuna as indigenous peoples played a role in restructuring the CCMPA management plan to be more socioeconomically driven. A new five-year plan was rolled out in 2008, a year earlier than expected because of the local discontent with the 2005–9 plan. The no-take fishing zone in the 2008–13 plan was reduced, and there were fewer temporally closed areas. Because we had found that the distribution of benefits was skewed toward individuals who had established contacts with the HCRF during the first phase of management within the CCMPA (2005–8), Bown and I ended that article with skepticism over the degree to which the revised management plan would indeed change the conditions under which the local population interacted with resources. When I returned in 2011 and encountered don Buelto in OFRANEH's office, our article was just coming out. The letter don Buelto drafted that day suggested that Büscher's (2008:230) statement that while "productive conservation-development outcomes can and do occur . . . they are rare and never straightforward" may be right. The challenge I take up in this chapter is to question whether there are possible configurations and partnerships that could create the basis for cultural sustainability, conservation, and control over economic development within a neoliberal development context. Could research voluntourism partnerships create a mechanism of support for rights-based conservation? Can the right to self-determination ever be protected under neoliberal conservation?

Doing Good for Whom?

The above questions are so critical because all signs indicate that the sector of humanitarian travel and volunteer tourism will only continue to grow. A Google search for "volunteer tourism" generated 113,000 hits in 2012, and "volunteer tourism organizations" generated 7,450 links. Most of these holidays are marketed to potential volunteers as opportunities to "make a difference" in the world (Ingram 2011:211), something that many individuals are eager to do in today's globalized world. In general, voluntourists are seeking an "alternative" tourism experience and are more likely to be interested in the three T's (trekking, trucking, and traveling [Mowforth and Munt 1998:125–155]) than the three S's (sea, sun, and sand) that consume mass tourists. Voluntourists are typically on a journey of discovery, learning more about themselves and others. Volunteer tourism has the potential to increase social, political, and environmental consciousness and participation in social activism among participants in these travel experiences (McGehee 2002; McGehee and Norman 2002; McGehee and Santos 2005). The results are a heightened consciousness and activism in a largely privileged set of individuals, those with the resources to undertake voluntourism to begin with.

With respect to conservation-related voluntourism, I propose that the growth of this subset of volunteer tourism is a symptom of the individualization of responsibility (Maniates 2002) that emerges under neoliberal conservation and development models. By *individualization* I refer to the tendency to ascribe responsibility for environmental protection and consumption-related problems to freestanding individuals. By depoliticizing resource depletion, and removing how power shapes and structures consumption choices and conservation measures, solutions become individualized, not structural. Consumer guilt arises—people feel personally responsible for global concerns, including natural resource depletion, poverty, climate change, and the like. People individualize responsibility for causing problems, and they create individual solutions to solve them. Michael Maniates (2002:45) cites the Lorax as the epitome of this phenomenon. We respond by planting a tree, by recycling, by taking reusable shopping bags; we "do our part." None of these are systemic changes, but individuals are thirsty for opportunities to feel like they are contributing to a solution. In a series of interviews with voluntourists in 2011, whenever I asked someone to talk about their relationship to and views on the environment, he or she responded with individual acts ("I recycle at home" or "I try to remember to switch off the light when I leave a room"). This desire to feel that one is "making a difference" through contributing to conservation efforts while on holiday drives the growth of conservation research tourism organizations like Opwall.

While individuals are embracing volunteer tourism for "feel-good" reasons, governments, nongovernmental organizations, and private operations support this sector on the basis that it may be "a creative and nonconsumptive solution to a wide range of social and environmental issues" across the globe (Lyons and Wearing 2008a:6). But is voluntourism truly nonconsumptive, or does it represent the commodification of poverty?

To best assess the degree to which volunteer tourism may in fact be a "sustainable" option, one must look beyond the economic impact on and infrastructural improvements of the experience to the host community, and beyond the take-aways of the guest. Unfortunately, even in 2011, a decade into the study of volunteer tourism, studies examining the effects of volunteer tourism on host communities were largely nonexistent (Ingram 2011:215). Some ethnographic studies were beginning to emerge, exploring voluntourism as a moral economy (Sinervo 2011a, 2011b) and development conundrums that emerge in humanitarian work (Freidus 2011). These works begin to look at nexus points where hosts and guest meet, although their focus rests in large part on volunteer relationships with youth in the global south. What is missing from this emerging literature is interaction with conservation volunteerism and indigenous rights.

Ingram (2011:216) suggests that the lack of attention to the effects of volunteer tourism programs on host communities may be viewed as an example of "post-colonial 'othering,' whereby the 'other' is of secondary importance to the volunteer's reading of the experience" (Ingram 2011:216). Problematically, marketing literature fails to include community-defined needs, emphasizing instead the role and importance of the volunteer, framing the volunteer and his or her knowledge and skills as vital to the host (Simpson 2004). Wearing's (2001) review of a variety of volunteer tourism organizations found several examples that fit this description. Companies that portray marginalized peoples as "authentic natives" for the tourists' consumption (or staging authenticity in MacCannell's [1976] terms), or that limit contributions to the local community, or that house control of operations with the company's own people (Wearing 2001:150–155) all illustrate forms of neocolonialism and have the potential to reinforce a dependent, subordinate position of developing nations vis-à-vis advanced capitalist societies.

Positioning a volunteer tourism experience in these ways quenches the individual's thirst to "do something good" or to "make a difference," but it does little to address structural causes of inequality, poverty, and unequal resource distribution. Hence, "the current volunteer tourism model externalizes development" (Ingram 2011:219), operating under a model of development that assumes an (often western) expertise that is delivered *onto* third world communities (Escobar 1995; Rist 1997). Host communities are positioned as passive recipients, as objectified "others," as waiting "in need" (Ingram 2011). The end effect of these opportunities is that the volunteers are satiated, as are the coordinating institutions, but the impact on the host community is limited. In this critique, the moral or ethical satiation of individual tourists and the monetary advancement of coordinating agencies are put ahead of localized needs and desires.

The Opwall Experience

To what extent does the above critique of the commodifying and neocolonial nature of voluntourism organizations apply to conservation research tourism experiences, such as those supported by Opwall? Brochure-wise, Opwall hits positive marks in terms of its stated conservation ethic, social and environmental responsibility, employment of locals, and communication with host sites and training of volunteers pre-departure. This is achieved through the institutionalization of a "social and environmental responsibility programme" that Opwall claims "meets (or exceeds in some aspects) the requirements of a Responsible Tour Operator." This policy includes operating all of their academic programs through host site NGOs, ensuring minimal environmental impact and minimal impact on local culture and customs, working with local communities to develop new revenue streams in conservation management, maximizing income to local communities, and engaging in proper recycling and waste disposal, among other objectives (Operation Wallacea 2012). Yet while on paper Opwall appears to be working hard to meet the three nodes of sustainability (social, economic, and environmental) and making strides toward a decommodified tourism agenda, grounded research suggests several improvements could be made to better align the organizational interests with local needs.

Opwall is somewhat unique in its structure, which shapes the interactions voluntourists have with the local population. Opwall is marketed as a "network of academics . . . who design and implement biodiversity and conservation programmes" and whose "research is supported by students who join the programme to strengthen their CV or résumé, gain course credit, or collect data for a dissertation or thesis" (Operation Wallacea 2012). The way the Opwall program works is that volunteer tourists sign up to work on a specific research project, supervised by a PhD whose area of expertise focuses on a conservation issue in the host site location (in the most perfect cases). Academics represent a broad array of disciplinary backgrounds, ranging from marine science, biology, herpetology, and environmental governance to anthropology and tourism studies, to name a few.

There are two avenues through which volunteer tourists connect with the academic supervisors and research programs at Opwall field sites. The first is by signing on to work on a senior honors thesis or undergraduate dissertation, or to join as a general research assistant. In this first option, students or volunteers select from a menu of projects listed on Opwall's website, and the academic adviser helps fold them into the broader research agenda. The second manner in which voluntourists link up with Opwall research programs is as "general surveyors." Sixth-form students from the UK, and high school student groups from the United States, Canada and Australia (ages 16–18) travel with their home school teachers on two-week expeditions. In Honduras these student groups begin with one week in the lowland cloud forest of Cusuco National Park and then move to the Cayos Cochinos for their second week. While in the Cayos Cochinos, these student groups complete full PADI Open Water dive training and Caribbean Reef Ecology courses. Once on site, sixth-form and high school student groups can also volunteer to assist on a small-scale academic project.

The relationship between the academic supervisor and Opwall is based on an exchange of resources: the academic is provided research clearance to a protected area (through the contract Opwall has negotiated with the host agency), travel to the field site, accommodations on site, and a budget to support his or her research project. In return Opwall receives shared ownership of the data collected on site, expanded legitimacy of the value of the voluntourism opportunities their organization provides (as measured by the scholarly publications that emerge), and an academic mentor to advise research voluntourists throughout the process. Academic mentorship is expected throughout the entire volunteer experience, from pre-departure advising, to onsite supervision, to thesis generation, and so forth.

In the early stages of development at the Cayos Cochinos marine site, the research program project scopes were developed by Opwall leadership and then staffed by an academic who responded to a job posting. Over time additional projects were added by Opwall academics as their research agendas evolved on site. When the program was launched in 2005, there were several programs offered in marine ecology, herpetology, and social science. While the early social science projects were conceptualized along economic and governance terms, Opwall senior staff were responsive to expanding their programmatic offerings based on feedback from 2005 and 2006. The following year (2007) Opwall added research programs of a more ethnographic nature, including one that explored Garifuna historical land rights and activism to negotiate the management of the CCMPA. To my knowledge, no students signed up for these newly added social science projects, possibly because they required proficiency in Spanish (not a requirement for the social science projects created by Opwall staff). The social science that continued under Natalie Bown's guidance between 2007 and 2009 focused on her area of expertise, protected area governance and fisheries management.

At first, Garifuna communities had almost zero interaction with Opwall research tourists. Each week Operation Wallacea student research groups changed over, with approximately one hundred student arrivals to replace departing groups. In 2004 and 2005 student groups arrived in La Ceiba and traveled by HCRF-staffed boats directly to the research station on Cayo Menor. Even the social science team lived full-time on Cayo Menor in 2004, traveling by HCRF boat to Chachahuate and East End to conduct daytime interviews with MPA residents. When I joined Opwall in 2005, we too began under the model where the social scientists were based on Cayo Menor and had to arrange boats to and from the Garifuna settlements. Social science boats were typically given lower priority than reef checks and open water training by the Opwall–HCRF boat coordinators. As the research season progressed, we negotiated with Opwall to create a mobile social science unit that would reside and eat in homestays, hire local boat captains for transportation, and locate translators for students who did not speak Spanish.

Several other activities were launched in the summers of 2004 and 2005, the ideas for which emerged from Opwall volunteer staff (i.e., the individuals who remain on Cayo Menor for the entire eight-week program) and research tourists. These activities were envisioned to continue as regular events that would enable direct income flow into the Garifuna communities located within the MPA, bypassing the HCRF. Enmeshed in the conservation-as-business model of Opwall and the protected area management strategy of the day, these new programs all targeted income generation, forsaking the social, cultural, and political implications of a forced transition in livelihood approaches. The three primary income-generating activities included day trips to Chachahuate, Tuesday barbeques, and direct school donations.

Figure 8.1 Opwall student group visiting Chachahuate. Photo by Keri Brondo

In 2005, responding to complaints from the Garifuna community that the HCRF took tourists only to Cayo Menor, thus limiting opportunities for the local population to earn income from arrivals to the CCMPA, we began to coordinate weekly field trips to Chachahuate, such as the one I described in the last chapter. During these visits, community members sold locally made jewelry, as well as food and beverages, and braided hair. Unfortunately, the amount generated during these trips was not systematically recorded. However, the Opwall team did observe and record the first trip of 45 volunteers to Chachahuate in 2005, and after the student research tourists' departure, we interviewed the community members who sold products or services to the community to get a sense of how income was spread among resident families. Thirteen community members earned money during the two-hour trip. Three women braided hair, and ten women and one man sold jewelry. The gendered distribution of earned income was quite drastic: the women earned between $6 and $30 apiece; the one man—Alonso—earned $70 selling his unusual sea product jewelry.

Additionally, every Tuesday for a period of seven weeks during the high season of Operation Wallacea's research program, community members from Chachahuate and East End were employed to cook barbeque-style lunches for the Opwall researchers. The lunch was followed by the performance of punta dancing. Over the course of the season, the community members earned approximately $4,200 (prior to subtracting costs). This money was raised by the community to benefit the local primary school. During these BBQs, Operation Wallacea provided a collection box alongside the buffet to encourage visitors to make additional, direct donations to the school. The sum varied each week, depending on the number of visitors present, their personal money allowances, their generosity, and the longevity of their stay in the Cayos Cochinos (i.e., whether/how much they had donated in previous weeks). According to Opwall staff, approximately $700 was collected and donated directly to the school. Some Opwall volunteers continued to support school donations upon their return home, leading to full educational scholarships to eight Garifuna youth (ages 14 and 18) in 2006.

Unfortunately, in 2006 the Tuesday barbeque program was discontinued, because a research tourist reported their wallet stolen. While there were at least a hundred 16–18-year-olds present on the island who could have been responsible for the stolen or misplaced wallet, the assumption was that someone from Chachahuate took it. From that point on, the Garifuna were forbidden from entering the island when Opwall tourists were present.

During the 2006 season the majority of temporary Opwall volunteer tourists (one-week visitors) never even knew that the Cayos Cochinos were inhabited. Not only were people surprised to meet our small team at the research station when we visited to charge our laptops, work in the air-conditioned and Web-connected research lab, or take a shower, but they were absolutely astonished that there were *people* living out in the beauty of the archipelago. In 2005 I had delivered weekly PowerPoint lectures to student groups, sharing what I knew of the Garifuna population and the social science research being pursued in the Cayos Cochinos and along the north coast of Honduras. By 2006 this program dissolved—primarily because Opwall agreed with our suggestion that the social science team must be mobile, living within the Garifuna communities and not stationed on Cayo Menor. In years to follow, while Opwall moved research tourist transport through Rio Esteban, once the Opwall tourists arrived within the MPA, they remained in a "natural" marine paradise, void of people.

By 2011 Opwall's website description of the Honduran expeditions had changed. They no longer offered opportunities for social science expeditions in the Cayos Cochinos, nor did they even mention the presence of the Garifuna community within the Cayos Cochinos. Staff from the organization shared in a group e-mail the rationale behind the decision to wipe out its social science agenda. The decision was based on the fact that the organization was disappointed with the inability to quantify the benefits that social science projects brought to the local community. In the late 2000s the objective of the advertised social science project was to identify and cost out alternative ecotourism projects for the Garifuna communities. The social science teams were expected to conduct market research to determine the likelihood of success for alternative projects, and to share this information with the MPA-dependent communities. Leadership at Opwall was disappointed by the lack of hard data regarding the potential development of ecotourism businesses. In contrast to Opwall's feelings about the benefits that ecotourism business plans and marketing research could bring, the organization felt the types of questions social science students had been asking over the years brought little to no benefit to the area, and the presence of these researchers served as impositions on the local community. In the end, Opwall decided that scrapping the social science projects would save the organization money, as the cost of logistics support for the social science teams exceeded the income generated for local residents as a result of their research. The question of impact is important—Opwall was correct in questioning whether the student research projects were doing any good for the community. Bown and I noticed research fatigue as, season after season, students would arrive asking quite similar questions, pursuing their own theses, and a systematic assessment was never fully formulated.

Opwall's very construction of what social science could offer—emerging from its market approach—was an *economic* evaluation of ecotourism. The collaborations Opwall imagined between researchers, volunteers, and the local community were all focused on income generation, just as was the relationship between researcher and the Opwall organization (Opwall sought to make a profit from the social science student expeditions). This business model can get in the way of real participatory, user-centered, rights-based conservation and resource management. It was also not representative of the kind of work that social scientists in the CCMPA were generally interested in pursuing.

The decision to eliminate social science was partly due to the way in which Opwall conceptualized social science, and the fact that the organization was not seeing enough direct profit from these studies. But this wasn't the only reason. From its very start in the Cayos Cochinos, Opwall had a difficult time locating a social scientist to lead research in this area. My sense is that when social scientists weighed the costs and benefits of the Opwall relationship in the CCMPA, the barriers outweighed the benefits, as compared to the marine ecology and herpetology work. Some of these challenges were in the area of mentoring and logistics, while others were linked to the historical and political context social scientists face when conducting research in the region.

Unlike the natural science research occurring in the CCMPA, where voluntourists do not leave the creature comforts of the research station on Cayo Menor (except to dive in the MPA's reefs), the social science team is mobile. The lead social scientist becomes responsible for a set of students with whom she or he had no prior experience, some of whom may have had very different expectations about what they were embarking on. In addition to this, the relationship between Opwall and the HCRF is confusing and even suspicious to the local population. Working under the auspices of these organizations makes it difficult to build trust and might even be considered an obstruction to collecting reliable social data. Furthermore, social scientists knowledgeable about Garifuna rights-based struggles in this region may shy away from association—at any level—with external organizations associated with the preservationist conservation policies that have diminished Garifuna rights to local resources. As a result, social scientists attracted to leading the CCMPA expeditions may be more likely to be focused on economics or governance than ethnography. Alternatively, one might be an activist-oriented researcher interested in "studying up" (Nader 1972), and committed to pushing for change within institutions of power.

Several have observed the long-standing gulf between the predominantly natural science–trained conservation planners and the largely social science–trained critics of conservation practices (e.g., Adams and Hutton 2007: 148; Redford 2011). But many are moving to bridge this gap (e.g., Brosius 1999, 2006; Igoe 2011; Mascia et al. 2003; Thornhill 2003). Research tourist organizations have the potential to bring together natural and social science in meaningful and game-changing ways, to work collaboratively with local communities to find creative solutions to threatened ecosystems. These partnerships are critical to move organizations like Opwall closer to a rights-based research tourism model. The other essential pieces in this transformation are leadership from the local Garifuna community and partnership with Honduran ethnic federations.

Opwall's "social and environmental responsibility programme" includes a clause to ensure that all field operations are run by local NGOs or host-country academic institutions. Opwall states that the purpose of this clause is to ensure that funding provided by the project stays in the host communities. As the managing agency for the CCMPA, the HCRF was a natural go-to organization for Opwall's expansion into Honduras. In the first years of the Opwall–HCRF contract, very little of the funding provided to the HCRF through Opwall volunteer fees was distributed to members of host communities. In the early years of the Opwall program in the CCMPA, the HCRF used its staff and boats to transport tourists directly from La Ceiba to Cayo Menor, where the voluntourists remained. This arrangement completely bypassed all six of the CCMPA-reliant Garifuna communities, and any income derived from accommodations, transport, and food for the voluntourists went to the HCRF. While possibly less cost-effective for Opwall and more time-consuming for travelers, by 2006 Opwall had moved all of its services to Garifuna communities, demonstrating their organizational commitment to "maximise the income from field operations to local communities" (Opwall 2012).

In addition to locating existing NGOs as partner institutions, Opwall also fosters the creation of new local NGOs. Grupo de Apoyo al Desarrollo (GAD) is one of those organizations that received early support from Opwall and now manages travel logistics and homestays for Opwall student volunteers passing through coastal Garifuna communities and to the Cayo Menor. This new arrangement means that some income derived from the Opwall–HCRF contract is now making its way into local communities. However, the income distribution is uneven, as indicated in the last chapter.

A critical barrier to achieving rights-based conservation tourism in the CCMPA is that neither the HCRF nor GAD has Garifuna leadership. Both organizations are led by educated professionals from the mainland and the United States. GAD was established by Opwall's local representative (an ex-Peace Corps member) and the HCRF's sustainable development coordinator. Unlike the HCRF, which continues to be perceived negatively by locals, GAD is generally fairly well received in the CCMPA communities.

In addition to coordinating homestay services for Opwall tourists, GAD established a scholarship fund available to local children and teenagers for all levels of education; it includes a monthly stipend. Further, in partnership with other lending institutions (e.g., WWF), GAD helped to establish the hotel that don Buelto described in chapter 7, training programs in tourism and business, and the development of a network of tour operators called La Ruta Garinagu (Garifuna Trail). Its website and tour packages are operated by GAD founder Anthony Ives, but the tours are designed to be community operated and owned. Interested households rotate meal preparation and housing for tourists.

The emergence of GAD and the transparent attitude of its founders toward the Garifuna community have begun to ease some of the tension and distrust of the HCRF that marks the CCMPA zone of influence, but not all community members realize the two are independent organizations. Even among those who do understand that GAD and the HCRF are distinct organizations, negative sentiments still exist; some fishermen are not interested in moving into tour operations (the focus to date of GAD projects) (see also Jimenez-Castro 2008:80–82). While GAD's initiatives may be positively received by the majority of community members and developed along the model of community-based tourism initiatives whereby residents have co-ownership, the lack of Garifuna leadership across the existing NGOs means that the CCMPA is seeing further consolidation and augmentation of the same institutions of power. The programmatic choices of NGO officials, however good-willed, retain the Garifuna community in service roles (accommodation, food service, transportation, and tour guides) to the expanding coastal tourism industry. Lack of Garifuna involvement is a problem and runs counter to a rights-based approach that recognizes and validates self-determination.

Blurred Boundaries: Commodified Conservation NGOs and the (Im)Possibility of Rights-Based Tourism

Can the CCMPA adopt a decommodified, sustainable and ethical approach to tourism, given the current makeup and organizational missions of the NGOs working in the region? In their attempt to understand the role of NGOs in the voluntourism industry, Lyons and Wearing (2008a:7) contrast what they call an "NGO approach" with a "corporate approach." They present NGOs as underlain by a decommodified agenda, and as placing a top priority on input from local communities and indigenous voices, supporting local communities through sustainable tourism development. Reliant on membership dues, and public and private funding granted to support organizational missions, NGOs should theoretically operate in a socially and environmentally sustainable manner. In contrast, corporate approaches are "fundamentally underpinned by capital accumulation in the logic of profit before people" (Lyons and Wearing 2008a:7). As a result, ethical decision making regarding environmental and social impacts can be overshadowed by a focus on profit. Unfortunately, this clean dichotomy does not fit the contemporary reality and blurred relationships that mark the voluntourism landscape.

In the case of the CCMPA, Opwall, a profit-driven volunteer research organization, partners with local NGOs, the HCRF and GAD, to achieve conservation objectives. Lyons and Wearing (2008a:9) argue that "as NGOs begin to develop partnerships with corporate entities, they run the risk of losing sight of their core activity of supporting local communities at all costs and instead become engaged in the gradual processes of the commodification of the alternative—and by extension, volunteer—tourism." Such concern is valid for the CCMPA, especially given that the HCRF's search for financial sustainability informed its initial contract with Opwall, allowing for island visitations beyond carrying capacity and damage to the reef ecosystem, and later, their controversial relationship with the reality show production. Furthermore, despite the increased attention to the Garifuna population within the revised management plan, the HCRF still continues to place first priority on management of resources and compliance with regulations. With its primary objective being the protection of natural resources, supporting local people was arguably never one of its core foci.

Given the relationship between the host CCMPA NGOs, the HCRF and GAD, and Opwall, a for-profit umbrella conservation expedition organization, the mechanisms through which voluntourists arrive in the region have all largely been commodified. Yet once on the ground, there is real opportunity for sustainable practice and meaningful relationships. Thus, as Lyons and Wearing (2008b:152) propose, it may not matter if voluntourism becomes commodified—so long as the experience still provides tangible benefit to local communities. The intervention point here is to establish creative alternative partnerships, within, through, or alongside the existing NGO–voluntourist–Garifuna-community relationships. Some possibilities include direct partnership between Garifuna-staffed organizations and local communities, especially ethnic federations that offer alternative development models to neoliberalism.

Tourism analysts have typically focused much of their attention on improvements to the tourist experience, a "positive" approach that often lacks engagement with the oversights, absences, and inequalities inherent in tourism (Botterill and Klemm 2005). This approach emerges from the hegemony of neoliberalism, whereby the tourism industry is focused on improvements to satisfy tourists' demands in order to improve profit. To decommodify tourism, and voluntourism in particular, we must look beyond the tourists' experience and turn to the host population to inform and shape the tourist experience.

A rights-based volunteer tourism experience would embed a cultural and ethical framework that promotes self-determination (see also Wearing 2001:158) and be developed under a conservation-with-justice model. Conservation with justice—or rights-based conservation—links conservation objectives and respect for people's rights, and especially those rights guaranteed under international and national doctrines (Greiber et al. 2009:vii). Transforming the CCMPA research tourism agenda under this model would meet the International Union for the Conservation of Nature (IUCN) Fourth World Congress on National Parks and Protected Areas recommendation to enhance collaborations between local communities and the tourist industry that move away from a market-oriented approach (Wearing 2001:156).

A central barrier to achieving rights-based conservation research tourism in the CCMPA is the lack of institutionalization of human rights (including indigenous rights) within its protected area management classification. In 2003 the CCMPA was classified as a Category III reserve for the protection of a specific outstanding natural feature and its associated biodiversity and habitats. As such, this categorization did not recognize processes or instruments to mitigate or avoid the negative impacts on human well-being and people's rights as the protected area management developed. Instead, the Category III status meant that the CCMPA as a multiple-use protected area included several levels of protection, with a no-take zone surrounded by several other areas of lower protection. Its protected status also meant that the area moved from open access to a privately owned and managed resource area. While Category III areas have as a secondary objective to "conserve traditional spiritual and cultural values of the site," in practice no measures were put in place to ensure this protection, producing significant unrest among the local population.

Coinciding with the revised CCMPA management plan (2008–13), the CCMPA was recategorized as Category V, which focuses on landscape/seascape conservation and recreation. Category V areas expect human intervention and emphasize long-term interactions of people and nature, with intensive uses of environmental products and service (typically agriculture, forestry, or tourism). The Garifuna's local and national resistance to the first stage of management may well have been responsible for this revised classification. Through the local resistance to the reality show up to the international human rights complaint with the IACHR, Garifuna turned back the promises of good governance, environmental stewardship, and local participation onto the HCRF and WWF to resist the original management plan and advocate for a revision. Thus, while cultural rights might be defined in ways consistent with elite development interests (i.e., Hale's [2005] neoliberal multiculturalism), the discourses inserted on participation can be picked up and used to articulate a counterargument. The revised management plan recognizes artisanal fishing practices and other subsistence-related activity within the CCMPA and puts in place measures for the Garifuna to capitalize from tourism developments (including reality show profits). However, it is questionable whether capitalizing from tourism development constitutes a rights-based approach. To what degree do tourism dollars mitigate the loss of historical managerial control of marine resources? Importantly, as the CCMPA continues to develop its protected area management strategies, the Garifuna move further away from their traditional role as resource managers in the region, and closer to service laborers within a tourism industry largely owned and operated by area NGOs.

The key to ensuring a holistic view of Garifuna "rights" within the CCMPA management is the institutionalization of these rights within international standards for protected area management. This form of advocacy might be a place for Garifuna activists to focus increased attention. For the most part, the IUCN protected area categories do not recognize human interests and people's rights, focusing instead on avoiding the negative impacts on natural resources (Janki 2009:90). A rights-based approach would provide *"processes or instruments* to assess and to mitigate, if not to avoid, negative impacts on well-being and people's rights in the context of developing and managing protected areas" (Janki 2009:90–91). While Garifuna activists might focus on these international, structural changes, in the meantime, on the ground, the CCMPA NGOs and Opwall could consider the adoption of a participatory action research (PAR) approach to embed rights-based research management within the voluntourism experience.

Influenced by Marxist and Gramscian ideas, as well as other theories of exploitation and dependence, PAR approaches aim to take power back through true participatory, direct, and self-managed democratic systems (Peet 1999:139). Power is defined as "the capacity of exploited peoples to articulate and systematize their own and others' knowledge so that they could become protagonists in defense of their class and in the advancement of their society" (Peet 1999:140). Current research practitioners of PAR advocate for local capacity building through partnerships between a community (or communities) and researchers whereby community members are actively involved in all phases of the research project, from defining the problem and designing the methodology, to collecting and analyzing the data, to sharing the findings (Center for Cultural Understanding and Change 2006; Institute for Community Research 2009; Schensul 2005). Bringing a PAR framework to rethink Opwall's research structure would move the organization closer to exploring questions that the local population deems of significance, enabling the identification of perceived gaps and moving closer to a rights-based model.[1]

NINE

Neoliberalism's Limit Points in Post-Coup Honduras

In 2009 the Honduran military orchestrated a coup d'état to depose President Manuel Zelaya. An enormous resistance movement emerged, at the core of which were the nation's indigenous and Afro-descendant peoples, women, labor parties, and other popular groups. Widespread international condemnation of the coup accompanied the strong and growing grassroots resistance. For instance, the United Nations General Assembly condemned the coup and advised states not to recognize any government other than President Zelaya's; the Organization of American States suspended its OAS membership; Latin American governments withdrew their ambassadors from the country; the European Union restricted political contacts with the de facto government; and the United States froze the visas of military and political actors as an attempt to pressure the de facto government to restore democratic rule to Honduras (Human Rights Watch 2010:9–10). Human rights abuses committed during the coup were of a serious magnitude and did not dissipate after the change of state. Security forces were responsible for thousands of illegal detentions, hundreds of injuries to peaceful protesters, dozens of murdered and disappeared individuals, and repeated uses of excessive force and intimidation against protesters, journalists, human rights defenders, and political activists (Human Rights Watch 2010).

The de facto government of 2009, headed by Roberto Micheletti of Honduras's Liberal Party, held elections in November 2009 in the face of this widespread condemnation and resistance. Editorials in the Honduran newspaper *El Tiempo* suggested that the electoral process was controlled by the coup regime with "2,000 troops, 14,000 police and 5,000 reservists in direct control of the polling," eliminating the possibility of free and fair elections (Center for Economic Policy and Research 2009). National Party candidate Porfirio Lobo won the election and came into power in January 2010 with a promise to restore democratic order to the nation. To the contrary, violent suppression of the resistance movement has continued to escalate since the change of state. Within just one month of Lobo coming to office, 254 human rights violations had been committed, or approximately nine cases per day (Honduras Human Rights 2010). By 2012 "at least 34 members of the opposition have disappeared or been killed . . . more than 300 people have been killed by state security forces . . . and at least 13 journalists have been killed" (Frank 2012).

From the moment of the coup, the Garifuna community was a target of repression. Within weeks, the first and only Garifuna-managed hospital in the country was taken over, and its founder—a Garifuna doctor (Dr. Luther Castillo)—was dismissed and forced into exile. The hospital had opened with support of Zelaya's administration in December 2007 and in accordance with an ILO covenant that supports locally managed health services of indigenous and tribal peoples.

Around the same time, Dario Euraque was dismissed from the director's role at the Honduran Institute of Anthropology and History. Euraque's work—which has influenced many anthropologists working in Honduras—has been instrumental in delineating the historical power imbalances and roots of the present conflict; and more recently (2004) he has written on Honduras's shift toward a pluralistic, multicultural society. As director of the institute under the Zelaya administration, Euraque was involved in challenging the "mayanization" inherent in the institute's approach to promoting Honduras's pre-Columbian past as largely Maya, making invisible the histories of other indigenous peoples (Honduras Culture and Politics 2010a). Euraque was seeking to expand the institute's view of history beyond this Maya-centric view when he was fired (Euraque 2010).

Replacing such leading scholars in Honduras's key cultural institutions were "political hacks" like Mirna Castro—the Micheletti-appointed minister of culture, arts, and sport (Schepers 2009). Castro went on record publicly denouncing the distribution of books throughout the country to what she called "vulnerable" populations, a patronizing word to describe the Garifuna and other indigenous peoples given the history of racism and oppression in the country (Umaña 2009). Such comments were not out of the ordinary for a member of the regime that dismissed the first Garifuna vice minister of culture, Salvador Suazo, who served in the Zelaya administration and had been in the process of producing a dictionary of the Garifuna language. This same regime appointed Enrique Ortez as chancellor of Honduras; Ortez defined President Barack Obama as "*Ese negrito que no sabe nada de nada*" (that little black man who doesn't know anything). Responding to the use of the term *negrito*, a universally racist and derogatory term—a Garifuna activist noted, "If those in power dare call the president of the first world a 'negrito,' what treatment would be expected for the poor Afro-Honduran on the ground?" What could be expected? In November 2010 the Garifuna community of Triunfo de la Cruz sent word to indigenous rights activists that relatives of a member of the National Congress (Diputado Antonio Fuentes) planned to seize its communal lands (Almendares 2009). Moreover, a few days before the de facto government left office, a radio station run by the vice president of OFRANEH was burned down (Anderson 2012:59). The coup—and subsequent election—sent a clear message to the Garifuna community. The Garifuna had supported the constitutional assembly proposed by Zelaya, and the cause for his removal. A constitutional assembly had the potential to institutionalize long-sought rights of this historically marginalized community, including proportional representation and legal title to communal and ancestral land.[1]

What is the relationship between Garifuna indigeneity, development agendas, gendered rights, and the coup d'état? Faced with the internationalization of Garifuna indigeneity and national legislation that opened spaces for mobilizations based on Garifuna cultural rights, the coup was a pushback by historical power holders against rising multicultural rights—a constitutional assembly represented a threat to the country's oligarchy and the potential redistribution of the country's scant resources in a more equitable manner. Yet, in the post-coup environment, multiculturalism as an official discourse of equality has become incorporated into a neoliberal development agenda to consolidate power along gendered lines and limit the possibilities for social change.

Limit Points, Neoliberal Multiculturalism, and Gendered Development

Hale (2005:13) coined the term "neoliberal multiculturalism" to refer to "an emergent regime of governance that shapes, delimits, and produces cultural difference rather than suppressing it." Hale (2005:13) argues that elites have embraced ethnic rights at the encouragement of multilateral institutions, defining them carefully within politics and programs such that they do not challenge the neoliberal paradigm of progress. In their study of broccoli's global commodity chain, Fischer and Benson (2006) introduce the concept of "limit points" to explain how social actors respond when affected by neoliberal structures. Limit points "limit the possibilities for social change by satiating desires and channeling energies toward what is practical and obtainable" (Fischer and Benson 2006:14). Ironically, one way in which rights are limited is through the co-optation of rights-based discourses on participation, good governance, and local ownership within national development models. Thus, what is "practical and obtainable" is not systemic change, but rather participation *within* a neoliberal, modernization approach to development. And this happens to be the development model accepted by ODECO, a male-headed organization that has made inroads into national and international development agendas.

A glaring example of neoliberal multiculturalism is the creation of the secretary for the development of indigenous and Afro-Honduran peoples and the promotion of politics of racial equality (secretaría para el desarrollo de los pueblos indígenas y afrohondureños y la promoción de políticas de igualdad racial). This position was created under the Lobo administration, and approved by National Congress on October 12, 2010. The Secretary position is intended to centralize government efforts to ensure antiracist development initiatives (Anderson 2012:60). It was filled by a man. Problematically, the new Secretary position is perceived by most indigenous and ethnic organizations to be an initiative of ODECO, and many organizations have come out strongly against its establishment.

The secretary's position was a campaign promise to ODECO, signed by the Lobo administration. Anderson (2012:61) reports that the research to learn about similar secretaries in other Latin American countries was conducted by ODECO president Celeo Álvarez; Luis Green, former treasurer of ODECO and the man tasked with creating the new secretary (who was later named its first minister); and Tulio Mariano Gonzalez, another Garifuna activist who runs a development NGO. The final meeting to consolidate the proposal for the secretary position was held in ODECO's offices in La Ceiba. Government press releases cited participation from other indigenous organizations, but Anderson's 2010 research with ethnic activists found evidence to the contrary—not only did activist organizations not participate in the development of this office, they stridently denounced it (Anderson 2012; Confederación de Pueblos Autóctonos de Honduras 2010). Early versions of the proposal to create the position defined the secretary as existing to promote the "inclusion and development of indigenous and Afro-Honduran peoples . . . obtaining resources for development programs and projects, and promoting affirmative action politics" (Anderson 2012:60–61). Such promises are remarkably similar to ODECO's own mission statements, which promote inclusion into a modernization as development model.

As Anderson argues, through the creation of the secretary position, the Honduran state institutionalized ODECO's discourse of racial equality. Doing so further spreads and perpetuates structural inequalities caused by neoliberalism, because ODECO's development model does not threaten the status quo. Thus, the secretary position serves as a "limit point" to equality even as it *invites* racial equality through discourses of multiculturalism. Economic models based on private investment and open markets can recognize differentiated cultural identities and subjects, selectively recognizing yet narrowly defining rights so long as they remain defined within market agendas (Anderson 2012:57–58). This centralization of representation of ethnic politics threatens and marginalizes ethnic organizations that counter the state, further limiting dialogue and counternarratives from reaching critical audiences (Anderson 2012).

Alongside ODECO's strong presence in this high-level position in the Lobo administration are other former ODECO members, such as Bernard Martínez, appointed as the minister of culture. Martínez was a presidential candidate for Partido de Innovación y Unidad Social Democratica, a conservative political party that supported the coup and ran on a platform calling for respect for private property, agricultural development, and national unity (Anderson 2012:60; Honduras Culture and Politics 2010b). The gendered nature of this consolidation of power is quite overt. Not only are all these individuals affiliated with ODECO, an organization that assumes modernization as development either has to or inevitably will take place, but all are male. Absent are activist Garifuna women and other ethnic activists from more oppositional organizations, federations, and popular movements. OFRANEH, for instance, a matriarchal organization, offers a counternarrative of development, falling into the "alternatives to development" perspective, which takes a critical stance against the discourse of modern development models and puts faith in grassroots social mobilization efforts to overcome the structures and discourses of modern development (Escobar 1991:675). OFRANEH's approach can also be characterized as informed by feminist critiques of development in highlighting the differential experiences that Garifuna women face as a result of national development policy.

The remainder of this chapter explores how the post-coup Honduran state has institutionalized a discourse of equality that actually serves as a "limit point" (Fischer and Benson 2006), limiting the possibilities for who 'wins' from the expansion of neoliberalism. As is often the case, those most affected are indigenous and Afro-descendant women. Gendered environmental activism responds to the limitations set by contemporary development models, yet it also competes with youth livelihood interests, interests shaped by transnational forces and a crisis in cultural identity.

REDs, Model Cities, and Land Grabs in Trujillo

On January 19, 2011, the Honduran National Congress passed an amendment to the constitution that gave the government the power to create special development regions, Regiónes Especiales de Desarollo (REDs). Pitched as a means to combat rising rates of migration where roughly seventy-five thousand Hondurans leave to look for work in the United States each year, these free-market "model cities" or "charter cities" are the brainchild of US economist Paul Romer. He defines a charter city as a "special economic zone . . . large enough to accommodate a city with millions of workers and residents." The Charter City website (http://chartercities.org), states that "the concept is very flexible, but all charter cities should share these four elements:

1. A vacant piece of land, large enough for an entire city.
2. A charter that specifies in advance the broad rules that will apply there.
3. A commitment to choice, backed by voluntary entry and free exit for all residents.
4. A commitment to the equal application of all rules to all residents."

These cities would be financed by foreign governments or investors and would have their own justice system, constitution, and private security forces, and not be subject to Honduran law.

Under Romer's model, charter cities are developed on "an uninhabited piece of city-sized land, provided voluntarily by a host government" (Charter Cities 2011). The "development authority that governs the new city could retain ownership of all land and use the gains in the value of the land to finance public expenditures . . . [and] lease land to private developers" (Charter Cities 2011). From the above, we see that the original concept for the REDs in which model cities could be built was in areas that were not already populated. Establishing in an unpopulated region, the RED would have the ability to freely experiment with new systems of governance, business, and civil society (Cáceres 2011). Yet on July 29, 2011, the National Congress passed new model city legislation, which subjected the RED territories to constitutional clauses regarding national sovereignty, territory, national defense, identity papers, and foreign relations (Honduras Culture and Politics 2011). Part of this new legislation was the decision that Congress could create a RED from either an unpopulated region *or urban regions* that request conversion through a binding local referendum (Honduras Culture and Politics 2011). The new legislation paved the way for powerful interest groups (i.e., those who stand to benefit from foreign investment) to influence an area's population to request a referendum.

The Honduran government identified the Trujillo area (from Puerto Castillo-Trujillo-Santa Fe to Betulia) for its first model city experiment. In December 2011, the Honduran public learned by way of an article published in the *Economist* that their government officials had signed preliminary memorandums of understanding (MOUs) with two US-based firms, Future Cities Development Corporation and Free Cities Institute, to develop their first model city experiments in the Trujillo area (*Economist* 2012). The former was cofounded by the libertarian economist Milton Friedman's grandson, Patri Friedman, who is a strong critic of democracy, arguing that it is inefficient and incompatible with libertarian models (*Economist* 2012). Friedman's belief is not in the freedom of voice that is central to democracy, but rather that people should be free to enter and exit the system (*Economist* 2012).

Prior to founding the Future Cities Development Corporation, Patri Friedman was the executive director of the Seasteading Institute, a non-profit group conducting research on and advocating for the creation of "seasteads"—or floating cities—where people could test libertarian ways of living. As early as 2002, this concept was being pitched on the coast—recall my conversation with Victor in chapter 4 about youth visions for the future and his critique of ODECO for not embracing the "floating city" concept.

The second US organization behind Trujillo's "model city" initiative is Free Cities Institute (FCI). FCI was founded by Michael Strong and Kevin Lyons. Strong is an educational entrepreneur who founded several charter schools and is the CEO of FLOW Inc., a social entrepreneurship nonprofit that he cofounded with John Mackey, the CEO of Whole Foods (Freedom Lights Our World, FLOW 2012). Less strident critics of democracy, Strong and Lyons emphasize the use of libertarian economic ideals to promote "peace, health, and happiness" (Free Cities 2012). The institute's vision has as its goal "the eradication of mass poverty and a dramatic reduction in global violence" (Free Cities 2012). These investment groups entered 2012 with plans to drastically remodel the Garifuna coastline using principles of innovation implemented in the Silicon Valley of California.

The projects were fiercely opposed by the Garifuna and several other civic groups in the country. On January 25, 2012, the attorney general of Honduras issued an opinion stating that the REDs (the "model cities") legislation is unconstitutional in that it violates national sovereignty and would thus be appropriate to repeal (*El Heraldo* 2012a). Because the opinion was nonbinding and the Supreme Court could discard it, when this book chapter was initially completed in the spring of 2012, all signs were that the model city projects would progress, with a May 8, 2012, *New York Times* article headlined "Who Wants to Buy Honduras?" (Davidson 2012).

On September 4, 2012, the first MOU was signed between the government's Commission for the Promotion of Public–Private Alliances (*Consejo de Alianzas Público–Privadas de Honduras*, or CoAlianza) and Grupo MGK, a newly announced consortium of business investors cofounded by Michael Strong and Kevin Lyons (*La Tribuna* 2012). According to their website, "most of their investors are based in Silicon Valley and know that innovation and entrepreneurship is the path to alleviating poverty and creating of broad-based prosperity" (Grupo MGK 2012a). Grupo MGK promised an investment of $15 million in basic infrastructure, the creation of 5,000 jobs within six months, and 200,000 more in the future, for the model city near Puerto Castilla, outside of Trujillo (*Honduras Weekly* 2012a). There was speculation over where the investment would come from, as the only investor profiled on the Grupo MGK website was *Calidad Inmobiliaria*, a Central American real estate group (Grupo MGK 2012a).

Upon announcement of the MOU signing, Paul Romer (the initial brains behind the charter city model) and the four other members of the "Transparency Commission" resigned and withdrew support for the project. One of the core principles of the charter city model is a foundational commitment to transparency and full disclosure. The MOU between CoAlianza and Grupo MGK was signed without knowledge and consultation of the Transparency Commission (Cowen 2012; Malkin 2012). Further, when Romer asked to review the agreement, he was denied (*El Heraldo* 2012b). The Honduran administration claimed that although President Lobo signed a decree naming the five members to the Transparency Commission in December 2011, the decree was never published in the *Gazette* and therefore did not legally exist. As a result, the administration could propose a RED directly to Congress for approval (Cowen 2012). The news of the MOU and Romer's reaction led to even more challenges to the Honduran Supreme Court regarding the RED legislation (Malkin

2012). By early October 2012, seventy-six separate legal challenges to the constitutional amendment had been filed (Stone 2012). OFRANEH was a leader in the opposition.

As this book hit the final copyediting stage, the model city land grab was all over national and international news, with heightened attention when one of the leading opposition lawyers, Antonio Trejo Cabrera, was gunned down in Tegucigalpa on September 22, 2012. The circumstances of his murder—shot while exiting a church after attending a wedding—suggested that the murder was targeted (Human Rights Watch 2012). Trejo had issued a constitutional complaint against the RED legislation on September 5, 2012. Trejo was also the lead lawyer for a peasant group in the Bajo Aguán Valley, where more than eighty people have died in connection with land disputes (Human Rights Watch 2012).

In early October 2012, a five-judge panel of the Supreme Court ruled (4–1) that the model city legislation was unconstitutional. Yet because it was not a unanimous decision, the case was sent to the full fifteen-member Supreme Court. Despite the Supreme Court ruling and public outcry, the websites for model city investment groups were optimistic that the projects would move forward. Days after the MOU between CoAlianza and Grupo MGK was signed, the Free Cities website was dismantled, replaced with an "under construction" tag. Michael Strong then quickly registered the Grupo MGK website on September 8, 2012; one of its first posts (on September 10, 2012) was that "Grupo MGK has recently been created to focus on the Honduran Special Development Region initiative. We have no relation to any other entities that may have similar sounding names. Please check back often for updates on Honduras' bright new future" (Grupo MGK 2012b). Updates to the website between September 8 and early October 2012 all centered on attempting to offset concerns that the MGK operated illegally or unethically in negotiating with CoAlianza, to address the perceived lack of transparency in this public–private partnership, and to maintain their commitment to the protection for human rights (Grupo MGK 2012b). Yet their frame for understanding human rights is quite narrow, with a promise that a "core value of Grupo MGK is respecting the rights of all people all of the time. Our belief is that the SDRs can immediately establish a *uniquely high standard of human rights in Latin America and become a beacon of entrepreneurship and economic freedom*" (Grupo MGK 2012b, emphasis added).

The Future Cities Development Corporation's (2012) website had not been updated since a 2011 post stating that their "first project is underway . . . within an uninhabited special development region in Honduras," and it was therefore unknown at the time this book was completed as to whether or not the group would end up signing a formal MOU with Honduras. Regardless, the core values they express on their webpage provide a further glimpse into how model city proponents conflate "human rights" with "economic freedom." The Future Cities career opportunities page states what they are looking for in the "disciplined idealists" whom they wish to employ, including individuals who "recognize the value of *self-determination* and personal growth" (emphasis added). Certainly, the founders have a different view of self-determination in mind than that which is affirmed through international indigenous rights conventions.

Even before the MOUs for model city development were signed for Puerto Castilla, Trujillo, megatourism projects were already well under way by 2011 and had displaced Garifuna from their lands. The central development projects are backed by Canadian investor Randy Jorgensen (aka the "King of Porn"), owner of Canada's biggest pornography retail chain, Adults Only Video (AOV). Jorgensen is the CEO of Life Vision Properties Company and Jaguar Construction; Life Vision is constructing four new gated-community housing developments that are being marketed to Canadian and US citizens, and Jaguar Construction is the building company (Spring 2011). Jorgensen is also a board member of the Grand Trujillo Authority Consortium, which is behind the development of the "Banana Coast" Cruise Ship Terminal being constructed in the Garifuna neighborhood of Río Negro. The Grand Trujillo Authority is a consortium between Jorgensen's Life Vision, the Miami tourism promotion company Global Destinations Developments, and the Municipality of Trujillo. Approval for the construction of the cruise port came on December 10, 2009, five days before Porfirio Lobo was elected president and while the country was still in political turmoil (Gill 2011). Honduran papers reported in February 2011 that the last Garifuna landowners who had refused to sell finally gave in, as they saw the surrounding land succumb to bulldozers, enabling the cruise port project to move forward (Spring 2011).

One of the housing developments is on the western side of Guadalupe, a small Garifuna community about an hour down the dirt road from Trujillo. Life Vision purchased land from within Guadalupe's communal land title for its Alta Vista housing project. According to human rights activists, 141 acres within the Guadalupe land title had been acquired by Life Vision Properties for their 292-acre Alta Vista project; the total price of purchase was 150,000 lempiras, or $7,500 (Spring 2011). Residents of Guadalupe reported that "the Canadians" or *testaferros* (i.e., Honduran nationals that act on behalf of the foreign investor and buy the land in their name) visited households on a regular basis, asking if they would sell their land (Spring 2011). As with land sales in Sambo Creek, the price tag Life Vision placed on ancestral territory was abusively low. Life Vision's blog reports that they have already sold over 55 percent of the lots in the development, and the plots are marketed as a "steal" in comparison to Bay Islands real estate. An ad from their website reads:

> Roatan is more developed and mature with a consistent level of economic activity, however the prices are also much higher there than Trujillo. *A serviced one acre lot with panoramic views of the Caribbean Sea in Alta Vista Mountain is under $50k.* Randy Jorgensen, the Developer, has suppressed values of property by more than 50% to comparable property in other parts of Honduras. This is so buyers can take advantage and be part of the emerging market in Trujillo.
>
> *But it can be for only so long! With Banana Coast Cruise Terminal coming into operation in the 2012–2013 cruise season, it is a matter of time before Trujillo property owners see the same economic activity as Roatan.*
>
> Compare buying a finished house in Roatan for a price of $300–450k, it is much cheaper to build your dream home in Trujillo. *A 3 bedroom home on the mountainside with a swimming pool can be built for under $200,000.* (Life Vision 2011).

While the Canadians who take advantage of early-bird construction rates will likely reap the benefits described by Life Vision, the Garifuna who were displaced through pressure to sell at extraordinarily low prices obviously will not. Who are the most affected by the development of these model cities? Women, who are less likely than men to migrate and are therefore present in larger numbers in Garifuna villages.

"There Is Nothing to Celebrate": Garifuna Activists Respond

As the model city and associated development projects continued to push forward, activists claimed they did so with little regard for their implications on Garifuna economy, subsistence, and cultural traditions. Spring (2011) quotes an activist from OFRANEH describing the lack of consultation with local communities regarding the ongoing developments.

> We have our own traditions, customs, but they [the Canadians] aren't respecting our traditions as an ethnic group. We, as an organization, are

in a process to rescue our culture and here [in Rio Negro], there is a process of cultural destruction going on. For example, the Canadians come here and buy up a huge amount of land that is part of our communities. Sociologically, development does not come from outside, it comes from within the community, is constructed locally and from the bottom up.

This activist points toward a stark contradiction in development approaches. As the country marches forward with its neoliberal development model, Garifuna continue to organize with other indigenous, peasant, and labor activists to offer "alternatives to development" (Escobar 1991).

On April 1, 2011, the 214th anniversary of the arrival of the Garifuna people in Honduras, more than three thousand Garifuna activists marched on the capital, declaring "THERE IS NOTHING TO CELEBRATE!" The statement released by a coalition of Garifuna organizations and communities in conjunction with the march cited the following, and many other, human and cultural rights abuses, and the problematic co-optation of participatory rights via official discourses of multiculturalism under neoliberalism. Excerpts from the statement read:

There is nothing to celebrate.
Because due to the stubbornness *of the current regime in maintaining a model as exclusive as the neoliberal one,* more than 200,000 brothers and sisters have had to emigrate from our communities risking their lives to go in search of an uncertain destiny, leaving behind parents, children, grandchildren and other loved ones, when *our youth find themselves forced to emigrate* due to the absence of opportunities and the *blackmail that says if we don't give up our territory it is because we are opposed to "development."*
There is nothing to celebrate.
Because even though the United Nations has declared the language, the music and the dance of the Garífuna people as an Oral Master Work and Intangible Asset of Humanity on May 18, 2011 and declared 2011 as the International Year of the Afrodescendants the *State has not made any effort to support the strengthening of our culture* which it *instead commercializes and labels as national folklore at the same time that it promotes cultural homogenization* through the media dictatorship taking place in Honduras. . . .
There is nothing to celebrate.
When the *conversion of the Garífuna community of Rio Negro into "Banana Coast" is the prelude to the expulsion of the Garífuna* from

Bahía de Trujillo, a *process which they seek to replicate in the whole coast in the name of uncertain tourism*, a pillar of an economy of dependence, as the agro-export model liquidates food security.

There is nothing to celebrate.

Because we unite the voices of the Organizations that today *condemn the celebration of a World Summit of Afro-descendants that legitimizes a regime that represses the black communities* as it showed the morning of this past Monday March 28th in the community of Triunfo de Cruz, Tela, Atlántida . . . [Black Workers for Justice 2011, emphasis added]

As 2011 continued to unfold, the alliance of black organizations, or Alliance 2-14, as it became known after the 214th anniversary March of the Drums, became more strident in its critiques of state-run multicultural initiatives that are becoming increasingly institutionalized and pervasive via ODECO (OFRANEH 2011b). First, the alliance uncovered a "security plan" to accompany the ODECO-sponsored World Summit, "with the objective of neutralizing any boycott of the state event" and discouraging participation in the counterevent, the Forum on the Usurpation of Territories in Africa and Latin America (OFRANEH 2011b). The security plan called for militarization of the city of La Ceiba by the Security Ministry and the Armed Forces of Honduras during the first World Summit for People of African Descent, which met in La Ceiba August 18–19, 2011.

The summit, which was organized by ODECO and the International Civil Society Committee, brought in approximately eight hundred representatives from organizations in 44 countries in America, Africa, Europe, and Asia. It was held to commemorate the United Nations and Organization of American States naming 2011 as the International Year for People of African Descent. The conference called for the creation of a permanent international forum—an International Coordination Committee—for the affairs of people of African descent throughout the world. This coordination effort would differ from the United Nation's Permanent Forum on Indigenous Issues, which operates within the UN's Economic and Social Council, by expanding its reach beyond the UN structure and into regional organizations like the Organization of American States, the Central American Integration System, and the Union of South American Nations, and the European Union (Social Watch 2011). The subtitle of the World Summit is informative—Integral and Sustainable Development with Identity—another sign of ODECO's model of development becoming the internationally institutionalized discourse on development and racial equality. Ironically, the photo on the UN's website (http://www.un.org/en/events/iypad2011/)

announcing the International Year for People of African Descent depicts a Garifuna man and baby from "a Garifuna community near Tela, Honduras," likely Triunfo de la Cruz, site of the proposed megatourist complex and the place OFRANEH leader Miriam Miranda was shot with a tear gas canister, arrested, and charged with sedition for her participation in the community land protest against the Los Micos development on March 18, 2011. This incident was referenced in the above excerpt from the 2-14 Alliance. In response to the "security plan" developed to accompany the World Summit, Alliance 2-14 wrote:

> It seems that Mr. *Celeo Álvarez has decided to shield himself behind the clubs and tear gas bombs that are used against his own people.* It is interesting to observe the reaction of Mr. Álvarez Casildo, director of the non-governmental organization *ODECO*, in relation to the Summit which from the very beginning *has excluded the participation of the Garifuna communities, limiting it only to professionals and foreign delegations.* . . .
>   . . . The *extreme violence of Honduras today stands in contrast to the official discourse of the administration* of Mr. Pepe Lobo who spared no words in his meeting with the Prime Minister of Canada, Steven Harper, in demonstrating his commitment to "respect the dignity of people, the common good, solidarity and participatory democracy."
>   However, *the current government* of Christian humanism continues to act in a secretive manner, restricting information and promoting the RED at an accelerated pace, a law that *in no way safeguards the common good, the integrity of people and much less participatory democracy.* We alert the authorities of national and international human rights organizations and call for an end to the threats against the Garifuna communities that will mobilize for the Forum on the Usurpation of Territories in Africa and Latin America, August 17–20th, 2011 and hold ODECO and the government of Pepe Lobo responsible for any attack or repression against the Garifuna people who mobilize toward the city of La Ceiba, exercising their rights to freedom of movement and expression, especially in the framework of the supposed International Year of Afro descendants declared by the United Nations.
>   Alliance of Black Organizations, 214—OFRANEH [OFRANEH 2011b, emphasis added]

As promised, Alliance 2-14 and several other organizations and communities representing people of African descent, indigenous peoples, peasant communities, and feminist organizations organized a countersummit, the

Forum on the Usurpation of Territories in Latin America and Africa (Foro sobre Acaparamiento de Territorio en África y América Latina), which they held at the same time as the World Summit. The main purpose of the Forum was to develop strategies to counter the "land grabbing" in Afro-descendant communities for the purposes of mega–development projects such as dams, mining, African palm plantations, tourism centers, housing developments, and model cities. Leading the forum, OFRANEH activists drew the analogy between William Walker, who attempted to create slave-holding colonies along the Central American coastline in the 1800s, and Randy Jorgensen, who "through the model city is repeat[ing] the tragedy of the twentieth century, when the banana companies seized the north coast." They wrote that, "seizing Garifuna territory, the planners of the neo-colonial empire wish to turn this country into a massive plantation of palm oil and sugarcane, a tax haven consecrated like Grand Cayman, located on a huge reservoir of hydrocarbons" (OFRANEH 2011a, author's translations).

Communiqués summarizing the forum linked land dispossession, climate change, exploitation of natural resources, and the privatization of public services to the growth of a "neoliberal model of capitalist exploitation and racist patriarchy" (OFRANEH 2011a). The activists denounced the law of Special Development Regions (RED), which enables the development of "model cities," as a neocolonial law that adversely affects all of Honduras and, in particular, the territories of the 20 Garifuna communities located between the Bay of Trujillo and Rio Sico. The gendered effects of neoliberalism became explicit within OFRANEH's communiqués from the forum. Activists declared that "Garifuna women are the bastion of village life and culture and therefore require respect for the autonomy of the territory" (OFRANEH 2011a). The statement continued that "[Garifuna women] are not ready to sell the land," thus calling for recognition of the gendered violations of neoliberal land legislation and respect for women's rights (OFRANEH 2011a).

Expressing their solidarity with the peoples of Africa who also suffer from the consequences of failed states, neocolonialism, and export-oriented development models, participants strongly opposed the agreements that came out of the ODECO-sponsored World Summit of Afro-Descendants (OFRANEH 2011a). They condemned the trend toward privatized health care, state support for commodity-driven food production, and promotion of biofuels with a lack of regard to national food security (OFRANEH 2011a), and they denounced the escalating violence that plagues Honduras due to a failed state that has been implemented since the coup. Participants also linked the rise in violent crimes to changes in youth attitudes as younger generations face a crisis in cultural identity, due to the loss of bilingual and cultural education in natal communities, and high drug use and teen pregnancy. As youth lack opportunities in their home communities, they continue to migrate at extraordinarily high rates.

Coming out of the forum, activists demanded that the right of consultation process identified in both ILO 169 and the UN Declaration on the Rights of Indigenous Peoples be respected, and thus development agendas proposed for indigenous territories be negotiated and developed with respect to indigenous peoples' right to healthy food, to water, to forests for foraging of native plants, access to natural assets, and ability to continue traditional small-scale agricultural customs (OFRANEH 2011a). Complete consultation never occurred, with the preliminary MOUs signed between model city developers and the Honduran government without full knowledge of Garifuna residing in the Trujillo area and both ethnic federations. Rather, OFRANEH activists argued that the Honduran right to free prior and informed consent had been distorted, citing the 2004 Ley de Propiedad chapter on the regulation of real estate for indigenous and Afro-Honduran people that has facilitated the sale of Garifuna ancestral coastal territory (OFRANEH 2012a). As this chapter was nearing completion, local activism in the area continued. On May 19, 2012, members of the Garifuna community Cristales, Trujillo, attempted to recover community land that had been usurped by the Crespo family for real estate speculation (OFRANEH 2012a). Julio Lino sustained injuries at the hand of Luis Crespo, and Crespo was released by authorities without their acknowledgment of any crime against the Garifuna community (OFRANEH 2012b).

Limiting Livelihoods

I want to end this chapter by returning to the ways in which neoliberal development structures operate as "limit points," limiting the possibilities for Garifuna who remain in coastal communities to reproduce cultural traditions within their ancestral territories, or even to merely earn a decent livelihood. Fischer and Benson (2006) call attention to "at least" statements as the place to look to locate this limiting nature of neoliberalism. For instance, when Barcelo (now Palma Real resort) was about to open in Sambo Creek in the early 2000s, Sambeños said to me, "At least we may now have a job." In 2012, Garifuna in the Trujillo area echo these calls— "At least we may have employment once the cruise ship arrives." These "at least" statements "provide a seemingly commonsensical resting place between what "is" and what "ought to be" (Fischer and Benson 2006:14). Yet they do little to mend the decades of inequality and abuse created by a heritage of conquest, colonization, slavery, land dispossession, and now neoliberal policy and the growing social problems that have been born in its wake.

Not only are we—as individuals—responsible for producing today's ecological disasters, but we can, the narrative goes, "save the world one act at a time." The individualistic, bootstrapping mentality of the neoliberal global order also means that communities that once shared communal resources to some degree also begin to negotiate their worlds as individuals. As don Buelto notes in his 2011 FIAN letter, "people are now in it for themselves." In this "race to the bottom" we should pay special attention to the winners and losers in Garifuna communities, and how these outcomes are gendered.

For instance, with specific regard to the Cayos Cochinos case, don Buelto was careful to state on two occasions in his letter that he does not speak for all of the community, and especially not for his daughters, who take no issue with the emerging tourism economy and indeed may benefit from it. Understanding the impact the transition from fishing to tourism has on gender relations will be an important focus for future work. Many of the tourism microenterprises in CCMPA-reliant communities have been dominated by women. Women run hotel and homestay operations, as well as small restaurants, and provide other services to tourists such as washing clothing or braiding hair.

The sale of traditional foodstuffs, hair braiding, jewelry sales, and women's dance performances are highly valued by tourists. Such transitions are certain to affect gender relations at the household level and beyond. In cases where similar transitions occurred, anthropologists have documented increases in women's overall status and power within and beyond the household level (e.g., Feng 2008; Ghodsee 2005). Women's economic liberation can also enable women to escape oppressive household relationships. Conversely, tourism can reinforce existing gender and racial hierarchies, relegating women and people of color to positions of servitude, limiting occupations of power and prestige to men of the dominant ethnic groups in emerging tourist economies (Bolles 1992; Stronza 2001). There is also potential for increased domestic violence when men feel their masculinity is threatened by losing their foothold as heads of households. Men are also taking on new roles in the tourism industry, especially as boat captains for organized tours. Men participate in cultural performances as musicians and work as tour guides, offering fishing trips and guided tours around the island networks; they also make artisan products.

Post-coup, OFRANEH stated that its efforts would focus on "two key sectors: women and youth." In an interview with delegates from La Voz de los de Abajo, a community-based organization from Chicago that works in solidarity with Hondurans and their migrant community in the United States, Miriam Miranda is quoted as saying, "Women pass our culture and identity to the youth. If women are not educated and prepared, they can't do that. Women are also the ones resisting in the community, and the role of youth is basic" (La Voz de los de Abajo 2011). The organization's emphasis on women and youth is important, because these two sectors of Garifuna society have been affected most drastically by decades of land privatization and the more recent mass-scale global neoliberal projects such as the model cities.

In chapter 3 I discussed the declining interest in traditional practices of fishing and agriculture among Garifuna youth. Bown (2010:212–214) also found that younger generations are disinterested in fishing and that older generations hope that their children will not have to rely on it for their livelihood. Bown observed that the decline in interest in fishing that has emerged alongside the growing reliance on migration and remittances will threaten environmental management, as interest in resource preservation and knowledge of the local ecology is on the decline. Future environmental leaders are not being fostered at the local level, and there had been no incentive to remain in the CCMPA or on the coast to steward the environment.

The public communications issued by Sambo Creek's patronato and Land Defense Committee during the effort to recuperate the Castillo plot in the early 2000s (chapter 4) revealed that what is most important in Garifuna communities is the ability of the youth to have a place to call home, where they can choose the type of livelihood strategy that they find most suitable to their needs. Despite the fact that the majority of interviewees claimed that people would plant crops if there were more land, this was not how people planned to use the land they recuperated. When asked in 2002, some 93 percent of those I formally interviewed in Sambo Creek (n = 67) stated that the recuperated land would be used to build homes for "the children of the community." Only five people noted that the area would be used to plant crops, but all of them mentioned that agricultural areas would be combined with housing. By 2011, my most recent return to Sambo Creek, the area had developed into another Colonia, with homes of varying sizes and quality. As with the development of Colonia Libertad,

Figure 9.1 New construction in Sambo Creek, 2011. Photo by Keri Brondo

Sambeños entered a lottery system to obtain a piece of the land to construct their home. And just as in Colonia Libertad, some Sambeños—including male activists who were intimately involved in recuperating the land—were selling off pieces of their newly obtained communal territory. One key activist from the 2002 land occupations was disparagingly labeled a "capitalist convert" by an OFRANEH staff member during my 2011 visit with the organization.

Perhaps OFRANEH offers a romanticized vision and interpretation of Garifuna communities. Perhaps neoliberal programs like Romer's charter city will keep Garifuna in their communities, and they will have to rely less on transnational migration as a livelihood strategy. After all, the "free city" business models claim to combine local knowledge with global technology, theoretically enabling Garifuna residents in coastal communities to maintain traditions while the coastline itself transforms into the Silicon Valley of the Caribbean. But which patches of culture will Garifuna maintain as their ancestral agricultural land transforms under neoliberal urbanization? The charter city model is based on free choice; people are free to choose to participate and free to leave. Options to leave are limited—unemployment throughout Honduras is rising, so national labor migration is reduced, and post-coup it has become increasingly difficult to obtain a visa to migrate for employment opportunities. While many still attempt to enter the US mojado, the number of youth within communities appears to be on the rise (Bown 2010). Those who "choose" to enter into working for Honduras's growing criminal networks and gangs, or in prostitution, face a premature death. To stay, or in "choosing" to participate in the charter city model, Garifuna effectively choose a life of limit points and "at least" statements. "Choice" in this regard is understood in the same way as choice in the discourse of the Free Cities career recruitment web page—it is a Machiavellian definition of self-determination, understood to operate within a specific political-economic system that runs counter to self-determination as conceptualized within the indigenous rights movement.

Visiting with Garifuna friends in 2011 in Sambo Creek was emotionally draining, leaving an emptiness one feels when there seems to be no way forward, when faced with a reality or resignation to "at least" statements. On the one hand, I visited with some friends who were getting by relatively well through the remittances they were receiving from abroad—some had enough to get through university, and many older residents had new, towering homes constructed through dollars earned in the United States. But others were not faring so well—several friends spent the last decade working at the neighboring Palma Real resort—"at least they had a job." Maybe so, but some had also formed a crack habit, spending the little they earned on drugs and parties with foreign tourists. "At least we now have a house of our own," some would say, because they obtained plots through the lottery of the recuperated Castillo plots. But even these homes may now go up for private sale to non-Sambeños. "At least we now have a secretary for the development of indigenous and Afro-Honduran peoples." But will this secretary work to resist the continued privatization of coastal territory? In the International Year for People of African Descent, are the existence of the secretary and the declarations coming out of the August 2011 World Summit mere rhetoric of inclusion, masking the growing exclusion and denial of indigenous rights to territory facilitated by neoliberal multiculturalism?

During the final copyedit of this book, there was a brief glimpse of hope to the contrary when—after a year of OFRANEH'S resistance to the model city land grabs—ODECO finally joined OFRANEH in critiquing the RED legislation as unconstitutional and infringing on national sovereignty. On October 8, 2012, ODECO hosted a conference entitled Model Cities, Garifuna Land, and the Feasibility and Implications for National Development, in which representatives from several national organizations and local Garifuna communities participated. Emerging from this conference was a declaration from ODECO that while they support efforts to generate investment opportunities that will drive economic growth, these efforts should be undertaken only if they do not compromise national sovereignty and the interests of Honduran people, especially those of Afro-Hondurans

(ODECO 2012). While it is still committed to economic development, that ODECO, the organization that has historically worked closely with the administration to carry out national development plans, issued a statement that called upon the Supreme Court to respect the October 2012 decision on the unconstitutionality of the RED legislation, is promising.

Perhaps ODECO tipped the scales—on October 17, 2012, the Honduran Supreme Court ruled that the Model City was unconstitutional in that it violated the nation's territorial integrity and sovereignty of the government. Regardless, the Lobo administration appears determined to find ways to move free zones forward. In early November 2012 President Lobo announced that his government would seek to establish a zone on the Pacific coast instead, working with El Salvador and Nicaragua (*Honduras Weekly* 2012b). Clearly, the post-coup administration will continue to back policies that include both ideological and territorial cartographies of erasure. As they do, what will come of afro-indigenous women's territorial rights?

Conclusion

Counterpunches to "Honduras Is Open for Business"

Zita, a friend from Sambo Creek, my husband, Daniel, and I took a *colectivo* (shared taxi) from Sambo Creek to La Ceiba one afternoon in the summer of 2011 to meet up with Miriam Miranda. It was going to be the first time in over five years that I would see Miriam. We exited the taxi and Zita and I made our way into the building while my husband went for a walk. Two staff members were waiting for us in the patio area and saw us pull up. Ruben (a pseudonym) apologized that Miriam had been called away on personal business, and he offered to meet with me in her place. He shared that while she — like many other Garifuna activists — is generally suspicious of anthropologists, she had warmed to me over the years and was honestly disappointed that she would miss me. After all, anthropologists (*antrópologos*) are easily confused with cannibals (*antrópofagos*). A former head of OFRANEH said the same when we met in 2001. We anthropologists feed off the Garifuna culture in order to climb our own career ladders. I could not, and still cannot, disagree. Being welcomed into the lives of Honduran Garifuna, non-Garifuna, and expatriates, has brought me to where I am today within the small world of anthropology.

Yet what brought me to the north coast in the first place was a commitment to social justice, and a desire to document abuses of power that occur in the wake of disaster. In 1999 I was inspired by the global news coverage of the Garifuna protests to the constitutional amendment to reform Article 107 and open the beaches to foreign ownership. This was a moment when the World Wide Web was just emerging as a powerful tool for both "witnessing at a distance" and "activism at a distance" (Ribeiro 1998). Armed with a background in theoretical debates on development and identity

189

politics, as well as feminist epistemological traditions and methods, I set off on a project of witnessing and documentation.

My white privilege made for easy (and uneasy) travel and research companions. I have tried in the practice of "doing ethnography" to be attentive to the rights afforded to me as a result of my positionality, and to respectfully represent the positions of others, as they emerged from their own situated statuses in the world. Feminist theories, and in particular the concept of situated knowledge, give us a way to go about recognizing and accounting for the various positionalities of our research subjects and ourselves. Sandra Haraway (2001:176) defined situated knowledge as a counter to relativism.

> The alternative to relativism is partial, locatable, critical knowledges sustaining the possibility of webs of connections called solidarity in politics and shared conversations in epistemology. Relativism is a way of being nowhere while claiming to be everywhere equally. The "equality" of positioning is a denial of responsibility and critical enquiry. Relativism is the perfect mirror twin of totalization in the ideologies of objectivity; both deny the stakes in location, embodiment, and partial perspective; both make it impossible to see well. Relativism and totalization are both "god-tricks" promising vision from everywhere and nowhere equally and fully, common myths in rhetoric surrounding Science.

Relativism, and cultural relativism included, one of the backbones of anthropology, states that all positions are equal. Haraway reminds us that such a position ignores power and the possibility (or reality) of exploitation. She also argues that the same is true for "objective science." Objectivity refuses to acknowledge that humans are interpreting what is or is not "the truth." The opening vignettes to this book were an effort to avoid "playing god." A counterapproach to relativism is feminist objectivity or situated knowledge, which recognizes that all of us are positioned—both researchers and subjects—and hence we each have a distinct "truth." But while the truth may look different for all, feminist scholars and poststructuralists acknowledge that some "truths" are legitimized, while others are dismissed or disregarded. The truths of those in power are made into objective knowledge and reproduced as reality (Foucault 1980). The ethnographic approach aims to unveil the complex dimensions of communities, households, and families that are built by individuals of varying positionalities and access to power. Such an approach pays attention to how access to land, for instance, is gendered and imbued with power, and could lead to the identification of more appropriate, locally based strategies for gender equality (Jackson 2003).

Haraway's influence provided two critical questions: (1) How did my situatedness affect my understanding of resource control, and (2) how did the situatedness of others shape their narratives of territorial control and resource management on the coastline and Cayos Cochinos? The book's opening vignettes offer some key insights into the first question. In the story of Francisco's death, the astute reader will have noticed the privileging of the mestizo and expatriate perspective. The entry opens with the account that Daniel heard when he walked out to the restaurant that morning, which is representative of the window through which I gazed at Sambo Creek's land struggle. While as an anthropologist I was dedicated to seeking out marginalized voices (presumably the voices and stories of the Garifuna), I woke up each day in a place of privilege—a nice home, with more amenities than many of those I encountered. Hotel staff and guests were usually the first people I spoke to each day, and their thoughts shaped what I heard and saw for the remainder of the day. Thus, these interpretations of events, like my husband's interpretations, shaped the research process as I went off each day to "seek the truth," which, influenced by Sandra Harding's (1991) standpoint theory, I presumed would be found among the most marginalized within the Garifuna community—women and other disempowered individuals.

Similarly in 2005, I spent my nights on the Cayo Menor with the other national and foreign researchers, distanced from the "other" by class, race, power, and space. In the mornings the social science team (four students and I) would boat over to Chachahuate and East End, spending the day on the cay interviewing households, conducting focus groups, and "hanging out." Arriving on the HCRF boat did little to promote our spoken message that we were indeed most interested, and prioritized, the local population's position on the establishment of the MPA and effects of recent regulations. These boats were the same ones used by navy patrols, staffed by armed soldiers who had confiscated equipment and shot individuals caught breaking fishing regulations. Residents had little faith in anyone attached to the managing agency—the agency responsible, in their view, for the demise of their livelihood, cultural traditions, and quite possibly their habitat.

In 2002, when I told a former leader of OFRANEH that we signed a rental agreement with a hotel/restaurant in Louba, I was warned about this distancing—"If you really want to understand the Garifuna community, you need to live with them, not separate, in a foreign or mestizo-owned dwelling." By choosing to remain in our rental, I had to be ever mindful of the potential to reproduce objective truth through the privileging of voices of those in power.

The choice to remain in a rental cabana also meant that my networks expanded, as did the scope of my project. Rather than exploring the construction of Garifuna indigeneity and its ties to the land struggle from solely the perspective of Garifuna community members and activists, I came to expand my study to explore the effects of the production of indigeneity and negotiation of land rights from the perspectives of all stakeholders within the region, including foreign expats, mestizo landowners, tourism workers, and recent mestizo immigrants in search of labor opportunities. I have tried, to the best of my ability, to represent their situated understandings of the world. The decision to expand the scope of my project, I believe, increased OFRANEH's early skepticism of the nature of my work.

When in 2005 I returned to the Cayos Cochinos without family, and thus better positioned to forgo the creature comforts offered by a rental cabana, the social science team and I insisted on living in homestays within the Garifuna communities reliant on the MPA. Opwall provided us with a budget to do so in all communities except Chachahuate—hence, why we remained on Cayo Menor the night of that party. By the following year, heeding our advice, Opwall made it a priority to arrange for us to be housed on Chachahuate if we so desired, which we did, and we resided there during the subsequent field season. Opwall also contracted a local boat owner to transport us across the island networks, and local translators to work with student research assistants, rather than having to rely upon the HCRF motorboats and networks.

What shifted in terms of my positionality and lens(es) into the exploration of resources and power between the 2002 study of Sambo Creek's land struggle, the 2005–6 work in Cayos Cochinos, and my 2011 return, was growing social, cultural, and economic capital, which subsequently shaped my networks, insights, and positions on resource allocation. My white skin, used car purchased through grant funding, and luxury of spending a year doing ethnographic work alongside a husband who also did not seem to have to work signaled an elite status to some Sambeños. Others understood our "student statuses" and related to us in this fashion, befriending us as equals or junior colleagues.

By 2005 I had a few years of experience in formalized research positions at Michigan State University. I was nearly through writing my dissertation and looking for an opportunity to return to the region. The increased pay and experience in my full-time university position afforded me a heightened sense of respect among conservation organization leadership and confidence that I could serve in a formal field supervisor role. By 2006 I returned as a doctorate and was introduced to new contacts by colleagues of the HCRF and Opwall as "*Profesora* or *Doctora*." It was not until 2006 that I began to experience and value the "traditions" that necessitated territorial access and control, practices that had waned significantly in Sambo Creek by 2002 but that still served as a cornerstone to the community's recuperation arguments. Being in the field without my family, with increased economic resources and logistical support from Opwall, and supervising students making their first trip abroad (filling a "teacher" status), I found myself invited to a variety of events to introduce my students to "Garifuna culture." In the teacher role, the students and I could cross gendered paths: we not only processed cassava and made *casabe* but also went out with male fishermen on cayucos in the CCMPA.

Between 2006 and 2011, I published a couple of articles on the territorial struggle. Ever aware of the partial truths associated with the perspectives I had access to, I tried in my writing to be as "true" to the data as possible, and attentive to how contemporary conditions and relationships to land and local resources have been shaped by power. Thus, the narratives I collected on land loss revealed a gendered, and ethnicized, loss of resources (e.g., Garifuna women to mestizo or foreign men), as well as the influence that politically connected individuals had on steering the direction of protected area management and territorial control (e.g., with the HCRF board comprised of CCMPA landowners). The written availability of these oral histories may serve to aid in the international court cases that OFRANEH has filed to reclaim Garifuna territory and, according to Ruben, was something that this organization appreciated. So in 2011 when Zita and I visited OFRANEH's office for the first time in years, despite Miriam's absence we were warmly welcomed and spoke with core staff for two hours about the contemporary state of Garifuna communities and the most critical environmental and territorial threats.

The same issues that plagued the coast at the turn of the millennium continued to play out in 2011, only now they seemed to have even more political-economic backing and to run the entire coastline. The on-again-off-again Tela project that I described in chapter 2 was under construction. Los Micos Beach and Golf Resort is located between the Garifuna communities of Miami and Tornabe and is planned to include an 18-hole golf course, 600 hotel rooms, a convention center, a marina, an equestrian center, a shopping plaza, and over 400 private villas (Loperena 2010). As Loperena (2011) writes, "Los Micos is a pillar of neoliberal economic reforms in Honduras; it is linked to the privatization of collectively owned coastal lands, the sale of prime coastal real estate to foreign investors, and capitalizes on natural and cultural resources for the benefit of private enterprise." Los Micos is not the only pillar of neoliberal reform along the coast: the REDs and model cities discussed in the last chapter are transforming the coastline further toward the Mosquitia, and the October 2010 congressional approval for concessions to build 41 hydroelectric dam projects along Honduras's rivers are others. The Patuca III project in Olancho is one of several of these megadam developments. The Patuca III project expects to build three dams along the Patuca River, financed through the Chinese company Sinohydro. While Honduran press reported that the 200 property owners whose land will flood as a result of the dam would be compensated for their relocation, no mention was made of compensation to the thousands of indigenous peoples (Tawahka, Miskitu, Pech, and Garifuna) living downstream of the dam site (Cultural Survival 2011). In October 2011, indigenous protesters were forcibly evicted from the site. By early December 2011 the Patuca III project was nearly 20 percent into its first phase of construction.

About an hour into my conversation with OFRANEH activists, Ruben asked "Was that your husband that I just saw walk by [pointing], going that way?" "Yes," I said, "he's going for a walk around town." Ruben shifted in his chair, concerned, and said he had just walked into a pretty dangerous area. He reminded me that the world has changed in Honduras. Post-coup, violence is rampant and crimes of opportunity prevail. Just two days prior a man had been shot and robbed walking into a shop around the corner in broad daylight. Daniel returned in time, unharmed, but the salient point is that this kind of warning was never something we heard in past years. In 2011 when Sambeño friends spoke of crime, they spoke of instability, unprovoked and indiscriminate violence, and fear. On our walk to catch the bus to Sambo Creek, Zita told me she was afraid to speak against the state in public, on phone lines and over the internet ("someone is always watching").

In 2002 when Sambeños spoke about violence, they associated it with the mestizo and foreign "other," as an action to protect what they felt rightfully belonged to them (e.g., purchased and privately titled land) or as act of retribution (mestizo rage). By 2011 many of the expatriates I knew in the early 2000s had returned to their home countries or were making plans to leave. By October that year Honduras had become the violence and murder capital of the world; the country's per capita homicide rate reached 82.1 homicides for every 100,000 inhabitants (United Nations Office on Drugs and Crime 2011). Femicides increased 257% over the last 10 years in Honduras, and every day at least one woman is murdered there (Collazo 2012). In January 2012 the United States pulled its Peace Corps volunteers due to rising security concerns but continued to back the corrupt military and police forces behind the country's "war on drugs." On May 11, 2012, during the final weeks of preparing this manuscript, machine-gun fire from officers on US Drug Enforcement Agency (DEA) helicopters killed four indigenous civilians (two of them pregnant women) and injured seven others. This "unintended" massacre occurred as this group of fishermen traveling the Patuca River to their home community of Ahuas in the Mosquitia region was confused with the DEA's target boat that was carrying drug traffickers (Kovalik 2012). Despite local protests and the request by 94 US House of Representative members "to suspend US assistance to the Honduran military and police given the credible allegations of widespread, serious violations of human rights and security forces" (US Congress 2012), as 2012 progressed the United States not only continued to back the Lobo regime but had increased its military funding, moving both its troops and counterinsurgency methods from Iraq and Afghanistan to form new military bases and wage an attack on drug trafficking (Shanker 2012). These decisions fuel conflict and insecurity on the ground by providing advanced weaponry that would inevitably get into the hands of the corrupt local enforcement and gangs involved in the drug trade.[1]

While those with resources were leaving in 2011, those without resources were finding it more difficult to get out of the country. And while those with resources were leaving, violence was not. And violence had changed. Now with the number of youth in natal communities on the rise, so too were crimes against one's own, emerging among what OFRANEH called "children of neoliberalism."

Despite the rising insecurity on the ground, the government's official discourse was "Honduras Is Open for Business." In an effort to offset the sharply declining economy and image of insecurity, early in 2011 President Lobo's administration approved a series of probusiness laws. In addition to the Ley de Ciudades Modelos (mentioned in the last chapter), other legislation included Ley para la Promoción de Alianzas Público-Privadas, Ley para la Protección y Promoción de Inversiones, and Ley de Empleo Temporal. In an American Anthropological Association panel dedicated to post-coup Honduras, Christopher Loperena classifies this event as an instance of "disaster capitalism," or "orchestrated raids on the public sphere in the wake of catastrophic events, combined with the treatment of disasters as exciting market opportunities" (Klein 2007:6)." Loperena (2011) writes: "Organized by the Ministry of Foreign Affairs, *Honduras Is Open* for Business (HOB) was essentially a coming-out party for the post-coup regime and a platform for business leaders who sought to showcase the immense opportunities awaiting international investors. Over the course of the two-day conference, the Lobo administration highlighted new laws designed to increase security and profitability for private investments." These political moves were eerily reminiscent of the middle-of-the-night congressional session in post-Mitch Honduras, when Congress voted to reform Article 107 and open the coast up for tourism development (chapter 2). Indeed, tourism then jumped to third place as a source of national revenue, up 18.3 percent between 1998 and 2001. In 2011, the Honduran press was estimating that the government would sell nearly 160 development projects, resulting in $15 billion in investments (La Tribuna 2011).

In spite of the country taking some serious turns for the worse, there may be grounds for optimism, given the theme of Garifuna resilience. Cutting across the chapters of this book is the power of indigenous peoples' resistance to the state's development model, even in the face of continuing state-sanctioned repression. From the 1954 Great Banana Strike to Sambo Creek's land occupations and the fishers' house meeting to protest the reality show in the CCMPA, Honduras's peasant, indigenous, and black communities are continuing to speak out against Honduras's oligarchy and unequal distribution of resources. On March 18, 2011, when Miriam Miranda of OFRANEH was abused, arrested, and charged with sedition at a peaceful protest against the Los Micos development, she described the violence with Loperena (2011): "In the process of getting arrested, they shot at me various times with teargas bombs, hitting me in the stomach . . . later I was dragged on the cement while the police continued to hit me and berate me with racial slurs."

As this book has shown, repression of this magnitude is nothing new to Garifuna activists. Neither is their fearless activism. While Garifuna mobilization is nothing new, what has changed in the new millennium is the solid (and growing) international backing of rights-based doctrines that recognize the Garifuna as indigenous and afro-descendant peoples with a "cultural heritage in need of safeguarding." Concomitantly, newly emerging and intensifying technologies are supporting social connectivity across diverse populations and interest groups, enabling witnessing and activism at a distance. Social mobilization is also expanding, and today marginalized peoples and communities are joined by the world's working and middle classes. While the new millennium marks a moment in history where the majority of the world's citizens are beginning to feel the squeeze of global austerity measures, importantly, indigenous and peasant communities have long felt the negative fallout of the structure of the global economy and have been organizing to protest for change. The social movements of the new millennium thus bring resource mobilization approaches that focus on power and emphasize social transformation, together with new social movement actors who represent a wide variety of individuals striving to renegotiate the social identities existent in civil society.

Moreover, as the gulf between the world's rich and poor continues to expand, the "target" has also changed. Eva and Aubert, the hotel owners in the book's opening vignette, and the foreign research tourists in the second, were distractions from the structural causes of social injustice on the north coast. They were the leaves on the tree of injustice, distracting Sambeños and Garifuna residents in the CCMPA from the root causes of resource loss. As these leaves begin to thin out, the trunk becomes visible, as do the symptoms eating away at its body (growing gang and drug-related violence, a heightened reliance on remittance economy), all rooted in the rampant spread of neoliberalism.

The potential for social transformation lies in expanding networks of mobilization, based on a combination of identity-oriented *and* resource mobilization approaches to social movements, supported by global-scapes. In this book, I have argued that categories of people, who are identified and positioned in particular ways, receive differential access to resources and opportunities. Garifuna identity categories have shifted over time, and these shifts are linked to the changing economic development approaches pursued in the coastal region. The Garifuna were excluded from Honduran national identity for a significant part of their time in the nation-state. They lived in a region (i.e., the north coast) where the people were not considered "Honduran"; its population was a mix of "foreigners" (or non-Hispanics) who were involved in the banana industry in one form or another. Since the 1990s, there have been state efforts to integrate the area and its people into the Honduran nation because both are seen as having economic potential. The region's natural and cultural landscapes have become represented as tourism attractions.

The successful production of global indigenous rights served to reinforce and legitimize particular identities and subject positions while delegiti-mizing others. Some Garifuna activists are organizing to make claims to resources as indigenous peoples and to push for democratization. With indi-geneity come increased rights, but it also produces new subject positions for Garifuna *as well as* non-Garifuna. Other (non-Garifuna) subjects in the Honduran state are beginning to frame their identity in response to the Garifuna "indigenous subject." In chapter 6 we saw how, as the Garifuna moved to reclaim ancestral territories that had fallen into mestizo hands, mestizo residents of "Garifuna communities" began to question their own identity as subjects within the State. Do mestizos have equal rights to coastal land? Do they belong on the north coast? Do foreign expats?

In this book I have shown how coastal communities are diverse, and how residents can and do unify across class and racial-ethnic boundaries in order to achieve their human right to livelihood and a basic standard of sociality. Carla, who joined the "children of the community" in the struggle to reclaim the community's ancestral territory, "belonged" in Sambo Creek. In the Cayos Cochinos, Garifuna fishers work closely with Tony Ives, the ex–Peace Corps member who directs the NGO GAD, to develop community-based projects. Tony maintains very strong relationships with the majority of individuals in the six CCMPA communities, so much so that he might also be said to "belong" on the coast. The voluntourists who come to the north coast to pursue a research agenda focused on the comanagement of resources or the effects of CCMPA management plan regulations on fishing for subsistence, for instance, might be said to have a "right" to visit and collaborate with locals on an evaluation of how the CCMPA's establishment has shaped the Garifuna's right to livelihood. In all of these cases, individuals are coming together to work toward solutions within the contemporary nature of society. These efforts are made within the current neoliberal economic structure. Where the power lies is in finding opportunities for eking out real, concrete alternatives to the status quo.

OFRANEH activists are serving out "counterpunches." I borrow this notion from the US website and newsletter *Counterpunch*, described on Wikipedia.com as "muckraking with a radical attitude." Articles in *Counterpunch* aim to expose political scandals, naming the names and calling out power in order to propose divergent ideas about democracy and development. These counterpunches blow holes within the structure, creating windows of opportunity. One window of opportunity that has occurred as a post-coup effort to demonstrate a "government of reconciliation" was a deal made between the Lobo administration and the Union Democrática (UD), which participated in the resistance to the coup, that the UD would head up the INA (Anderson 2012:64). Under new leadership, the INA has agreed to work with OFRANEH toward the creation of a "multicommunal" land title that would incorporate 15 Garifuna communities into a single title, expanding the registered land and expanding the possibilities for land reclamation (Anderson 2012:64). Part of framing Honduras as "open for business" is convincing others that the state is working toward reconciliation and inclusion. The expansion of INA's budget and new leadership, like local activists turning the rhetoric of participatory conservation management planning back onto the HCRF, may create windows of opportunity and possibilities for change.

In sum, the trends that transformed the coastal and island landscapes take root in a deep history of ethnic and racial discrimination tied to national development policy. The shift toward neoliberal conservation and development policies and the focus on tourism growth as a primary source of foreign revenue primarily benefited foreign expat entrepreneurs in the short run, and global capitalists and Honduras's elite in the long run, while further limiting Garifuna autonomy, self-determination, and control over ancestral territories. Hardest hit have been women, consistent with the ways in which environmental rights and responsibilities are refashioned in a damagingly gendered manner under neoliberal agrarian reforms. The contemporary global development model (development as modernization) ensures the continued and accelerated control of local resources by powerful nations and individuals. Now the smaller-scale expatriate entrepreneurs are being pushed out of coastal development as massive, government-backed development projects like the Model Cities, Patuca III, and Los Micos complex begin to take shape. As these trends continue, the uneasy relationships of "harmonious racism" (Anderson 2009:61–69) that once characterized coastal communities may disappear completely, as those with slightly more resources return to their home countries or the capital city. Among those who remain, and those who continue to volunteer their areas of technical and research expertise, we may see further consolidation of interests and increased solidarity, but the verdict is still out.

Notes

Introduction

1. Pseudonyms are applied in all cases for individuals quoted or discussed, except in cases where individuals and their actions have been previously identified in the news media.

2. In 2000 a German owner of lands in the center of Sambo Creek was jailed because his watchmen shot and killed a Garifuna resident who walked on his lands. The German was given the option of leaving Honduras permanently or spending a set amount of time in a Honduran prison. The man opted for the latter.

3. By the time I returned the following year, the Garifuna had been fully prohibited from entering Cayo Menor when research tourists were present. Significantly, the largest Garifuna population in the Cayos Cochinos resides on an island cay without water (called Chachahuate), and Cayo Menor serves as one of their water sources, as well as potential hunting grounds and location for timber.

4. With this growth in mind, some have argued that the desire to become competitive within the global tourism market creates an urgency to develop protected areas (Büscher and Dressler 2007).

Chapter One: Identity, Labor, and the Banana Economy

1. On April 12, 2002, I attended the 205th anniversary celebration of Garifuna presence on the coast, at the headquarters of the Organización de Desarrollo Étnico Comunitario (ODECO) in La Ceiba. The keynote speaker was Santos Centeno García, Garifuna historian and author (Centeno García 1997). There were approximately a hundred individuals present, Garifuna men and women from surrounding communities, a group from a local high school (all mestizo youth), three music and dance troupes from nearby communities who were to perform that evening, and several activists and ODECO supporters from Honduras and abroad. In recounting Garifuna history, Centeno García spoke of a Portuguese shipwreck, describing how Africans who were destined for slavery swam to freedom on the island of St. Vincent, where they became integrated into Carib society. Varieties of shipwreck accounts circulate, with differing ports of origin and dates of the shipwreck. The significance of this origin narrative—like the pre-Columbian account—is that it sets up the Garifunas' history of resistance to enslavement and oppression.

2. There has not been sufficient research on how the Garifuna viewed their position in this time period. In his discussion of ethnic politics, Anderson (2009:89–91) cites a letter written by a Garifuna man named Sixto A. Cacho, in which he identifies commonalities between the Garifuna and the mestizo population. Cacho writes that the Garifuna share a history of racial intermixture that dates back to the pre-Columbian inhabitants of the Americas. His letter emphasizes the shared oppression of Garifuna and mestizos ("*latinos*") under the fruit companies, and he advocates solidarity of Hondurans against foreign domination (Anderson 2009:90–91). He points out that despite phenotypic similarities, the Garifuna share more in common with the mestizo worker than with the West Indians, who were the foreign companies' "preferred workers" and received the better jobs. As he does mestizo Hondurans, Cacho asserts the Garifuna as authentic Hondurans and argues that they are entitled to the same rights and privileges.

Chapter Two: Development and Territorialization on the North Coast

1. The war became known as the Soccer War, because it was triggered by abusive treatment of the Honduran team during a World Cup qualifying game in San Salvador. Although the war lasted only five days, it had serious effects, including Honduras's withdrawal from and the subsequent collapse of the Central American Common Market, as well as continued border incidents.

2. The 1954 Great Banana Strike is often cited as igniting popular organizing in Honduras. The strike began when Honduran banana workers for United Fruit were refused overtime wages for loading a boat on a Sunday. Nearly thirty thousand workers at other American-owned enterprises later joined them. The strike lasted for three months and eventually shut down 60 percent of the national economy (Norsworthy and Barry 1993).

3. While Garifuna organizations and their media supporters often talk about Article 107 as if it was written to protect Garifuna lands, this constitutional article was not established for that purpose. More likely, it was created to protect the nation's sovereignty after a century of wars with neighboring countries. Within the last century, Honduras has been at war with all three of its neighbors, the most recent of which was the infamous Soccer War in 1969. This constitutional prohibition against foreign ownership existed in both the 1956 and the 1965 constitutions.

4. Individuals purchasing land for residential purposes must register their purchase with the Ministry of Tourism and complete construction of the residence within 36 months from the date of purchase or pay an annual penalty worth 20 percent of the value of the property until the construction is complete. Foreign individuals or companies interested in purchasing property for tourism or other development projects must complete an application with the Honduran Tourism Institute (IHT) at the Ministry of Tourism. The application procedure includes personal information, proof that a contract to buy a specific property exists, proof that said property is registered with the Honduran Tourism Institute, and a plan for how the proposed development project will generate economic benefits for Honduras.

5. In fact, this was how I first heard of the Garifuna land struggle—reading an Internet posting about the impacts that repeal of Article 107 could have on Garifuna territorial control. I later saw an article about it in *Chicago Streetwise*, a paper that

I was handed on the street during the 1999 American Anthropological Association's annual meetings.

6. The jaguar symbolized the guardians of ancient Maya temples.

7. This project did not come to fruition until the 2000s, under the name Los Micos Golf and Beach Resort, and is briefly described in the concluding chapter.

Chapter Three: Mestizo Irregularities, Garifuna Displacement, and the Emergence of a "Mixed" Garifuna Community

1. Anderson (2009) drew upon the following database, cited as follows in an endnote: "Data derived from the database of the 2001 Honduran census, at the Instituto Nacional de Estadística, http://www.ine-hn.org (accessed August 11, 2008)." The website address no longer links to Honduran census data.

2. The role of religion and churches is not something I have sufficient data on and do not discuss in this book. However, I will note that the influx of Christian (non-Catholic) churches in the area is likely linked to the decline in the practice of *Dügü*, the ancestral religious rituals. Catholicism is tolerant of *Dügü*, but other denominations—and the Evangelical church in particular—find ancestral rites to be sacrilegious.

3. I use *urban* to refer to the paved road area, which the bus from La Ceiba services.

4. Phytoplasma ("lethal yellowing") follows wind damage and high humidity and is carried by insect hosts. Once infected, coconut and other palms die within three to six months of the first symptoms.

5. Remittances are the largest source of foreign income in Honduras, most of which come from the approximately one million Hondurans living in the United States. In 2009 remittances totaled $2.8 billion, which was a reduction of 11.8 percent from 2008, likely related to the global economic decline (US Department of State 2012).

6. The Sambo Creek household sample (n = 55) was designed to sample each geographic section of the community. What was important at the time of sampling was to obtain representation from every section of the community, not necessarily a representative sample of adults. This was of interest because the various settlements expressed class distinctions, but also because the surrounding areas of the community had unique histories in their transformation from cultivation land to living space. Interviewees were recruited in approximately every fifth household. Within these household interviews, representation by age, gender, and ethnicity was ensured through a strategy of rotating interviews by gender and then by age group (three age groups were sampled: ages 20–29; 30–50; and over 50). Despite an attempt to rotate between female and male adult members of the household, Sambo Creek has far more female permanent residents than men, and the sample was therefore weighed more heavily with women (i.e., 35 women and 20 men). This is because in certain areas of the community there were several consecutive houses without a male resident. Rather than leaving out large sections of the community, the woman head of household was interviewed.

Chapter Four: Gendered Rights and Responsibilities

1. In this excerpt, landowners are not replaced with pseudonyms. While the account of how land passed from Buity to Fernandez is speculative, the records on Fernandez's and then Castillo's ownership for this plot are public.

Chapter Five: Representing the Garifuna

1. See Anderson 2007, 2009; Greene 2007a, 2007b; Hooker 2005; and Safa 2005 for scholarly discussions of afro-indigenous multiculturalism.

2. These organizations are: the National Garifuna Council of Belize, the National Creole Council of Belize, La Organización Negra Guatemalteca (ONEGUA) of Guatemala, the Black Women's Organization of Guatemala, Asociación de Mujeres Garifunas Guatemaltecas of Guatemala, the Nicaraguan Garifuna Organization, Asociación de Desarrollo y Promoción Humana de la Costa Atlántica (ADEPHCA) of Nicaragua, the Afro-Latin American/Afro-Costa Rican Women's Network, INSCA of Costa Rica, the Caribbean Project of Costa Rica, the Association of Friends of the Ethnic Caribbean Museum of Bocas del Toro of Panama, the Afro-Panamanian Response, the Afro Panamanian Women's Network, the Southern Diaspora Research and Development Center of Panama, the Coalition Garifuna US, and Hondurans Against AIDS of the United States.

3. The Nuestras Raíces (Our Roots) Program was created in 1995. The program was developed in response to ethnic mobilization and protests citing the government for inadequate infrastructure and poor access to basic public services. The program was originally financed through domestic funds from 1995 to 1997, and beneficiaries received nominal pay to open and rehabilitate small tertiary roads and paths. The primary beneficiaries (72 percent) were Lenca, one of Honduras's seven indigenous and ethnic groups. The World Bank was invited to finance the program under the Social Investment Fund Project (FHIS) in 1997. Ethnic organizations have consistently issued complaints regarding the lack of participation, information, transparency, and politically biased targeting (Traa-Valarezo and Rodriguez 2003).

4. OFRANEH's denunciation of ODECO became far more strident in recent years, discussed in chapter 9.

5. A report by the Central American and Caribbean Research Council states that nearly five thousand people were present at the protest. This would be nearly all of the population of Sambo Creek, including people living abroad. My interviews with those present at the demonstration reported far fewer, perhaps a couple hundred, which is still a substantial turnout.

6. That the judge ruled at this time signaled that he was a friend of Castillo. Moreover, the details of this event were delayed from the news—and the judge was in fact a major shareholder in the news media (personal communication with local activist).

7. La Confederación de Pueblos Autóconos de Honduras (CONPAH) is credited for the establishment of this accord with the government.

Chapter Six: Roots, Rights, and Belonging in Sambo Creek

1. At the height of the Mosquito Kingdom (1790–1820), the Miskitu controlled an expansive region along the coast of eastern Nicaragua and Honduras (Hale 1994:39), including the area that is now Sambo Creek, giving rise to the name Sambo Creek.

2. *Moreno* means "brown" and is used by Garifuna to refer to themselves, although most state a preference for the term *negro*.

Chapter Seven: "Businessmen Disguised as Environmentalists"

1. The low estimate assumes all Honduran visitors paid $2, the 831 foreign visitors associated with Opwall paid $10 (which we know they did), and all other foreign visitors were brought in by a local tour operator and paid the minimum payment of $5. The high estimate assumes all foreign visitors arrived in boats not operated by a local tour operator, and thus each paid $10. These estimates do not include a fee for the 34 individuals recorded in the NA category (i.e., reflecting that either the fees were not applicable or the information was not available to log).

2. Sea turtle breeding beaches face north; the principal nesting beach is the uninhabited side of Cayo Menor.

Chapter Eight: Research Voluntourism as Rights-Based Conservation

1. There are also computer technologies and software packages available to assist in a participatory approach to fisheries management within the CCMPA, which the HCRF might consider. Participatory Fisheries Stock Assessment (ParFish) is particularly well suited for comanaged fisheries and involves fishers at all levels of management (data collection, assessment, and decision making).

Chapter Nine: Neoliberalism's Limit Points in Post-Coup Honduras

1. While Garifuna activists did support Zelaya's push for a referendum on constitutional reform, they were not necessarily supporters of the Zelaya administration. In fact, prior to the coup, OFRANEH issued several communiqués denouncing the Zelaya administration for its inadequate support for collective property rights, for supporting large-scale tourist development projects, and for firing Garifuna professionals in education (Anderson 2012: 58–59).

Conclusion

1. As the writing of this book came to a close, human rights abuses were unfortunately on the upswing. I point readers to the blog of anthropologist Adrienne Pine for coverage of the rising instability and violence against indigenous peoples in post-coup Honduras: Quota.net.

Bibliography

Adams, William M., and Jon Hutton
   2007   People, Parks and Poverty: Political Ecology and Biodiversity Conservation. Conservation and Society 5(2): 147–183.

Almendares, Juan
   2009   Urgent: Assault on Garifuna Communal Lands. Quotha (blog of Adrienne Pine). November 18. http://www.quotha.net/node/559.

Amnistía Internacional
   2006   Documento—HONDURAS. Temor por la seguridad. Accessed October 13, 2012. http://www.amnesty.org/es/library/asset/AMR37/005/2006/es/530bfb1e-d402-11dd-8743-d305bea2b2c7/amr370052006en.html.

Anaya, James S.
   1996   Indigenous Peoples in International Law. New York: Oxford University Press.

Anderson, Mark
   2000   Garífuna Kids: Blackness, Modernity, and Tradition in Honduras. PhD dissertation, Department of Anthropology, University of Texas at Austin.

   2001   ¿Existe el racismo en Honduras? Discursos garífunas sobre raza y racismo. Mesoamérica 22(42):135–163.

   2007   When Afro Becomes (like) Indigenous: Garifuna and Afro-Indigenous Politics in Honduras. Journal of Latin American and Caribbean Anthropology 12(2): 384–413.

   2009   Black and Indigenous: Garifuna Activism and Consumer Culture in Honduras. Minneapolis: University of Minnesota Press.

   2012   Garifuna Activism and the Corporatist Honduran State since the 2009 Coup. In Black Social Movements in Latin America: From Monocultural Mestizaje to Multiculturalism. Jean Rahier, ed. Pp. 53–73. New York: Palgrave Macmillan.

Andraka, Sandra, Claudia Bouroncle, and Carlos García-Saez, eds.
   2004   Plan de manejo del monumento natural marino archipiélago Cayos Cochinos, Honduras 2004–2009.

   n.p.   WWF centroamérica/Fundación Hondureña para la Protección y Conservación de los Cayos Cochinos, Honduras.

AVINA
    2011   WhoWeAre.AVINA.http://www.informeavina2010.org/english/que-hacemos
            .shtml.

Black Workers for Justice
    2011   March of Drums: There Is Nothing to Celebrate. Black Workers for Jus-
            tice, accessed October 28, 2011. http://blackworkersforjustice.org/article
            .php?id=144.

Bolles, Lynn A.
    1992   Sand, Sea, and the Forbidden. Transforming Anthropology 3(1): 30–34.

Bookbinder, Marnie P., Eric Dinerstein, Arun Rijal, Hank Cualey, and Arup Rajouria
    1998   Ecotourism's Support of Biodiversity Conservation. Conservation Biology
            12(6): 1399–1404.

Botterill, David, and Mary Klemm
    2005   Introduction: Tourism and Social Inclusion. Tourism, Culture, and Com-
            munication 6(1): 1–6.

Bourgois, Philippe
    1989   Ethnicity at Work: Divided Labor on a Central American Banana Plantation.
            Baltimore: Johns Hopkins University Press.

Bown, Natalie K.
    2010   Contested Models of Marine Protected Area (MPA) Governance: A Case
            Study of the Cayos Cochinos, Honduras. PhD dissertation, School of Geog-
            raphy, Politics and Sociology, Newcastle University.

Brockington, Dan
    2002   Fortress Conservation: The Preservation of the Mkomazi Game Reserve,
            Tanzania. Bloomington: Indiana University Press.

Brockington, Dan, Rosaleen Duffy, and Jim Igoe
    2008   Nature Unbound: Conservation, Capitalism and the Future of Protected
            Areas. London: Earthscan.

Brondo, Keri Anne
    2006   Roots, Rights, and Belonging: Garifuna Indigeneity and Land Rights on
            Honduras' North Coast. PhD dissertation, Department of Anthropology,
            Michigan State University.

Brondo, Keri Vacanti
    2007   Garifuna Women's Land Loss and Activism in Honduras. Journal of Inter-
            national Women's Studies 9(1): 99–116.
    2010   When Mestizo Becomes (like) Indio . . . or is it Garifuna? Negotiating Indi-
            geneity and 'Making Place' on Honduras' North Coast. Journal of Latin
            American and Caribbean Anthropology 15(1): 171–194.

Brondo, Keri Vacanti, and Natalie Bown
    2011   Neoliberal Conservation, Garifuna Territorial Rights, and Resource Man-
            agement in the Cayos Cochinos Marine Protected Area. Conservation and
            Society 9(2): 91–105.

Brondo, Keri Vacanti, and Laura Woods
   2007   Garifuna Land Rights and Ecotourism as Economic Development in Hon-
          duras' Cayos Cochinos Marine Protected Area. Ecological and Environ-
          mental Anthropology 3(1): 1–18.

Brosius, Peter J.
   1999   Analyses and Interventions: Anthropological Engagements with Environ-
          mentalism. Current Anthropology 40(3): 277–310.
   2006   Common Ground between Anthropology and Conservation Biology. Con-
          servation Biology 20(3): 683–685.

Brown, Pete
   2002   Pantelhó: History-Making and Identity in Highland Chiapas. Journal of
          Latin American Anthropology 7(1):104–127.

Burns, Alan F.
   2005   Honduras. Afro-Tropical: A World on Fire. Accessed May 19, 2011. http://
          www.clas.ufl.edu/users/afburns/afrotrop/Honduras.htm.

Büscher, Bram
   2008   Conservation, Neoliberalism, and Social Science: A Critical Reflection on
          the SCB 2007 Annual Meeting in South Africa. Conservation and Society
          22(2): 229–231.

Büscher, Bram, and Wolfram Dressler
   2007   Linking Neoprotectionism and Environmental Governance: On the Rap-
          idly Increasing Tensions between Actors in the Environment–Development
          Nexus. Conservation and Society 5(4): 586–611.

Büscher, Bram, and Webster Whande
   2007   Whims of the Winds of Time? Emerging Trends in Biodiversity Conservation
          and Protected Area Management. Conservation and Society 5(1): 22–43.

Cáceres, Marco
   2011   Congress Opens Door for Model Corruption in Honduras. Honduras Weekly,
          August 7. Accessed October 24, 2011. http://www.hondurasweekly.com/
          congress-opens-door-for-model-corruption-in-honduras-201108073946/.

Calderón, Manuel Torres, Thelma Mejia, Dan Alder, Paul Jeffrey, with Jack Spence
   2002   Deciphering Honduras: Four Views of Post-Mitch Political Reality. Cam-
          bridge, MA: Hemispheric Initiatives.

Cayetano, Sebastian B., and Fabian B. Cayetano
   1997   Garífuna History, Language and Culture of Belize, Central America and
          the Caribbean. Bicentennial Edition, April 12, 1797–1997. Belize.

Centeno Garcia, Santos
   1997   Historia del movimiento negro hondureño. Tegucigalpa, Honduras: Edito-
          rial Guaymuras.

Center for Cultural Understanding and Change (CCUC)
   2006   Collaborative Research: A Practical Introduction to Participatory Action
          Research (PAR) for Communities and Scholars. Chicago: Field Museum.

Center for Economic Policy and Research (CEPR)
2009   US Group That Supported Overthrows of Democratically Elected Govern-
        ments in Haiti and Venezuela Will Observe Elections in Honduras. http://
        www.cepr.net/index.php/press-releases/press-releases/group-that-supported-
        overthrow-will-observe-honduras-elections, accessed December 13, 2011.

Central American and Caribbean Research Council (CCARC)
2002   Informe Comunidad de Sambo Creek. Honduras. Unpublished report pre-
        pared by CCARC. In the possession of the author.

Charter Cities
2011   Frequently Asked Questions. http://chartercities.org/faq/11/faq, accessed
        October 24, 2011.

Cobo, José R. Martínez
1983   Final Report on the Study of the Problem of Discrimination against Indig-
        enous Populations, United Nations. Accessed October 5, 2012. http://social
        .un.org/index/IndigenousPeoples/Library/Mart%C3%ADnezCoboStudy
        .aspx.

Collazo, Abigail
2012   As Drug Wars Intensify, Violence against Women Soars: Announcing Tweet-
        chat 6/6 at #Defensoras. Fem 2.0. Accessed October 12, 2012. http://www
        .fem2pt0.com/2012/06/04/as-drug-wars-intensify-violence-against-women-
        soars-announcing-tweetchat-66-at-defensoras/.

Confederación de Pueblos Autóctonos de Honduras (CONPAH)
2010   Día Internacional de Pueblos Indígenas. La Tribuna, Ecomentarios,
        August 16. Accessed October 2, 2012. http://old.latribuna.hn/2010/08/16/
        dia-internacional-de-pueblos-indigenas/.

Cooke, Bill, and Uma Kothari
2001   Participation: The New Tyranny? London: Zed Books.

Cowen, Tyler
2012   Paul Romer on What Happened in Honduras. Marginal Revolution. Sep-
        tember 24. Accessed on October 12, 2012. http://marginalrevolution.com/
        marginalrevolution/2012/09/paul-romer-on-what-happened-in-honduras
        .html.

Cultural Survival
2011   Campaign Update—Honduras: Dam Construction Speeds Ahead in Viola-
        tion of Indigenous Rights. Cultural Survival. Accessed December 3, 2011.
        http://www.culturalsurvival.org/news/honduras/campaign-update-honduras-
        dam-construction-speeds-ahead-violation-indigenous-rights.

Davidson, Adam
2012   Who Wants to Buy Honduras? New York Times, May 8, 2012. Accessed May
        31, 2012. http://www.nytimes.com/2012/05/13/magazine/who-wants-to-buy-
        honduras.html?pagewanted=all.

Deere, Carmen Diana, and Magdalena León
2001a   Empowering Women: Land and Property Rights in Latin America. Pitts-
        burgh: University of Pittsburgh Press.

2001b Institutional Reform of Agriculture under Neoliberalism: The Impact of Women's and Indigenous Movements. Latin American Research Review 36(2): 31–63.

2001c Who Owns the Land? Gender and Land-Titling Programmes in Latin America. Journal of Agrarian Change 1(3): 440–467.

Derman, William, Rie Odgaard, and Espen Sjaastad, eds.
2007 Introduction. *In* Conflicts over Land and Water in Africa. William Derman, Rie Odgaard, and Espen Sjaastad, eds. Oxford: James Curry.

Duffy, Rosaleen
2002 A Trip Too Far: Ecotourism, Politics, and Exploitation. London: Earthscan.

Durham, William
1979 Scarcity and Survival in Central America: The Ecological Origins of the Soccer War. Stanford: Stanford University Press.

Echeverri-Gent, Elisavinda
1992 Forgotten Workers: British West Indians and the Early Days of the Banana Industry in Costa Rica and Honduras. Journal of Latin American Studies 24(2): 275–308.

Economist
2011 Honduras Shrugged: Two Start-Ups Want to Try Out Libertarian Ideas in the Country's New Special Development Regions. Economist, December 10, 2011. Accessed June 5, 2012. http://www.economist.com/node/21541391.

Edelman, Marc, and Angelique Haugerud, eds.
2005 The Anthropology of Development and Globalization: From Classical Political Economy to Contemporary Neoliberalism. Malden, MA: Blackwell.

Eide, Asbjørn
1995 Economic, Social and Cultural Rights as Human Rights. *In* Economic, Social and Cultural Rights: A Textbook. Asbjørn Eide, Catarina Krause, and Allan Rosas, eds. Pp. 21–40. Dordrecht, the Netherlands: Martinus Nijhoff.

England, Sarah
2006 Afro-Central Americans in New York City: Garífuna Tales of Transnational Movements in Racialized Space. Gainesville: University Press of Florida.

Escobar, Arturo
1991 Anthropology and the Development Encounter: The Making and Marketing of Development Anthropology. American Ethnologist 18(4): 658–682.

1992 Imagining a Post-Development Era? Critical Thought, Development and Social Movements. Social Text 31/32:20–56.

1995 Encountering Development: The Making and Unmaking of the Third World. Princeton: Princeton University Press.

Euraque, Dario
1998 The Banana Enclave, Nationalism, and Mestizaje in Honduras, 1910s–1930s. *In* Identity and Struggle at the Margins of the Nation-State: The Laboring Peoples of Central America and the Hispanic Caribbean. Aviva Chomsky and Aldo Lauria-Santiago, eds. Pp. 151–168. Durham: Duke University Press.

2003   The Threat of Blackness to the Mestizo Nation: Race and Ethnicity in the Honduran Banana Economy, 1920s and 1930s. *In* Banana Wars. Steve Striffler and Mark Moberg, eds. Pp. 229–252. Durham, NC: Duke University Press.

2004   Negritud gárifuna y coyunturas políticas en la Costa Norte Hondurena, 1940–1970. *In* Conversaciones históricas con el mestizaje y su identidad nacional en Honduras. Dario Euraque, ed. Pp. 165–264. Honduras: Centro Editorial.

2010   El golpe de estado del 28 de junio de 2009, el patrimonio cultural y la identidad nacional. San Pedro Sula, Honduras, CA: Central Impresora, SA.

Feng, Xianghong
2008   Gender and Hmong Women's Handicrafts in Fenghuang's "Tourism Great Leap Forward," China. Anthropology of Work Review 28(3): 17–26.

Fischer, Edward F., and Peter Benson
2006   Broccoli and Desire: Global Connections and Maya Struggles in Postwar Guatemala. Stanford: Stanford University Press.

FLOW (Freedom Lights Our World)
2012   Homepage. Accessed June 4, 2012. http://www.flowidealism.org/index-project.html.

Fortwangler, Crystal
2007   Friends with Money: Private Support for a National Park in the US Virgin Islands. Conservation and Society 5(4): 504–533.

Foster, Byron
1987   The Politics of Ritual: The Development of the Garifuna Cult of the Dead on St. Vincent. First Annual Studies on Belize Conference, Belize City.

Foucault, Aubert
1973   The Order of Things: An Archaeology of the Human Sciences. New York: Vintage Books.

1979   Discipline and Punish: The Birth of Prison. New York: Pantheon Books.

1980   Power/Knowledge: Selected Interviews and Other Writings, 1972–1977. Vintage Press.

Frank, Dana
2012   In Honduras, a Mess Made in the U.S. New York Times, January 26. Accessed June 5, 2012. http://www.nytimes.com/2012/01/27/opinion/in-honduras-a-mess-helped-by-the-us.html?_r=1.

Free Cities Institute (FCI)
2012   Homepage. Free Cities. Accessed June 4, 2012. www.freecities.org.

Freidus, Andrea Lee
2011   Raising Malawi's Children: AIDS Orphans and a Politics of Compassion. PhD dissertation, Michigan State University, East Lansing.

French, Jan Hoffman
2011   The Power of Definition: Brazil's Contribution to Universal Concepts of Indigeneity. Indiana Journal of Global Legal Studies 18(1): 241–261.

2009   Legalizing Identities: Becoming Black or Indian in Brazil's Northeast. Bloomington: University of North Carolina Press.

Future Cities Development Corporation
  2012   Homepage. www.futurecitiesdev.com, accessed June 18, 2012.

Gass, Vickie
  2002   Democratizing Development: Lessons from Hurricane Mitch Reconstruction. Washington, DC: Washington Office on Latin America.

Ghodsee, Kristen
  2005   The Red Riviera: Gender, Tourism, and Post-Socialism on the Black Sea. Durham, NC: Duke University Press.

Gill, Rosalind
  2011   "Porn King," Developer of Projects in Trujillo. La Prensa. March 6. Accessed November 30, 2011. http://www.laprensa.hn/Apertura/Ediciones/2011/03/07/Noticias/Empresario-de-la-pornografia-dirige-proyectos-en-Trujillo.

Giovarelli, Renee, and Susana Lastarria-Cornhiel
  2006   Study on Women and Property Rights: Project Best Practices. USAID. Accessed May 19, 2011. http://pdf.usaid.gov/pdf_docs/PNADJ420.pdf.

González, Nancie L.
  1969   Black Carib Household Structure. Seattle: University of Washington Press.
  1988   Sojourners of the Caribbean: Ethnogenesis and Ethnohistory of the Garifuna. Urbana: University of Illinois Press.

Greene, Shane
  2007a   Introduction: On Race, Roots/Routes, and Sovereignty in Latin America's Afro-Indigenous Multiculturalisms. Journal of Latin American and Caribbean Anthropology 12(2): 329–355.
  2007b   Entre lo indio, lo negro, y lo incaico: The Spatial Hierarchies of Difference in Multicultural Peru. Journal of Latin American and Caribbean Anthropology 12(2): 440–474.

Greiber, Thomas, Melinda Janki, Marcos Orellana, Annalisa Savaresi, and Dinah Shelton, eds.
  2009   Conservation with Justice: A Rights-Based Approach. Gland, Switzerland: IUCN.

Griffin, Wendy
  1997   Garifunas Prepare Second March on Tegucigalpa. Honduras This Week. July 21. Online Edition 63. Accessed October 7, 2012. http://www.marrder.com/htw/jul97/national.htm.
  1999   March of Honduran Indians and Blacks Met with Bullets. Honduras This Week, October 25, 1999. Online Edition 180. Accessed October 8, 2012. http://www.marrder.com/htw/oct99/national.htm.

Grupo MGK
  2012a   Updates. Grupo MGK. Accessed October 12, 2012. http://www.grupomgk.com/english/updates.html.
  2012b   FAQ. Grupo MGK. Accessed October 12, 2012. http://www.grupomgk.com/english/about.html.

Guerrón-Montero, Carla
  2005   Marine Protected Areas in Panama: Grassroots Activism and Advocacy. Human Organization 64(4): 360–372.

Gupta, Akhil, and James Ferguson
    1997   Beyond "Culture": Space, Identity and the Politics of Difference. *In* Culture, Power, Place: Explorations in Critical Anthropology. Akhil Gupta and James Ferguson, eds. Pp. 33–52. Durham, NC: Duke University Press.
Hale, Charles R.
    1994   Resistance and Contradiction: Miskitu Indians and the Nicaraguan State, 1894–1987. Stanford: Stanford University Press.
    2005   Neoliberal Multiculturalism: The Remaking of Cultural Rights and Racial Dominance in Central America. PoLAR: Political and Legal Anthropology Review 28(1): 10–28.
Hanson, Paul W.
    2007   Governmentality, Language Ideology, and the Production of Needs in Malagasy Conservation and Development. Cultural Anthropology 22(2): 244–284.
Haraway, Sandra
    2001   Situated Knowledges: The Science Question in Feminism and the Privilege of Partial Perspective. *In* The Gender and Science Reader. Muriel Lederman and Ingrid Bartsch eds. Pp. 169–188. London: Routledge.
Harborne, Alastair, R. Daniel, C. Afzal, and Mark J. Andrews
    2001   Honduras: Caribbean Coast. Marine Pollution Bulletin 42(12): 1221–1235.
Harding, Sandra
    1991   Whose Science? Whose Knowledge? Thinking from Women's Lives. Ithaca, NY: Cornell University Press.
Harvey, David
    2005   A Brief History of Neoliberalism. Oxford: Oxford University Press.
El Heraldo
    2012a   Fiscalía dictamina que ciudades modelo son inconstitucionales. El Heraldo, February. Accessed May 31, 2012. http://www.elheraldo.hn/Secciones-Principales/Pais/Fiscalia-dictamina-que-ciudades-modelo-son-inconstitucionales.
    2012b   Romer: Han desviado las normas de transparencia en ciudades modelo. El Heraldo, September 23. Accessed October 12, 2012. http://www.elheraldo.hn/Secciones-Principales/Al-Frente/Romer-Han-desviado-las-normas-de-transparencia-en-ciudades-modelo.
Higgins-Desbiolles, Freya, and Gabrielle Russell-Mundine
    2008   Absences in the Volunteer Tourism Phenomenon: The Right to Travel, Solidarity Tours and Transformation beyond the One-Way. *In* Journeys of Discovery in Volunteer Tourism. Kevin D. Lyons and Stephen Wearing, eds. Pp. 182–194. Wallingford, UK: CABI International.
Hitchcock, Robert K.
    1995   Centralisation, Resource Depletion, and Coercive Conservation among the Tyua of the Northeastern Kalahari. Human Ecology 23(2): 168–198.
Hoffman, David M.
    2009   Institutional Legitimacy and Co-Management of a Marine Protected Area: Implementation Lessons from the Case of Xcalak Reefs National Park, Mexico. Human Organization 68(1): 39–54.

Honduras Culture and Politics
    2010a Dario Euraque: Required Reading. Honduras Culture and Politics (blog). December 8, 2010. (9:13 a.m.) Accessed October 24, 2011.http://hondurasculturepolitics.blogspot.com/2010/12/dario-euraque-required-reading.html.
    2010b Cultural Diversity and the Ministry of Culture. Honduras Culture and Politics (blog). February 1 (12:14 p.m.) Accessed October 24, 2011. http://hondurasculturepolitics.blogspot.com/2010/02/cultural-diversity-and-ministry-of.html.
    2011 Model Cities Law. Honduras Culture and Politics (blog). August 1 (1:00 a.m.). Accessed October 24, 2011. http://hondurasculturepolitics.blogspot.com/2011/08/model-cities-law.html.

Honduras Human Rights
    2010 254 Human Rights Violations under the Pepe Lobo Regime. February 24. http://hondurashumanrights.wordpress.com/2010/02/24/254-human-rights-violations-under-the-pepe-lobo-regime, accessed October 24, 2011.

Honduras Weekly
    2012a Model Cities Set to Begin? September 11, 2012. Accessed October 15, 2012. http://www.hondurasweekly.com/model-cities-set-to-begin?-201209115712/.
    2012b Gulf of Fonseca Offered as Free Economic Zone. November 2, 2012. Accessed November 13, 2012. http://hondurasweekly.com/money/.

Hooker, Juliet
    2005 Indigenous Inclusion/Black Exclusion: Race, Ethnicity, and Multicultural Citizenship in Latin America. Journal of Latin American Studies 37(2): 285–310.

Human Rights First
    2006 Human Rights First Report to the Human Rights Committee on Its Consideration of the Initial Report by the Government of Honduras under the International Covenant on Civil and Political Rights (ICCPR), October 16–17, 88th Session. Accessed October 12, 2012. http://www.humanrightsfirst.org/wp-content/uploads/pdf/061212-hrd-report-honduras-hrc.pdf.

Human Rights Watch (HRW)
    2010 After the Coup: Ongoing Violence, Intimidation, and Impunity in Honduras. HRW. Accessed October 9, 2012. http://www.hrw.org/sites/default/files/reports/honduras1210webwcover_0.pdf.
    2012 Honduras: Investigate Murder of Rights Lawyer—Killers of Antonio Trejo Should Be Brought to Justice. HRW, September 24. Accessed October 12, 2012. http://www.hrw.org/news/2012/09/24/honduras-investigate-murder-rights-lawyer

Igoe, Jim
    2004 Conservation and Globalization: A Study of National Parks and Indigenous Communities from East Africa to South Dakota. Riverside, CA: Wadsworth.
    2011 Rereading Conservation Critique: A Response to Redford. Fauna & Flora International, Oryx. 45(3): 333–334.

Igoe, Jim, and Dan Brockington
    2007   Neoliberal Conservation: A Brief Introduction. Conservation and Society 5(4): 432–449.

Igoe, Jim, and Beth Croucher
    2007   Conservation, Commerce and Communities: The Story of Community-Based Wildlife Management Areas in Tanzania's Northern Tourist Circuit. Conservation and Society 5(4): 534–561.

Ingram, Joanne
    2011   Volunteer Tourism: How Do We Know It Is 'Making a Difference'? *In* Volunteer Tourism: Theoretical Frameworks and Practical Applications. Angela M. Benson, ed. Pp. 211–222. New York: Routledge.

Institute for Community Research (ICR)
    2009   The Institute for Community Research: Research Partnerships for Healthy Communities. Participatory Action Research. ICR. Accessed June 23, 2009. http://www.incommunityresearch.org/research/research.htm.

Instituto Hondureño de Turismo (IHT)
    1993   Estudio socioeconomico y de mercado para el projecto turistico Bahia de Tela, Honduras. August.

Inter-American Commission on Human Rights (IACHR)
    2003   IACHR Pleased at Presentation of Title Deed to Garífuna Community. IACHR. Accessed December 13, 2011. http://www.cidh.org/Comunicados/English/2003/20.03.htm.
    2007   Admissibility Report N 39/07, Petition 1118-03, Garifuna Community of Cayos Cochinos and Its Members. Honduras. July 24. Accessed October 9, 2012. http://www.cidh.oas.org/annualrep/2007eng/Honduras1118.03eng.htm.

International Ecotourism Society, The (TIES)
    2011   What Is Ecotorism? International Ecotourism Society. http://www.ecotourism.org/what-is-ecotourism. Accessed October 2, 2012.

International Labour Organization (ILO)
    1989   C169, Convention concerning Indigenous and Tribal Peoples in Independent Countries, 1989. Accessed January 9, 2006. http://www.ilo.org/wcmsp5/groups/public/—asia/—ro-bangkok/—ilo-jakarta/documents/publication/wcms_124013.pdf.

Jackson, Cecile
    2003   Gender Analysis and Land: Beyond Land Rights for Women? Journal of Agrarian Change 3(4): 453–480.

Janki, Melinda
    2009   A Rights-Based Approach to Protected Areas. *In* Conservation with Justice: A Rights-Based Approach. Thomas Greiber, ed. Pp. 87–111. Gland, Switzerland: IUCN.

Jimenez-Castro, C.
    2008   Management of a Marine Protected Area by a Local NGO in Honduras: Its Implications for Local Communities. Master's thesis, Lincoln University.

Accessed December 9, 2011. http://researcharchive.lincoln.ac.nz/dspace/bitstream/10182/1237/3/Jimenez-Castro_mapplsc.pdf.

Jones, Jeffrey R.
1990   Colonization and Environment: Land Settlement Projects in Central America. Tokyo: United Nations University Press.

Keck, Margaret, and Kathryn Sikkink
1998   Activists beyond Borders. Ithaca: Cornell University Press.

Kerns, Virginia
1983   Women and the Ancestors: Black Carib Kinship and Ritual. Urbana: University of Illinois Press.

Klein, Naomi
2007   The Shock Doctrine: The Rise of Disaster Capitalism. New York: Metropolitan Books.

Kovalik, Dan
2012   US DEA Kills Innocent Civilians in Honduras—US Media Silent. Huffington Post, May 16, 2012. Accessed June 5, 2012. http://www.huffingtonpost.com/dan-kovalik/honduras-civilians-dead_b_1521177.html.

Laclau, Ernesto, and Chantal Mouffe
1985   Hegemony and Socialist Strategy: Toward a Radical Democratic Politics. New York: Verso.

Lâm, Maivân Clech
2004   Remembering the Country of Their Birth: Indigenous Peoples and Territoriality. Journal of International Affairs 57(2): 129–150.

Lee-Smith, Diana, and Catalina H. Trujillo
2006   Unequal Rights: Women and Property. In Women and Gender Equity in Development Theory and Practice: Institutions, Resources, and Mobilization. Jane S. Jaquette, Gale Summerfield, and Louise Fortmann, eds. Pp. 159–172. Durham, NC: Duke University Press.

Lemos, Maria C., and Arun Agrawal
2006   Environmental Governance. Annual Review of Environment and Resources 31: 297–325.

Life Vision Properties
2011   Lot Sales up 238 percent in 2010 in Roatan. Life Vision Properties (blog). June 2. Accessed August 31, 2011. http://lifevisionproperties.wordpress.com/2011/06/02/lot-sales-up-238-in-2010-in-roatan/.

Liverman, Diana M., and Silvina Vilas
2006   Neoliberalism and the Environment in Latin America. Annual Review of Environment and Resources 31(1): 327–363.

Loperena, Christopher
2010   Financiamiento del BID, enclave turístico y pérdida de la tierra Garífuna en la Bahía de Tela. May 10. CIP Americas, Megaproyectos del BID, desplazamiento y migración forzada. CIP Americas. Accessed December 8, 2011. http://www.cipamericas.org/archives/2222.

2011 Honduras Is Open for Business: Assessing the Democratic Transition and Resistance in the Post-Coup Period. Paper presented at the Annual Meeting of the American Anthropological Association in Montreal, Canada, November 14–18, 2012.

López, Arriola
2000 Purificación "Popo" Arriola López: Garífuna Dance Troupe Director. Interview and transcription by InCorpore Cultural Association. Triunfo de la Cruz, Honduras. July 1998. K. Stevens, ed. and trans. Stanford Center for Latin American Studies.

Lyons, Kevin D., and Stephen Wearing
2008a Volunteer Tourism as Alternative Tourism: Journeys beyond Otherness. *In* Journeys of Discovery in Volunteer Tourism. Kevin D. Lyons and Stephen Wearing, eds. Pp. 3–11. Wallingford, UK: CABI International.
2008b All for a Good Cause? The Blurred Boundaries of Volunteering and Tourism. *In* Journeys of Discovery in Volunteer Tourism. Kevin D. Lyons and Stephen Wearing, eds. Pp. 147–154. Wallingford, UK: CABI International.

MacCannell, Dean
1976 The Tourist: A New Theory of the Leisure Class. New York: Schocken Books.

Macintyre, Martha, and Simon Foale
2007 Land and Marine Tenure, Ownership, and New Forms of Entitlement on Lihir: Changing Notions of Property in the Context of a Goldmining Project. Human Organization 66(1): 49–59.

Malkin, Elisabeth
2012 Plan for Charter City to Fight Honduras Poverty Loses Its Initiator. New York Times, September 30. Accessed October 12, 2012. http://www.nytimes.com/2012/10/01/world/americas/charter-city-plan-to-fight-honduras-poverty-loses-initiator.html.

Malkki, Liisa H.
1997 National Geographic: The Rooting of Peoples and the Territorialization of National Identity among Scholars and Refugees. *In* Culture, Power, Place: Explorations in Critical Anthropology. Akhil Gupta and James Ferguson, eds. Pp. 52–74. Durham, NC: Duke University Press.

Maniates, Michael
2002 Individualization: Plant a Tree, Buy a Bike, Save the World? *In* Confronting Consumption. Thomas Princen, Michael Maniates, and Ken Conca, eds. Pp. 199–236. Cambridge: Massachusetts Institute of Technology Press.

Manor, James
1999 The Political Economy of Democratic Decentralization: Directions in Development. Washington, DC: World Bank.

Mascia, Michael B., J. Peter Brosius, Tracy A. Dobson, Bruce C. Forbes, Leah Horowitz, Margaret A. McKean, and Nancy J. Turner
2003 Conservation and the Social Sciences. Conservation Biology 17(3): 649–650.

McAfee, Kathleen
  1999 Selling Nature to Save It? Biodiversity and Green Developmentalism. Environment and Planning D: Society and Space 17(2) :133–154.

McDonald, David A., and Greg Ruiters
  2005 Theorizing Water Privatization in Southern Africa. *In* The Age of Commodity: Water Privatization in Southern Africa. David A. McDonald and Greg Ruiters, eds. Pp. 13–42. London: Earthscan.

McGehee, Nancy
  2002 Alternative Tourism and Social Movement. Annals of Tourism Research 29:124–243.

McGehee, Nancy G., and William C. Norman
  2002 Alternative Tourism as Impetus for Consciousness-Raising. Tourism Analysis 6(3–4): 239–251.

McGehee, Nancy G., and Carla A. Santos
  2005 Social Change, Discourse, and Volunteer Tourism. Annals of Tourism Research 32(3): 760–779.

Medina, Laurie Kroshus
  1998 History, Culture, and Place–Making: "Native" Status and Maya Identity in Belize. Journal of Latin American Anthropology 4(1): 134–165.
  2004 Negotiating Economic Development: Identity Formation and Collective Action in Belize. Tucson: University of Arizona Press.

Merrill, Tim, ed.
  1993 Honduras: A Country Study. Washington, DC: Federal Research Division, US Library of Congress.

Morris, Saul, Oscar Neidecker-Gonzalez, Calogero Carletto, Marciel Munguia, Juan Manuel Medina, and Quentin Wodon
  2002 Hurricane Mitch and the Livelihoods of the Rural Poor in Honduras. World Development 30(1): 49–60.

Mowforth, Martin, and Ian Munt
  1998 Tourism and Sustainability: New Tourism in the Third World. London: Routledge.

Moya, Ruth
  1987 Educación y mujer indígena en el Ecuador. Paper presented to the Regional Office for Education of UNESCO, Quito, March.

Muehelbach, Andrea
  2001 "Making Place" at the United Nations: Indigenous Cultural Politics and the U.N. Working Group on Indigenous Politics. Cultural Anthropology 16(3): 415–48.

Nader, Laura
  1972 Up the Anthropologist: Perspectives Gained from Studying Up. *In* Reinventing Anthropology. Dell H. Hymes, ed. Pp. 284–311. New York: Pantheon Books.

N'gweno, Bettina
  2007   Can Ethnicity Replace Race? Afro-Colombians, Indigeneity and the Colombian Multicultural State. Journal of Latin American and Caribbean Anthropology 12(2): 414–440.

Niezen, Ronald
  2003   The Origins of Indigenism: Human Rights and the Politics of Identity. Berkeley: University of California Press.

Norsworthy, Kent, and Tom Barry
  1993   Inside Honduras: The Essential Guide to Its Politics, Economy, Society, and Environment. Albuquerque: Inter-Hemispheric Education Resource Center.

Occhipinti, Laurie
  2003   Claiming a Place: Land and Identity in Two Communities in Northwestern Argentina. Journal of Latin American Anthropology 8(3): 155–174.

Office of the UN High Commissioner for Human Rights (OHCHR)
  2007   Declaration on the Rights of Indigenous Peoples. OHCHR. Accessed October 8, 2012. http://www.ohchr.org/EN/Issues/IPeoples/Pages/Declaration .aspx.

Operation Wallacea (Opwall)
  2012   Social and Environmental Responsibility Programme. Operation Wallacea Accessed June 18, 2012. http://www.opwall.com/About/responsibletourism .shtml.

Organización de Desarrollo Étnico Comunitario (ODECO)
  2002   What Are ODECO's Principal Objectives? Accessed January 6, 2006. http:// www.caribe.hn/odeco/page2.html.
  2012   Declaración de la Conferencia Nacional sobre las Ciudades Modelos. Accessed October 12, 2012. http://odecohn.blogspot.com/.

Organización Fraternal Negra Hondureña (OFRANEH)
  2002a   Comunicado Público, Sambo Creek. November 7. In possession of the author.
  2002b   Comunicado Público, Sambo Creek. GarifunaWeb, November 21. Accessed December 13, 2011. http://garifunaweb.com/ofraneh/ofraneh11-21-02 .htm.
  2002c   Chronology of the Garifuna Community's Right to Land in Sambo Creek. La Ceiba (Honduras).
  2005   Persecution of Garifunas. La Ceiba (Honduras), March 28.
  2011a   LaCumbreAfroylasCiudadesmodelodeneocolonialismo.OFRANEH,August 12. Accessed December 13, 2011. http://ofraneh.wordpress.com/2011/08/12/ la-cumbre-afro-y-las-ciudades-modelo-de-neocolonialismo.
  2011b   Honduras: Threats of Repression from Organizers of the state sponsored Summit of Afrodescendants and Garifuna People. Friendship Office of the Americas, August 16. Accessed December 13, 2011. http://friendshipamericas .org/afro-descendant-communites-threatened-model-cities-issue- alert.

2012a Más de lo mismo: Libre agresor que disparó a Garífuna en la recuperación en Trujillo. OFRANEH, May 22, 2012. Accessed June 4, 2012. http://ofraneh .wordpress.com/2012/05/22/mas-de-lo-mismo-libre-agresor-que-disparo-a-garifuna-en-la-recuperacion-en-trujillo/.

2012b Honduras: La Biosfera del Rio Plátano, Represas hidroeléctricas y el catastro en comunidades Garífunas. OFRANEH, May 30. Accessed June 4, 2012. http://ofraneh.wordpress.com/2012/05/30/honduras-la-biosfera-del-rio-platano-represas-hidroelectricas-y-el-catastro-en-comunidades-garifunas/.

Organización Negra Centroamericana (ONECA)
2002 Declaración de San Jose VIII asamblea de la Organización Negra Centro-americana — 5, 6, y 7 de diciembre de 2002. GarifunaWeb. Accessed August 22, 2011. http://garifunaweb.com/oneca/oneca12-7-02.html.

Peet, Richard
1999 Theories of Development. New York: Guilford Press.

Peet, Richard, and Michael J. Watts
1993 Introduction: Development Theory and Environment in an Age of Market Triumphalism. Economic Geography 69(3): 227–253.

Phillips, James
2011 Resource Access, Environmental Struggles, and Human Rights in Hondu-ras. In Life and Death Matters: Human Rights and the Environment at the End of the Millennium. 2nd ed. Barbara Rose Johnston, ed. Pp. 209–232. Walnut Creek, CA: Left Coast Press.

Proceso Digital
2011 CN aprueba ley que regula las Ciudades Modelos. Proceso Digital, July 29. Accessed October 24, 2011. http://proceso.hn/2011/07/29/Nacionales/CN.aprueba.ley/40381.html.

Puntenney, Pamela J.
1990 Defining Solutions: The Annapurna Experience. Cultural Survival Quar-terly 14(2): 9–14.

Redford, Kent H.
2011 Misreading the Conservation Landscape. Fauna & Flora International, Oryx 45(3): 324–330.

Reed, Bob, Scott Boback, Steve Green, and Chad Montgomery
2007 Cayos Cochinos Boa Constrictor and Ctenosaur Population Monitoring and Conservation. In Operation Wallacea Science Programme 2007, Timothy Coles, David J. Smith., and Richard Field, eds. Pp. 96–98. Lincolnshire, UK: Operation Wallacea.

Ribeiro, Gustavo Lins
1998 Cybercultural Politics: Political Activism at a Distance in a Transnational World. In Cultures of Politics/Politics of Cultures: Re-visioning Latin Amer-ican Social Movements. Sonia E. Alvarez, Evelina Dagnino, and Arturo Escobar, eds. Pp. 325–352. Boulder, CO: Westview Press.

Richards, Patricia
    2005   The Politics of Gender, Human Rights, and Being Indigenous in Chile. Gender and Society 19(2): 199–220.

Rist, Gilbert
    1997   The History of Development: From Western Origins to Global Faith. London: Zed Books.

Robinson, William I.
    2003   Transnational Conflicts: Central America, Social Change, and Globalization. London: Verso.

Rocheleau, Dianne, Thomas-Slayter, Barbara, and Esther Wangari, eds.
    1996   Feminist Political Ecology: Global Issues and Local Experiences. London: Routledge.

Rostow, W. W.
    1960   Stages of Economic Growth: A Non-Communistic Manifesto. Cambridge: Cambridge University Press.

Ruhl, Mark J.
    1984   Agrarian Structure and Political Stability in Honduras. Journal of Interamerican Studies and World Affairs 26(1): 33–68.

Safa, Helen
    2008   Challenging Mestizaje: A Gender Perspective on Indigenous and Afrodescendant Movements in Latin America. Critique of Anthropology 25(3): 307–330.
    2006   Racial and Gender Inequality in Latin America: Afrodescendent Women Respond. Feminist Africa, no. 7: 49–66.

Schensul, Jean
    2005   Strengthening Communities through Research Partnerships for Social Change: Perspectives from the Institute for Community Research. *In* Community Building in the 21st Century. Stanley Hyland, ed. Pp. 191–218. Santa Fe: SAR Press.

Schepers, Emile
    2009   Honduras Update. Peoples World (blog). September 13. Accessed September 13, 2009. http://peoplesweeklyworldblog.blogspot.com/2009/09/honduras-update-september-13-2009.html.

Secretaría de Estado en los Despachos de Recursos (SEDR)
    2004   Meeting Minutes regarding Régimen Tarifario del Monumento Natural Marino Archipiélago Cayos Cochinos. October 14.

Sen, Amartya
    1999   Development as Freedom. New York: Alfred A. Knopf.

Shanker, Thom
    2012   Lessons of Iraq Help U.S. Fight a Drug War in Honduras. New York Times, May 5. Accessed June 5, 2012. http://www.nytimes.com/2012/05/06/world/americas/us-turns-its-focus-on-drug-smuggling-in-honduras.html?ref=honduras.

Shiva, Vandana
　　1989　Staying Alive: Women, Ecology, and Development. Boston: South End Press.

Simpson, Kate
　　2004　Doing Development: The Gap Year, Volunteer-Tourists and a Popular Practice of Development. Journal of International Development 16(5): 681–692.

Sinervo, Aviva
　　2011a　Appeals of Childhood: Child Vendors, Volunteer Tourists, and Visions of Aid in Cusco, Peru. PhD dissertation, Department of Anthropology, University of California, Santa Cruz.
　　2011b　Connection and Disillusion: The Moral Economy of Volunteer Tourism in Cusco, Peru. Childhoods Today 5(2): 1–23.

Social Watch
　　2011　African Descent Summit calls for permanent space at the UN. Social Watch: Poverty Eradication and Social Justice. August 26. Accessed October 28, 2011. http://www.socialwatch.org/node/13572.

Spring, Karen
　　2011　Canadian Porn Kings, Tourism "Development" Projects, Repression & the Violations of Indigenous-Garifuna Rights in Honduras. Siga Adelante (blog). March 11 (8:30 a.m.). Accessed November 30, 2011. http://siga-adelante.blogspot.com/2011/03/canadian-porn-kings-tourism-development.html.

Stone, Hannah
　　2012　Honduras "Model City" Plan in the Spotlight. Council on Hemispheric Campaigns, October 5. Available online at Common Dreams. Accessed October 12, 2012. https://www.commondreams.org/view/2012/10/05-7

Stonich, Susan C.
　　1993　"I Am Destroying the Land!" The Political Ecology of Poverty and Environmental Destruction in Honduras. Boulder, CO: Westview Press.
　　2000　The Other Side of Paradise: Tourism, Conservation, and Development in the Bay Islands. New York: Cognizant Communication Corporation.

Stronza, Amanda
　　2001　Anthropology of Tourism: Forging New Ground for Ecotourism and Other Alternatives. Annual Review of Anthropology 30: 261–83.

Tela News (TN)
　　2000　Tela Bay. Tela News, May 25.

Thompson, Margaret
　　2011　Resistance to Political and Business Assaults on Indigenous Land and Resources in Honduras. Upside Down World: Covering Activism and Politics in Latin America, July 15. Accessed July 5, 2012. http://upsidedownworld.org/main/honduras-archives-46/3127-resistance-to-political-and-business-assaults-on-indigenous-land-and-resources-in-honduras.

Thorne, Eva T.
　　N.d.　　Honduran Garifuna Women and Land Rights. Unpublished manuscript.
　　2005　　Land Rights and Garifuna Identity. NACLA 38(2): 21–25.
Thornhill, Alan
　　2003　　Social Scientists and Conservation Biologists Join Forces. Conservation Biology 17(6): 1475–1476.
Traa-Valarezo, Ximena, and Jorge Rodríguez
　　2003　　Empowering Autochthonous Peoples in Honduras: The Nuestras Raíces (Our Roots) Program. En Breve, no. 29: 1–4.
La Tribuna
　　2011　　Infraestructura, energía y agro negocios acaparan interés de los inversionistas. La Tribuna, May 6. Accessed December 5, 2011. http://old.latribuna.hn/2011/05/06/infraestructura-energia-y-agro-negocios-acaparan-interes-de-los-inversionistas/.
　　2012　　Plan de "ciudades privadas" en Honduras, estancado. La Tribuna, October 2. Accessed October 12. http://www.latribuna.hn/2012/10/02/plan-de-ciudades-privadas-en-honduras-estancado/.
Tsing, Anna Lowenhaupt
　　2005　　Friction: An Ethnography of Global Connection. Princeton: Princeton University Press.
Umaña, Helen
　　2009　　An Authentic Cultural Inquisition. Honduras Coup 2009 (blog). Translation from Spanish posted by RAJ, July 25 (11:55 p.m.). Accessed October 27, 2011. http://hondurascoup2009.blogspot.com/2009/07/authentic-cultural-inquisition.html.
UNAIDS (Joint United Nations Programme on HIV/AIDS)
　　2004　　Honduras: Epidemiological Fact Sheets on HIV/AIDS and Sexually Transmitted Infections. UINAIDS. Accessed November 15, 2005. http://www.unaids.org/en/geographical+area/by+country/honduras.asp.
United Nations
　　2004　　The Concept of Indigenous Peoples. Background paper prepared by the Secretariat of the Permanent Forum on Indigenous Issues. Workshop on Data Collection and Disaggregation for Indigenous Peoples. United Nations Educational, Scientific, and Cultural Organization (UNESCO). New York, January 19–21.
　　2005　　Intangible Heritage. United Nations Educational, Scientific, and Cultural Organization (UNESCO). Accessed December 13, 2011. http://www.unesco.org/culture/ich/index.php?pg=00006.
United Nations Office on Drugs and Crime (UNODC)
　　2011　　2011 Global Study on Homicide. United Nations Office on Drugs and Crime (UNODC). Accessed June 5, 2012. http://www.unodc.org/documents/data-and-analysis/statistics/Homicide/Globa_study_on_homicide_2011_web.pdf.
United Nations World Tourism Organization (UNWTO)
　　2011　　Facts & Figures. UNWTO. Accessed December 13, 2011. http://www.unwto.org/facts/menu.html.

US Congress
    2012   Letter to Secretary of State Hillary Clinton. Just Foreign Policy. Accessed June 6, 2012. http://www.justforeignpolicy.org/sites/default/files/signed_honduras_letter.pdf.

US Department of State
    2010   Honduras (08/18/10) [Country Profile]. US Department of State, August 18. Accessed October 12, 2012. http://www.state.gov/outofdate/bgn/honduras/172098.htm.
    2012   U.S. Relations with Honduras. Bureau of Western Hemisphere Affairs Fact Sheet. June 19. US Department of State. Accessed October 12, 2012. Accessed October 19, 2012. http://www.state.gov/r/pa/ei/bgn/1922.htm.

Van Sertima, Ivan
    1976   They Came before Columbus. New York: Random House.

Vivanco, Luis A.
    2001   Spectacular Quetzals, Ecotourism, and Environmental Futures in Monte Verde, Costa Rica. Ethnology 40(2): 79–92.

La Voz de los de Abajo
    2011   OFRANEH—Honduras: "We Are in Permanent Resistance." Papeles de Sociedad.info, July 8. Accessed October 28, 2011. http://www.herbogeminis.com/OFRANEH-Honduras-We-are-in.html.

Vreugdenhil, Daan X, Paul R. House, Carlos A. Cerrato, Ricardo A. Martínez, and Ana C. Pereira
    2002   Rationalisation of the Protected Areas System of Honduras, vol. 1. Honduras: World Institute for Conservation and Environment, 2002.

Warren, Kay B.
    1998   Indigenous Movements and Their Critics: Pan-Maya Activism in Guatemala. Princeton: Princeton University Press.

Warren, Kay B., and Jean E. Jackson
    2002   Introduction: Studying Indigenous Activism in Latin America. *In* Indigenous Movements, Self-Representation, and the State in Latin America. Kay B. Warren and Jean E. Jackson, eds. Pp. 1–46. Austin: University of Texas Press.

Wearing, Stephen
    2001   Volunteer Tourism: Experiences That Make a Difference. Wallingford, UK: CABI International.
    2002   Re-centering the Self in Volunteer Tourism. *In* The Tourist as a Metaphor of the Social World. Graham S. Dann, ed. Pp. 237–262. Wallingford, UK: CABI International.

Wearing, Stephen, Matthew McDonald, and Jess Ponting
    2005   Building a Decommodified Research Paradigm in Tourism: The Contribution of NGOs. Journal of Sustainable Tourism 13(5): 424–439.

West, Paige, and James Carrier
    2004   Ecotourism and Authenticity: Getting Away from It All? Current Anthropology 45(4): 483–498.

Woost, Michael
　　1997　Alternative Vocabularies of Development? "Community" and "Participa-
　　　　tion" in Development Discourse in Sri Lanka. *In* Discourses of Develop-
　　　　ment: Anthropological Perspectives. Ralph D. Grillo and R. L. Stirrat, eds.
　　　　Pp. 229–253. Oxford: Oxford University Press.

World Bank
　　2001　Honduras: World Bank Supports Sustainable Tourism Project for the Carib-
　　　　bean Coast. Press release. July 26. World Bank. Accessed October 15, 2005.
　　　　http://web.worldbank.org/external/default/main?pagePK=34370&
　　　　piPK=34424&theSitePK=4607&menuPK=34463&contentMDK=
　　　　20013449.
　　2004　Sustainable Coastal Tourism Project. World Bank. Accessed December 13,
　　　　2011. http://web.worldbank.org/external/projects/main?pagePK=104231&
　　　　theSitePK=40941&menuPK=228424&Projectid=P057859.

World Database on Protected Areas (WDPA)
　　2010　Coverage of Protected Areas. WDPA. Accessed December 9, 2011. http://
　　　　www.wdpa.org/resources/statistics/2010BIP_Factsheet_Coverage_of_
　　　　Protected_Areas.pdf

Index

activists, activism, 17–18, 109–10, 173, 196, 198–99. *See also various organizations*
Act of Compromise, 49
Afro-Hondurans, 14, 34, 53, 97, 171–72
agricultural sector, 9, 14, 47, 48, 66, 81; Garifuna, 25–26, 86–87; land loss &, 99–100; modernization of, 36, 37, 41, 42–43; in Sambo Creek, 58, 68, 85
Alliance 2-14, 180, 181–83
Álvarez, Celeo, 95, 99, 105–6, 143, 171, 181
Alvarez, Gustavo, 25
ancestral rights, 112, 115–16, 118
Andino, Tiburcio Carías, 66
Arawaks, 20, 118, 121
Article 107, 42, 47, 48–49, 79, 137, 202n3; amending, 51, 196
autochthony, 38–39
AVINA Foundation, 135, 136

"Banana Coast" Cruise Ship Terminal, 177, 178, 179–80
banana production, 14, 25, 31, 33, 34, 47, 57, 64; labor, 26, 28, 29–30; plantations, 36–37; US, 23–24
Bay Islands tourism zone, 48, 55
blacks, 15, 21, 28–29, 30, 34, 35, 38–39. *See also* Afro-Hondurans; Garifuna; West Indians

Callejas, Rafael, 40–41
Canadians, 1, 3, 4, 120, 121, 177–79

capitalism, 24; disaster, 195–96
Caribs, 20–21, 118
Castillo, Miguel, 113–14
Castillo family, 77–78, 100
Cayo Bolaño, 57, 101, 137
Cayo Mayor, 6, 133, 135
Cayo Menor, 5, 152, 191, 201n3, 205n2; HCRF ownership of, 134–35, 138; Opwall &, 158–60
Cayo Paloma, 149, 150, 151
Cayos Cochinos, 5, 13, 48, 57, 101
Cayos Cochinos Marine Protected Area (CCMPA), 6, 201n3; communities, 132–34, 184; fishing, 141–44, 149, 205n1; HCRF, 135–36; landowners, 134–35; management, 15–16, 129–30, 131, 136–38, 139–41, 153, 166, 198; tourism, 130–32, 144–48, 164–67, 184
Central American Afro-descendant Organizations, 106
Central American Commission of Environment & Development (CCAD), 106
Chachahuate, 6, 101, 129, 137, 141(fig.), 144, 160, 191, 192; residents of, 132–33, 145
class, 9; & activism, 123–24
CoAlianza, 175, 176
Cobo, José Martínez, 90–91
coconut production, 47, 98, 203n4
Colonia Libertad, 66, 69, 70, 76
Colonia Suazo, 66, 67, 69, 76

About the Author

Keri Brondo is Assistant Professor of Anthropology at the University of Memphis. Her teaching and research interests include gender, development and social justice, indigenous identity politics, tourism, environmental anthropology, and applied, practicing, and engaged anthropology. She received her PhD in Anthropology from Michigan State University in 2006, with specializations in Culture, Resources, and Power and Latin American and Caribbean Studies, and she has spent the last decade researching and writing about Garifuna land rights, women's activism, and conservation policies in Honduras. In the United States, Brondo's work focuses on gender equity, applied and practicing anthropology, and collaborative research on the relationship between parks, people, and conservation, and green infrastructure and social justice.